how to do
media &
cultural
studies
Jane Stokes

SAGE Publications
London • Thousand Oaks • New Delhi

First published 2003
Reprinted 2003

 SAGE Publications Ltd
6 Bonhill Street
London EC2A 4PU

SAGE Publications Inc.
2455 Teller Road
Thousand Oaks, California 91320

SAGE Publications India Pvt Ltd
32, M-Block Market
Greater Kailash – I
New Delhi 110 048

British Library Cataloguing in Publication data
A catalogue record for this book is
available from the British Library

ISBN 0 7619 7328 1
ISBN 0 7619 7329 X (pbk)

Library of Congress control number 2002104222

Typeset by Mayhew Typesetting, Rhayader, Powys
Printed and bound in Great Britain by Athenaeum Press,
Gateshead

how to do
media &
cultural
studies

For Rose

Acknowledgements

Thank you to Kembrew McLeod, Andrea Millwood Hargrave and the Independent Television Commission for permission to use extracts from their work.

Contents

Introduction

How To Do Media and Cultural Studies is aimed at undergraduate students undertaking independent research and their lecturers. Most courses require students to write a long essay which they must research independently at some time during their university careers. Whether it is called a long essay, a dissertation or a thesis, the project usually occurs in the final year and forms an important part of the final assessment. *How To Do Media and Cultural Studies* gives guidance on designing and executing independent research for degree-level students. It can be used by students working on their project alone or in class to prepare students for their project. This book provides a practical overview of the principal methods available to students in an accessible and direct way, which will be useful in classes on research methods. The reader's knowledge of research methodology is expanded through detailed case studies of previous research and discussion of the range of work conducted using each of the main methods. The examples discussed are all from media, cultural or film studies, but the principles underlying the methods are applicable to a broader range of fields within the humanities or social sciences. Primarily aimed at media, film and cultural studies students, *How To Do Media and Cultural Studies* will also be useful to those on humanities and social science courses who wish to research media or culture.

How To Do Media and Cultural Studies emphasizes throughout the importance of treating research methods as a fundamental element of the design of a research project and an integral part of the curriculum. I believe that research methods, an area which is frequently neglected or side-stepped in the literature, should be central to the teaching of media and cultural studies. Serious questions of epistemology have been elided by the long-term neglect of research methodologies. So, although *How To Do Media and Cultural Studies* is a textbook which will have practical applications for teachers and researchers, it is also a call for more thoughtful reflection on how research is conducted. In almost any other field, this would not be a controversial statement: research methodology is a central part of the curriculum in most academic disciplines. However, within media and cultural studies, many people are reluctant to tackle the teaching of methods, with the consequence that the rules of evidence by which we conduct our research are rarely explicitly spelled out. This book provides students and lecturers with a clear, direct presentation of the main paradigms of research.

One of the great strengths of media and cultural studies is its diversity. There are multiple potential avenues for research and hundreds of variations in the approaches taken by previous scholars. Research into media, culture and film uses a range of paradigms borrowed from disciplines such as psychology, sociology, history, anthropology, literary studies and ethnomethodology among others. The multidisciplinarity of the field allows the researcher a great deal of freedom, but it can seem daunting to students embarking on their first piece of major research. Lecturers also may find the wealth of methods a problem when designing the curriculum for methods or project teaching. When teaching independent, research lecturers may not have the time to cover the full range of methods that all the students in a class might like to use. The consequence for students is often that they are unaware of the full range of methods available. *How To Do Media and Cultural Studies* presents an overview of the principal methods that can be used by undergraduates. It presents a broad range of methods for use by lecturers and students.

The kind of research undertaken (and the method employed) should depend entirely on the kind of question being asked. The basic assumption of this book is that, although it is possible to use almost any research method to study our field, it is not possible to use any method to study any topic. There are epistemological reasons for choosing particular methods, depending on the nature of the subject and the precise research question. In the opening chapter we discuss how to *operationalize* your research question – that is, how to design a research project which addresses your question – in more detail.

Quantitative and qualitative methods

It has become commonplace to think about methods of research as belonging to two separate categories. The terms *qualitative* and *quantitative* are used to refer to these seemingly discrete sets of methods. These two broad paradigms of research are both used to investigate media and cultural studies and are often seen to be distinct and mutually exclusive. Table 0.1 summarizes the two general paradigms in broad outline.

Quantitative research is the term used to describe approaches developed in the natural sciences and now used widely in social science research. Quantitative methods are those which are based on *numerical information* or *quantities*, and they are typically associated with statistical analyses. Within media and cultural studies, *quantitative* methods are most typically associated with the American tradition of mass communication. These methods embrace several different kinds of research traditions, including survey research, network analysis and mathematical modelling. Within media and

TABLE 0.1		*Quantitative*	*Qualitative*
The Two	Concerned with:	Number	Meaning
General	Roots in:	Social science	Humanities
Paradigms of	Epistemology:	Positivist	Humanist
Research		Empirical	Interpretive
	Most typical of:	Mass communication	Cultural studies
	Archetypal method:	Survey	Hermeneutics

cultural studies, quantitative methods include *content analysis, survey research* and certain kinds of *archive research*. Quantitative research is often discounted by its opponents as being overly concerned with numbers and as being untheoretical and uncritical.

Qualitative research, in contrast, is the name given to a range of research paradigms that are primarily concerned with *meaning* and *interpretation*. These methods are more typical of the humanities, and many, such as *narrative analysis* and *genre analysis*, have been developed for the study of literature. These *interpretive* approaches sprang from *literary studies* and *hermeneutics*, and are concerned with the critical evaluation of texts. Qualitative approaches which include methods such as *focus groups* and *interviews*, investigate how audiences understand media and cultural texts. These methods are subject to criticism from supporters of quantitative methods for their lack of objectivity.

Unfortunately, the labels 'quantitative' and 'qualitative' have become associated with stereotypical notions of what each means, with the consequence that researchers sometimes overlook the opportunities each method holds. Academics become entrenched in support of one or the other set of methods. But the separation of methods into this distinct opposition has, I believe, been harmful to the understanding of methods of research and analysis. Scholars of cultural studies are often particularly vociferous in attacking quantitative approaches, which they condemn as vulgar and clumsy. In what James D. Halloran calls 'the tyranny of the absolutism of non-absolutism' (1998: 30), many researchers refuse to contemplate the possibility that quantitative research might offer them some insight. At the same time, scholars from the quantitative tradition find the rules of evidence employed by cultural studies researchers to be non-existent. They criticize cultural studies for being subjective and lacking any rigour. In truth, researchers from both traditions work with commitment, diligence and integrity to answer questions that they consider to be important. Prejudice, bias and ignorance can prevent supporters of one paradigm from seeing the value of the other.

However, many books about research methods perpetuate the false distinction between quantitative and qualitative, and insist on treating these two ways of thinking as completely divergent approaches. I believe that the distinction is an artificial one which is harmful to our understanding of the field. Most studies of the media and culture are concerned to some extent with both number and meaning. As Fred Inglis says, 'even train-spotters *mean* something by their numbers' (Inglis, 1990: 50). Several other commentators have observed the baneful lack of debate across and between these two ways of thinking (see also Halloran, 1998; Jensen, 1991a; Curran, 2000a).

How To Do Media and Cultural Studies discusses both quantitative and qualitative methods together. In Chapter 1, we look in more detail at the various paradigms operating within the study of media and culture and argue for a more integrated approach to the use of research methods. In Chapters 3–5, research methods are categorized according to whether they are suitable for studying *texts, industries* or *audiences*, and readers are presented with a discussion which includes empirical and interpretive methods as appropriate. This may lead to repetition at times; for example, interviews are discussed as a method for investigating both *audiences* and *producers*. But this approach is designed to stress the importance of putting the object of analysis first. This book is about methods – and therefore about *how* to study – but it is predicated on the belief that the method should be selected to suit the topic of investigation, and not the reverse. When beginner researchers have a broad knowledge of the methods available, they will be bolder, more adventurous researchers equipped to tackle the questions they genuinely want to ask. Students will be able to add to their own knowledge and make a worthwhile contribution to the field only if they are enabled to make questions drive research rather than methods. Researchers of all levels can benefit from improved knowledge of research methods. *How To Do Media and Cultural Studies* aims to enable readers to answer the questions they want to ask, not just the ones they know how to answer.

About this book

How To Do Media and Cultural Studies presents a selection of methods for studying media and culture aimed at the beginner researcher. The first chapter gives some ideas on how to get started – often the most daunting part of any project. Students are encouraged to use their own interests and experience to develop their research ideas. Chapter 1 offers advice on how to develop your area of interest into a workable research question and provides some general guidelines for matching the research question to the appropriate method of analysis. The main paradigms of research in media, film and cultural studies are discussed and categorized according to their usefulness in researching our three categories of objects of analysis: texts, industries and audiences. In this chapter we also consider briefly what happens when your research interests do not fit neatly into these categories or when you want to investigate the relationships between these objects of analysis. In subsequent chapters, these issues are discussed in more detail. The first chapter leads the reader through all the stages in designing a research project up to and including the design of a *research proposal*.

Chapter 2 presents the range of sources available to the researcher with a discussion of relevant trade and academic publications and websites. Chapters 3, 4 and 5 focus on the practicalities of carrying out research, each one concentrating on a general topic area.

In Chapter 3, several methods used to investigate *texts* are presented with an emphasis on those most readily accessible to students. These include one of the most quantitative methods, *content analysis*, and one of the most qualitative, *semiotics*. We look at some methods typically used in film studies but which have useful applications for the study of many other media forms: these are *genre*, *auteur* and *star studies*. Chapter 3 groups these together under the heading 'typological approaches' – meaning methods which analyse texts as belonging to a group or genus. Primarily associated with film studies, these approaches have many applications to broader areas of media and culture. In this chapter, we have several suggestions for students' own projects. We apply genre analysis to the television drama *The Sopranos* to exemplify one approach to the study of texts.

In Chapter 4, we look at how to conduct research into media and cultural *institutions and industries*, including *archive research*, the *interview* and *participant observation*. The advantages and disadvantages of each method are discussed and examples of research considered. This chapter briefly discusses oral history as a method for investigating the media and culture industries, although this is covered in more detail in Chapter 5, where it is included as a key method for investigating audiences.

Chapter 5 examines the different approaches the student researcher can take to *audiences*. The methods presented here include the *interview* and the *survey*, as in Chapter 4, but here we look at the special considerations involved in applying these methods to members of the public, rather than media professionals. This chapter also gives guidance on conducting your own focus group. There are many commercial companies and state organizations that collect data on audiences and media consumption, some of these are discussed here.

Each of Chapters 3–5 guides you through the stages involved in executing the relevant method and provides you with lots of examples and ideas to follow up in your own research. These chapters also include discussion of how to combine methods in your research. The last chapter looks at the presentation of the final essay and includes examples of tables of contents. Here you are given guidance on how to present your research in a professional academic manner. The two appendices identify, respectively, *libraries and archives of relevance* and *websites of interest to researchers in media and culture.*

Throughout, *How To Do Media and Cultural Studies* presents case studies and examples of key work published in the field to encourage students to think about how previous scholars have used certain methods in their work. In the space of a single volume, it would be impossible to cover all the methods available; the methods selected have been carefully chosen to suit the ability and resources of a beginner researcher. I hope that students will find this book a useful and practical guide to conducting their own research, and that lecturers will find the book a valuable addition to the literature on research methods.

Getting Started 1

Chapter overview

This chapter is designed to guide students through the early stages of developing a research project, from designing a question to submitting a proposal. It begins with a discussion of how to decide upon a subject. Students are encouraged to think about the field and about their own interests and networks before settling on a research area. The range of possible topics is discussed and some tips for coming up with ideas are given.

The design and development of the research question is a crucial stage in the development of any research project. In this chapter we give advice and ideas on how to develop a workable research question by thinking about the object of analysis and the theoretical paradigms you wish to work within or develop. The emphasis throughout is on thinking about how to find the right method for your research interests. We discuss the main paradigms of research in media, cultural and film studies. In this chapter we discuss which methods are appropriate to the study of texts, industries and audiences. Of course, it is always possible to combine research methods, although you have to be wary of conducting two different research projects – here we look briefly at when it is appropriate to combine research methods. Phrasing your research question is a very important part of the project, too. We give some examples of how to phrase your question here. Table 1.1 shows the main stages in designing a research project to be discussed in this chapter.

You should be wary of beginning your research project before you have positively determined that you have access to the necessary material: included in this chapter is a section on identifying sources as well as reviewing previous literature. We also discuss how to design your proposal, note taking and working from an outline or proposal.

TABLE 1.1	1.	Think about what interests you most from your studies so far
Stages in	2.	Think about what areas of media or culture interest you the most
Designing a	3.	Read (or reread) literature which relates to your area of interest
Research	4.	Decide on a subject area
Project	5.	Discuss the topic with colleagues and lecturers
	6.	Define your object of analysis
	7.	Design your research question

Introduction

Most courses require students to conduct an original piece of work towards the end of their degree. While a lot of people are energized at the opportunity offered by the project, others find the idea daunting. This chapter will help you to decide what topic you are going to investigate and guide you through the necessary stages in designing a project up to the stage of writing the research proposal.

Deciding on a subject

The areas covered by media, film and cultural studies sometimes seem so broad that the task of deciding what to research can seem overwhelming. You may wonder, 'What is an appropriate subject for academic research in a field where all areas of culture seem open to study?' Remember that our fields of study were largely originated by people who were prepared to study what others considered to be unworthy of academic investigation. Media and cultural studies would not exist as a field of academic research if people had not been prepared to take risks and to challenge conventional notions of what is appropriate to study. So do not worry too much about whether what you want to study is legitimate or not; as long as it is fundamentally to do with the media or culture, it will probably be fine. The most important factor in your selection of a topic is that you find a subject engaging enough to sustain your interest throughout the time you will be working on it. Settling on a subject area is one of the most important decisions you will make in designing your project, so it is worth spending some time thinking carefully about what you want to do.

In general, the project should bring together your academic and your personal interests, so try to match your own experience with your studies. You need to think about what interests you, but this must be informed by your knowledge of what other people in the field have done and what it is feasible for you to investigate.

TABLE 1.2

Self-Administered Questions for Generating Ideas for the Project

About yourself

What medium or media do I enjoy using?

Do I belong to a cultural group which I could study?

What motivates me to study media or cultural studies?

Could my family or friends make interesting subjects of research?

About your studies

What subject areas have I especially enjoyed studying?

Is there a researcher whose work I especially admire? What do I like about his/her work?

Did a specific lecture or seminar particularly interest me?

Which assignment for a previous class did I particularly enjoy?

Is there any area of my studies so far which I would like to look at in more depth?

About the subject

What current developments in media technology, industry or culture do I find especially interesting?

Is there an important event in the history of the field about which I would like to find out more?

Do I have access to an institution (through work experience or personal networks) which could be useful to me in conducting the project?

Reflect on your interests

A good way to start thinking about the topic for your research is to reflect on your personal interest in the field. Ask yourself what areas of culture or media interest you the most. Think about your own personal use of the media: for example, do you spend more time watching television, listening to music or reading books? Which is your favourite medium and why? Would you describe yourself as a fan or a connoisseur of any particular media form or genre? Many excellent projects are written by students about programmes, films or music that they admire. If you are part of a subculture or scene, perhaps you could research the attitudes and behaviour of fellow members of your group? If you are a member of a fan club, your co-members can make an excellent resource: after all, they share your passion and are probably keen to talk about their interest. Perhaps you have experience of working in the media, or access to people who work in the media and who would be amenable to being interviewed. Your own knowledge, experience, contacts and interests are invaluable resources in conducting original research. If there is some aspect of media or culture about which you want to know more, this is a good starting point. Listing all of the subject areas you are interested in on a piece of paper will help you to appreciate the range of areas on which you could draw. Table 1.2 provides some ideas to get you started.

Think back on your studies

By now you will probably have taken several modules in the field. The project is a good opportunity for you to pursue areas of interest which you did not have time for during your course. Go through your notes, reflecting on classes or lectures you found especially interesting. Spend some time with your course and module guides to remind yourself of what you have been studying. When you look through your folders, you will probably be surprised at the range of topics you have studied so far. You should find that one of these is interesting enough to give you some ideas for your own research project.

Build on studies you have read

One excellent starting point is to ask yourself what has interested you the most about the research you have read on your course? Most research is generated by testing theories of previous scholars in new situations: is there any work that you have read which you can build on in your own research? For example, David Morley's book *Family Television* studies how the structure of the family is reflected in the way people watch television (Morley, 1986). One of his main conclusions is that patriarchal power structures are reflected in television viewing habits, but Morley acknowledges the limitations of his study, which is based on a narrow demographic range of mainly white, middle-class families. You might be inspired by Morley to ask whether members of other demographic groups use television in distinctive ways. For example, your own family background may differ in interesting ways from those Morley researched. A study of the decision-making processes around television viewing in extended or single-parent families, for example, would make an interesting comparison with Morley's research. Alternatively, you could ask: 'Who controls television viewing in households which are not based around family relations as in student accommodation or when groups of friends live together?' Is it the owner of the television? Are decisions about television viewing made by the person who is most similar to the *patriarch* in the group (the person who earns the most perhaps)? Or are such matters determined by the person who watches television the most? You could use the same methods as Morley, but by applying his ideas to a different situation you could come up with some new ways of thinking about how we watch television.

Another way to build on Morley's research would be to interview groups of people about their collective media habits, as Morley does, but apply that method to other areas of media use. For example, you might interview a group of friends who frequently socialize together about the decision-making process involved in choosing what film they are going to see.

You could find out more about media use by understanding the group dynamics involved in deciding what to do in leisure time. Or you could look at the family unit, as Morley did, but investigate how families decide which channels they are going to receive on their subscriber television service. Morley's focus on the dynamics of group decision making around the media is very productive of new ideas. There are numerous ways in which you could apply a method of research that has been used by previous researchers to new situations or media. Start by rereading research which you found particularly interesting, and this time pay close attention to the method used. Think about how the researcher's approach may be adapted to new situations or environments.

Think about current developments

Your research should be original, and one of the best ways of ensuring that you avoid already well-trodden ground is to study the latest developments in the field. These may be

- *technological* – looking at the implications of the latest media technology
- *regulatory* – looking at how recent governmental legislation or decisions (for example, the granting of a new BBC charter) may influence the media system
- *social* – examining how new cultural phenomena are forming.

Each of the above is constantly changing. Our field is often at the forefront of examining the impact of new technology. Don't be put off by the fact that 'nothing has been written' about a new technology – there is a large literature on the impact of new technology which you can exploit in your project. Likewise with the changing political or economic environment: there are always points of comparison you can make with past events. Think about how new changes will impact a well-documented industry or institution. Current events are well tracked in trade and industry publications and on the Internet – don't be afraid to use a variety of sources as long as your background and theoretical approach are founded on academic research.

Use your contacts

If you have contacts within the industry – perhaps through work experience or personal networks – could you base your study on these? Employers may be willing to allow you to use the workplace as the focus for your study. You

TABLE 1.3	The African-American man in Hollywood cinema
Examples of	Beatles fan culture
Subject Areas	Benetton advertisements
for Research	Black British culture
Projects	Boy bands
	Contemporary British cinema
	Cosmopolitan magazine
	Disabled people in the media
	The films of Quentin Tarantino
	Football coverage in British newspapers
	Game shows
	Home improvement television
	Indian cinema
	Internet shopping
	Men's magazines
	New technology in publishing
	Sindy doll marketing
	Teenage magazines
	Television advertising
	Webzines

may be permitted to sit in on meetings (on your own time!), where decisions are made, or to observe at first hand how some aspect of the business is conducted. Chapter 4 gives some more discussion of using your work experience (see pages 122–25). Family and friendship contacts can also be helpful; for example, they may be useful in recruiting interviewees or subjects for survey research (see Chapter 5).

Think carefully about your studies, your interests and your contacts, and you will probably be able to think of several subjects you could choose for your project. Look again at Table 1.2 and write down your own responses to these questions.

The range of topics for student projects

Table 1.3 shows some of the subject areas that students of mine have used for their projects. As you can see, this is a wide range of subjects, and I am sure you could come up with some ideas that would not look out of place among these. Note that these are not *questions* but *subject areas*; there is a big difference between them which we will discuss in the section on 'Developing your research question'. You might want to read the appropriate chapters of the rest of this book before you settle on an idea. You should read through the rest of this chapter when you have come up with a general topic area in order to hone down your subject to a researchable question.

Brainstorming

Brainstorming is a great way of generating ideas and a useful technique for helping you to think about what you really want to do. When you have thought about the questions raised in Table 1.2, allow yourself the time to indulge in a brainstorming session. You can do this alone, in a study group or in class. First get a very large piece of paper and some marker pens. Give yourself a set period of time – ten to fifteen minutes, depending on how many of you there are – to cover it with writing. Write down each and every topic that you *could, would* or *might* like to study. Don't edit your ideas – be spontaneous and write everything down, almost like automatic writing. Make sure you keep writing, as quickly as you can, for the whole time. When the time is up, go and have a cup of tea or take a walk. Come back to the sheet of paper after about ten minutes and read it. Now, think about what connections you can make. Take a different coloured pen and draw lines between similar ideas and try to come up with categories for your ideas. Can you identify common themes? Is there one idea which seems to dominate everything else? Do you have several distinct ideas? Once you have gone over the sheet of paper and covered it in new writing, make a list of any ideas which are potential research subjects. Next think about how you could put these ideas in order of what interests you the most. Is there one topic which seems more appealing than the others? You may have several different ideas at this stage or you may still be stuck; don't worry: talk through your concerns with other students in your class or with your tutor. By the end of your brainstorming session, you should have at least a couple of ideas which are worth pursuing further and you will have thought more about what interests you and why.

How high is your brow?

The debates about the 'highbrow' and 'popular' cultures are very well rehearsed elsewhere, and I will not get into them now (see, for example, Storey, 1993, 1994; Inglis, 1990, 1993; Turner, 1996). Suffice it to say that although there is a general acceptance of the distinction between 'media' and 'culture' in academic and popular debate, in this book we are going to consider them equally valid areas of study. The distinctions we need to make for our present purposes are not of the brow level of the various forms, but of the kinds of work which can be done in researching media and culture. However, although the method for researching Covent Garden opera may not be any different from that used to research Carlton television, whether one chooses to study the opera or popular television can in itself be a highly political decision. In planning your research, you should feel equally entitled to study the so-called 'elite' or 'popular' forms – all have equal currency in the market place of cultural forms and ideas.

Use your supervisor

You should talk to your tutor or supervisor at an early stage in the design process to get guidance on how to approach your chosen subject area. Each university will have its own expectations and criteria: your tutor will be able to advise you on these. Your tutor will also know if there are any special resources available to you locally relating to your topic. Early discussions can save you from going down false paths, so make an appointment to see your tutor as soon as you have an idea. Make regular appointments to meet your supervisor and stick to them. Students who discuss their project regularly with their supervisor do much better in the final assessment than those who don't. Supervisors constitute a valuable resource provided for you – make the most of them!

Developing your research question

Once you have decided on a subject area, and you have discussed it with your tutor, you need to work on developing your *research question*. The research question is what will guide your project, so it is crucial that you define it very carefully. Begin to do this by thinking about what it is about the subject that you find interesting. Read as much as you can about the topic to find out what kinds of research have been done in this area before. Think about *theory*; how could you apply the findings of particular theorists to your own interests?

Define your object of analysis

The next stage in the design process is to define exactly what you are going to take as your *object of analysis*: that aspect of the subject which you are going to study in detail. The object of analysis specifies the precise set of phenomena you will examine and is a description of your particular area of enquiry. What do you want to say about British films of the 1990s, game shows or digital music? Try to be as precise as possible. Narrow your focus to a single aspect of the subject, or to one key relationship. Your object of analysis should be *manageable* – sufficient to keep you busy but not too much to handle. It should also be *accessible*; you will be wasting your time trying to research films if you can't get hold of viewing copies, for example.

If your subject area was one of those in Table 1.3, let's say contemporary British cinema, there are several narrower areas you could select for your project, depending on the exact area you are interested in. Table 1.4 gives some ideas of how this subject may be narrowed down further.

If you want to look at issues of representation in British films, you could choose to look at how a particular social group is depicted in a certain set of films. Let us take as an example representations of the Asian community in films such as *East is East, Bhaji on the Beach* or *Bend it Like Beckham*. The representation of British Asian culture in these films would provide a clear object of analysis. Another recurrent theme in contemporary British cinema is the East End villian. You could take as your object of analysis films such as *Lock, Stock and Two Smoking Barrels* which use the mythology of the East End of London as a theme, building on stereotypes of that community as villainous and dangerous. If, however, you were struck by the popularity of *Billy Elliot* and think the film bears all the hallmarks of a classical musical, while also being a typically *British* movie, you could study it in the context of a history of the British musical and determine for yourself the extent to which this film conforms to type.

All of the above examples involve focusing on *texts*. However, contemporary British cinema could be narrowed to an industry-focused study, if you took as your object of analysis the health of the cinema industry. If that were the case, you could cull information about the financial well-being of the industry from the pages of the trade journals such as *Variety* and *Screen Finance*. Here you would be conducting primary analysis not on the films, but on company reports and industrial information found in press releases and financial news coverage. Potential titles for such a study could be 'The Rise of the British Film Industry since the 1990s' or 'The Impact of the Multiplex on Cinema Attendance'.

Alternatively, your object of analysis might lean towards the social uses of cinema-going. In this case you might be more interested in what people get out of going to the cinema, and wish to focus on audiences. If you looked at what people get out of a night out at the cinema, perhaps interviewing your own friends or colleagues at university, you would have the basis of an interesting investigation into the social uses of the cinema. Here you would be taking cinema-going as a social phenomenon and studying it from the perspective of the pleasures people get from the social aspect; the content of the texts themselves and of the industry which produced them might be completely irrelevant.

	Subject area	Focus of analysis	Examples of potential objects of analysis
TABLE 1.4 Moving from Subject Area to Object of Analysis	Contemporary British cinema	Texts	The representation of British-Asian culture in *Bhaji on the Beach*, *East is East* and *Bend it Like Beckham*
			The East End of London as location for gangster movies
			Billy Elliot as British musical
		Industry	The rise of the British film industry since the 1990s
			The impact of the multiplex on cinema attendance
		Audience	What people like about going to the movies
	Men's magazines	Texts	Analysis of the representation of women in men's magazines
			Comparison of product reviews in men's and women's magazines
		Industry	The rise and fall of the 'lads' mag': a case study of *Loaded*
		Audience	What do readers and non-readers think about men's magazines: a focus group study
	Television advertising	Texts	Advertisements and the representation of place: landscape as a signifier in television advertisements
		Industry	The impact of the expansion of commercial television on the advertising industry: comparing the 1950s with today
		Audience	Recall and impact of advertisements. What advertisements do people recollect and does it have an impact on purchasing?

The examples in Table 1.4 include various approaches to other topics given in Table 1.3, men's magazines and television advertising. The object of analysis for any study can be narrowed down by deciding on the focus of analysis. Both of these general subject areas lend themselves to multiple potential objects of analysis, depending on whether the researcher defines their main interest as primarily concerned with *texts*, *industries* or *audiences*. Table 1.4 offers some examples of objects of analysis under each category.

When you are narrowing your subject area to a workable object of analysis, it might be useful if you think about which of these areas interests you most. When you have decided whether it is the texts themselves, the ways the texts are produced or the ways the audiences understand and receive them, you will be on the way to developing your research question. The categories of *text*, *industry* and *audience* are those which are used in later chapters of this book.

Read around your subject area

When you have settled on your object of analysis, you should begin to read as much as you can about it. Read any key literature, but also read *around* your subject area; investigate related areas or similar topics for ideas on thoretical approaches and methods of analysis. The research project is an opportunity for you to add to the knowledge which already exists, but you can't do this until you are aware of what is already known and written about your subject (see Chapter 2 Sources and Resources). If you find that there are hundreds of books and articles on your object of analysis, you have probably not narrowed it sufficiently. Read the most frequently cited and/or recent books and articles on the topic and find out which are the main areas of contention. Could you find out something about these? Is there an area which the literature seems to have missed? Or a new phenomenon which the research hasn't caught up with yet? If, however, you find nothing has been written, you are probably not looking in the right place or you are being much too specific. Redefine your search terms and try again. As you read, take careful notes on what research has been done in your area of interest and by whom; you will need this information when you come to write your literature review (see Chapter 6, pages 159–60).

Think about theory

When you have settled on your object of analysis, the next stage is to consider *why* you are studying it. The matter of *why* brings in the central topic of *theory*. The importance of theory as a tool to help us think about things cannot be overvalued or overlooked. In doing original research at this level, we are unlikely to be developing new theoretical models or having dramatically profound theoretical insights. Our use of theory, then, is purely pragmatic: theories provide us with ways of thinking about our object of analysis. The purpose of theory is to help us.

In defining your object of analysis, I asked you to hone it down by thinking about what exactly interested you about your research area. In defining the theory, you are thinking about *why* you are interested in your object of analysis. What is it about your chosen subject that you find interesting? What theoretical approaches can you bring to bear on your investigation? This might be glaringly obvious or incredibly difficult to unpack depending on the exact nature of your question. But spending some time reflecting on why you are interested in this topic will bring to the fore the crux of your study. You need to draw on the existing literature, too; to think about how previous scholars have justified their research in this area. What theoretical approaches have been taken to your object of analysis? How have previous researchers explained why they are interested in the topic? Do their explanations have any resonance with your own interest in the area? What approaches have not been taken? Can you find a new coupling of object of analysis with theory that has not been tried before? The theoretical basis may be taken from key writers within the field such as Stuart Hall or David Morley. Alternatively you might choose to apply theories developed by leading intellectuals such as Jürgen Habermas or Michel Foucault. The theoretical paradigm is what gives you the *rationale* for your research. It should help you to justify your selection of subject and your method of analysis. The theoretical paradigm will help to explain *why* you are undertaking your project.

Choosing the right method

We have discussed the *what* and the *why* of your research project. The next stage in your planning is to think about *how* you are going to conduct your research. You will improve the overall quality of your work if you spend as much time thinking about *how* you are going to approach your subject as you did settling on the subject itself. The method of research you are going to adopt will depend largely on the object of analysis and the theoretical approach you are going to take (the *what* and the *why*). But before you can make a decision about what method to use, you need to be aware of the various paradigms for studying media and culture.

In the introduction, we briefly discussed the way research paradigms are typically categorized into *quantitative* and *qualitative* methods (see pages 2–4). The literal definitions of these are simple: a *quantitative* method is any kind of inquiry which uses numerical values, such as statistical research, certain kinds of survey research or any method which generates numbers. These are largely about measurement of one kind or another. In contrast, *qualitative* research is based on the interpretation of the world according to concepts which are typically not given numerical values, such as ethno-methodology or certain kinds of interview. These methods are considered to be interpretive (see Table 0.1, page 3 and discussion). Whether a researcher conducts quantitative or qualitative research has become a highly charged issue in social science, and the two sets of paradigms are typically presented as separate and distinctive (see, for example, Burns, 2000). The difference between qualitative and quantitative research methods may be great, but the differences in the kinds of questions asked are not always great – it is important to realize that *most research topics in media and cultural studies involve some measurement and some analysis – the two do not exist independently of each other.* Klaus Bruhn Jensen argues that 'for purposes of theory development as well as applications of media studies, it is crucial that researchers assess the relevance of different methodologies with reference to the purposes and objects of analysis, asking *what* and *why* before asking *how*' (Jensen, 1991a: 6).

While the main focus of this book is on *how* to do your research project, it is essential that your choice of method is fully predicated on *what* you want to study and *why*: the object of analysis and the theoretical approach should be the primary determinants of the method. In the subsequent chapters, we examine the methods of analysis available to the student according to the main object of analysis and try to avoid perpetuating the unhealthy distinction between 'quantitative' and 'qualitative' methods.

Rules of evidence in media, cultural and film studies

Every area of enquiry, whether it be in the natural or social sciences or in the humanities, has its own *rules of evidence*. This refers to the way in which arguments are made and evidence gathered. The underlying ideology behind the rules of evidence is sometimes referred to as the *epistemology*: the study of knowledge. How we can know anything, and, moreover, how we can prove what we know, are essential questions in any academic discipline. Within the classic scientific model, for example, knowledge is built through the observation of replicable experiments. The 'scientific method' has been applied to some areas of social science, but the rules of evidence are by no means fixed. In the fields of media and cultural studies, there is no consensus among scholars as to what the rules of evidence should be: some people (largely those with training in mass communications) tend towards using the models derived from the social sciences in which quantitative and qualitative methods are used fairly rigorously. Scholars within the cultural studies tradition, who may come from a background in the humanities, would be more likely to use hermeneutic methods of analysis typical of those employed in literary analysis. Whatever our background, we all aim to prove a point in our research: we have to have something to say, and we use our analysis of the media and of culture to support our claims. We have to present our work in such a way that any reasonable person reading it would agree with our conclusions based on the evidence we have presented. We talk about a project being *valid* if it is a well-designed piece of research which does what the researcher wants it to. Roger Sapsford puts it neatly when he says:

> To ask whether a study is valid – or rather, the *extent* to which it is valid –
> is to ask about the status of the evidence. We are asking whether what is
> presented as evidence can carry the weight of the conclusions drawn from
> it, or whether there is a logical flaw (in measurement, in sampling, in
> comparison) which makes the conclusions doubtful or at least detracts
> from our belief in them. (Sapsford, 1999: 9)

A valid piece of work should demonstrate the relationship between the object
of analysis and the method: the researcher should show that the choice of
method was the correct one to make the desired point. Regardless of whether
our work falls into the category of quantitative or qualitative research as
discussed above (see pages 2–4; 18–19). It should be both *valid* and *reliable*.
Reliability is a measure of how well the research is actually done and the
consistency of the findings. Research is said to be *reliable* when it has been
accurately and appropriately conducted.

Paradigms of research in media, culture and film studies

Although the categories of 'quantitative' and 'qualitative' may not be very
useful in a multidisciplinary field such as ours, we do need a way to define
different kinds of research. It is useful to think about the various ways we
conduct research according to two separate dimensions, which I have
labelled '*objective/interpretive*' and '*instrumental/abstract*'. Table 1.5
presents a schematic outline of these two dimensions of research, and it is
possible to position research on this map according to the extent to which it
is characteristic of these dimensions.

Let's start with the *objective/interpretive* dimension. This relates some-
what to the qualitative/quantitative distinction. It is useful to think about
research according to the kinds of claim the researcher is making for it. Some
researchers argue that their work is totally objective and not open to interpretation. They base their conclusions on scientifically argued grounds
relating to the design of their study: their findings are the product of the
method, and their own opinions or interpretation have little to do with
the outcome. Their work is judged according to the criteria of the *validity*
of the question, the *reliability* of the study and the *integrity* of the researcher
as *impartial*. In our field, this kind of research focuses on *factual* information
and tends to be largely descriptive. Examples of 'objective' research include
analysis of large sets of statistical data, such as audience numbers used in
gathering ratings data.

However, many researchers conduct enquiries which are fundamentally
interpretive. In this kind of research, scholars acknowledge that their findings

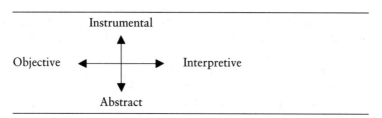

FIGURE 1.1
Dimensions of
Research
Paradigms in
Media and
Cultural Studies

depend on how the work is interpreted and may not be particularly valid according to researchers steeped in the objectivity of some social science research. Interpretive research acknowledges the limitations of enquiry and does not aspire to be all-knowing (a criticism sometimes made by such researchers of the more objective approach). The interpretive scholar relies on insight and judgement. The persuasiveness of an interpretive study depends on the rhetorical force with which the case is made. Examples include analyses of television programmes which focus on the themes and character portrayals. 'Interpretive' studies are less factual and more analytical in focus than their 'objective' counterpart.

In practice, these distinctions are very rough. Most research contains elements of both – even the most interpretive work will contain statements of fact which are objectively true. In recent years, the use of interpretive research has been accepted as an industry standard, with focus groups, for example, forming a mainstay of the market researchers' armament.

It is necessary to make a further distinction, which I have labelled '*instrumental/abstract*' (see Figure 1.1). For we need to distinguish between research which is done mainly for business or bureaucratic reasons, which we could call *instrumental* and research which has as its aim only the pursuit of abstract knowledge. In practice, these dimensions, too, are caricatures: most research has a functional, bureaucratic aim, even if that is only to expand the researcher's CV. But there is research which is more highly theoretical and has no particular business application. There is not necessarily a discrepancy between critical work (that is politically engaged) and empirical work (working with numbers and statistics). The Glasgow Media Group have engaged in what Greg Philo has called 'a critical media studies' for some time (Philo, 1999). Their research is 'empirically based and critical', according to Philo (1999: ix).

Because media and cultural studies take as their object of analysis a topic, there is no one method of research that you can use. Many disciplines in the sciences, for example, have a preferred method and canon of texts which everyone trained in that specialism must learn. This is one of the definitions of a discipline. Neither media nor cultural studies is a discipline in this sense: our field is a topic which we can use any method to study. However, the method must be appropriate to the particular area of the topic. For example, if you want to study the *representation* of gay people in soap operas, your method would be a *textual analysis* based on the analysis of images of lesbian and gay men in particular soaps. If you want to know what gay and lesbian people *think* about their representation in soap operas, you would base your research on *surveys and/or interviews*. It would be inappropriate to use interviews to analyse texts or to use textual analysis to study attitudes and opinions. Which method of analysis you use depends largely on your object of analysis. In analysing the portrayal of any group of people in any genre of programme (or film, book, or other form), you would use techniques appropriate to the study of texts. Matters of how frequently something is represented are best understood through *content analysis*, while questions of what those representations *mean* would be more directly answered by *semiotic analysis*. If you are interested in gay people's attitudes towards and opinions about the representation of their communities on television, you would be most concerned, not with the texts themselves, but with the audience – you would probably choose the focus group or the interview if you wanted to take this approach. However, if you think the appointment of a particular executive to the position of commissioning editor for that division has led to a change of policy regarding the representation of gay people, you should look at methods appropriate for the study of industry.

Research into media and culture can be divided into three broad areas, each with its own preferred paradigms of research: *texts*, *industries* and *audiences*. Within each of these areas, it is theoretically possible to employ any method used in the humanities or social sciences, but, in practice and by convention, each of these three areas has a different set of methods associated with it (see Tables 1.6, 1.7, and 1.8). Sometimes the use of a particular method to study a specific phenomenon is based on sound epistemological principles; sometimes it is simply a convention.

Studying media texts

If you are primarily interested in studying particular films, television programmes, pieces of music or museum exhibits, these can all be considered texts for our present purposes. The paradigms most frequently used in the analysis of texts derived initially from the study of literature. The field of hermeneutics is the classical precursor, although in modern times it is to the subject of English literature that we can look to see the most direct antecedents of textual analysis. Many approaches to media and cultural output have a great deal in common with analyses of novels and other forms of literature. In some cases, the analysis of texts has changed little since the development of English literature as a field in the early part of the twentieth century: methods which analyse the themes, plot or characterization of texts

	Object of analysis	Method	Example
TABLE 1.6 Methods for Studying Texts	How much of something occurs in a set of texts	Content analysis	Glasgow University Media Group (1976; 1980; 1982), *News studies*; Greg Philo (1996, 1999); Jane Stokes (1999a), 'girls' magazines'
	The meaning of a text or set of texts	Semiotics	Roland Barthes (1990), *Fashion*; Judith Williamson (1978), *Decoding Advertisements*
	The narrative structure of a text or set of texts	Narrative analysis	Vladimir Propp (1968); Arthur Asa Berger (1982), *The Prisoner analysis*
	A group of texts of the same kind or genre	Genre study	Jane Feuer (1982), *The Hollywood Musical*; Will Wright (1979), *Six-Guns and Society*
	A group of texts by the same 'author'	Auteur study	Lawrence S. Friedman (1999) on Martin Scorcese
	A group of texts featuring the same performer	Star study	Dyer (1982), *Stars*; (1987) *Heavenly Bodies* Holmes (2001) on Joan Crawford

derive from the study of the novel or poetry. Since the 1960s, there has been a strong influence from film studies and an expansion in the approaches available to analyse texts.

Table 1.6 shows the methods to be discussed in Chapter 3. Content analysis is the most empirical of the methods we will consider in our discussion of textual analysis: it is a method which relies on the gathering of numerical information about texts under examination. In Table 1.5, it would be located at the 'objective' end of the 'objective/interpretive' dimension, although there are many aspects of it which are interpretive, as we shall see in Chapter 3. You should choose this method if you are interested in *how much* of something occurs in a text or set of texts. Whenever you need quantitative values relating to the occurrence of particular phenomena in texts, content analysis is the best method to adopt. Content analysis should be used if your object of analysis is texts of some kind, and your theoretical question is about quantities. It has been used most widely to study how many news items cover what kinds of issues by the Glasgow University Media Group, who are perhaps the most prolific users of this method (Eldridge, 1993; Glasgow University Media Group, 1976, 1980, 1982; Philo, 1996, 1999).

If, however, you are primarily interested in the *meaning* of texts or images, semiotics is more appropriate to your needs. This method allows you to develop your own interpretation of your object of analysis by breaking down the text into its component units of meaning, or *semes*. This is often used in conjunction with content analysis to gain a multifaceted analysis of a set of texts: content analysis can give a value to how many of something occur, and semiotics can supply some interpretation as to what those occurrences mean. For example, we hypothesize that men's magazines cover sports less and in a less informed way than news magazines. We are interested in theories of masculinity and think that the images of sportsmen vary significantly in both media. A content analysis of how much sport coverage there is in men's magazines as opposed to news magazines would give you facts to support an argument about the relative coverage of sport in these two kinds of publications. You would be able to categorize the different representations of men to a certain extent by content analysis. A semiotic analysis of the nature of the coverage, the kinds of images carried and the types of features and stories these images support would give you an interesting study of the representation of sporting heroes.

If you were interested in studying the nature of the stories told about sportsmen in various publications, a very good method would be narrative analysis. This embraces a range of methods for looking at the structure of narratives in any media: it can be applied to film, television, songs, advertisements – any medium in which stories are being told. If your interest is mainly in the plot or storyline, in how it is that 'boy meets girl' in a particular set of texts, you should choose narrative analysis. The set of methods discussed in Chapter 3 under the rubric of 'typological methods' all derive from film studies and provide valuable insights into other media; these are *genre*, *auteur* and *star* studies. Table 1.6 gives examples of studies employing each of the main methods of investigating texts.

Studying the culture industries

The media industries have provided the object of analysis for research by media sociologists, economists, and critical scholars. There are many hundreds of different ways in which the media industries have been studied, deriving from almost every discipline; here I concentrate on those that students are most likely to research. These are presented in outline in Table 1.7.

The most typical method is *archive research*, which is used to investigate the contemporary and historical status of the culture industries. If you are interested in the history of a particular company or industry, archive research will probably be your primary method. Documents pertaining to, or produced by, the organizations you are studying will form your primary source.

	Object of analysis	Method	Example
TABLE 1.7 Methods for Studying Industries	History of specific institutions; history of media technologies; past policy debates; history of legislation	Archival research	Asa Briggs (1961–1995), *History of Broadcasting in the United Kingdom*
	History of broadcasting; social impact of media	Social history	Paddy Scannell and David Cardiff (1991), *A Social History of Broadcasting*; John Corner (1991), *Popular Television in Britain*
	Opinions and attitudes of industry workers	Interview	Lesley Henderson (1999), 'Producing serious soaps'; Kembrew McLeod (1999) 'Authenticity in hip-hop'
	Working practices of a company or organization; behaviour of workers in industry	Participant observation	Philip Schlesinger (1987), *Putting Reality Together*; Jackie Harrison (2000) *Terrestrial TV News in Britain*

If, however, you are interested in the history of industries from the point of view of the audiences, you will be conducting *social history*. In this case, your primary sources would also include documents pertaining to how the industry was understood in the broader society, perhaps through contemporaneous magazine and newspaper reports. The example of social history discussed here is Scannell and Cardiff's (1991) study of broadcasting as a cultural phenomenon. Most academic research based on archive research is fairly interpretive – the researcher must determine the significance of the documents being investigated.

Industries are not researched through archives alone; people are frequently excellent sources of information about the industries in which they work. If you are able to *interview* people in industry about their work, they can often provide interesting and important insights into the culture industries, as in Lesley Henderson's (1999) study of soap opera workers or Kembrew McLeod's study of workers in the hip-hop industry. The interview is a good method for getting at people's perceptions of what they are doing and to finding out about their attitudes towards and opinions of their work. Your main interest might be in what actually happens rather than what people tell you happens, in which case you should consider *participant observation*. This is a more intensive method than interviews in general, and depends on your being able to get access to the workplace itself and observe people in their normal work. Participant observation was the method employed by Philip Schlesinger in his (now) classic study of BBC newsroom workers, *Putting Reality Together* (1987), and by Jackie Harrison in her study (2000).

Most research projects can benefit from an understanding of the economic reality of the culture industries, and Chapter 4 includes some discussion of the type of information available for researchers in this area. Academic research is usually done in the interests of knowledge for its own sake, but that is not the case for the vast majority of research undertaken into the culture industries. Most of the documents which the researcher analyses will have been written for purely instrumental reasons by companies and organizations to gain a strategic advantage in the market place. The credibility of such documents is not necessarily reduced by their instrumentality, but you need to be aware of why information has been collected in order to discount any potential bias in the material you find.

Studying audiences

Audience research is another area of our topic which is extensively pursued by the culture industries for their own instrumental reasons. Indeed, the vast majority of audience research is not academic but bureaucratic in motivation. Television companies need to know how many people are watching which programmes; companies with products to advertise need to know what magazines their potential customers are likely to read. The kinds of research undertaken to investigate audiences' use of media and culture are presented in Table 1.8.

TABLE 1.8
Methods for
Studying
Audiences

Object of analysis	Method	Example
Behaviour of people in own environment	Observation	James Lull (1990), *Inside Family Viewing*; Liebes and Katz (1990) on *Dallas* viewers
People's responses to questions	Survey	Guy Cumberbatch (2000), *Television: The Public's View*
Audiences' reports of behaviour	Interview	David Morley (1986), *Family Television*
Attitudes, opinions and behaviour of groups	Focus group	Janet Wasko et al (2001) *The Global Disney Audiences Project* on Millwood Hargrave (2000) *Delete Expletives*
Memories of past behaviour and attitudes	Oral history	Tim O'Sullivan (1991), 'Television memories . . .'

Most academic research concerns the impact of the media on the people who use it, on the meanings and interpretations people get out of the media. One of the methods adopted by media scholars to the study of audiences is participant observation. As in the study of industries, this involves studying the behaviour of people in their natural environment – in this case, usually their own home. James Lull (1990) has concentrated on the observation of audiences watching television, and he uses methods derived from ethnography. This very labour-intensive method is relevant only if your research question is about precisely how people use the media, and it is applicable only to certain kinds of media use. *Survey research* is a more adaptable method for studying audiences, although it relies on subjects' reports of their own behaviour, attitudes and opinions. Survey research is widely used by the industry, too, and the case study used in this chapter is from Guy Cumberbatch's work, which was commissioned by the Independent Television Commission (ITC) (Cumberbatch, 2000). Within media and cultural studies, a more typical method of studying audiences is the *interview*, and David Morley's (1986) work offers several examples of how this approach can provide interesting insights into the audiences of the media. More recently, the *focus group* has found favour with researchers at the instrumental and the abstract end of the research scales. Focus groups have become widely used by the industry and also by academics. The example given here is from Andrea Millwood Hargrave's work, which includes focus groups among its methods (Millwood Hargrave, 2000). Audience research usually concentrates on people's current use of the media and culture, but there is no reason why this should be so: there has been some very interesting research on the history of audience by the method of *oral history*. If you are interested in people's memories of their past use of media or culture, this is an ideal method to use (and the past does not have to be the distant past – you could interview people in your class about their memories of television in their school years, for instance).

Your method of analysis, then, will differ according to the nature of your object of analysis – if you are interested in people's ideas and opinions you will use different methods than if you were interested in their behaviour. This book covers only those methods which it is feasible for a final-year undergraduate to undertake, so not all paradigms are covered.

Combining research methods

By conducting two or more methods of research, you can often achieve a more textured understanding of your object of analysis. The idea of 'triangulation' is that one method confirms or reinforces another. Thus, interviews can provide a reinforcement of what one suspects from reading archives. Here we look at the ways in which methods of analysing texts, industries and audiences can be combined and discuss some examples from the literature of how this has been done in the past.

There are times when you might want to combine methods of audience research to get a more nuanced picture of a phenomenon. Many researchers have used surveys followed up by in-depth interviews: the survey generates data of a broad scope but little context; interviews are then used with a smaller subset of the original sample to get more detailed, contextual information. Andrea Millwood Hargrave's study of attitudes towards offensive language, for example, used both surveys and interviews (Millwood Hargrave, 2000). In the first phase of the study, surveys were administered to find out how people ranked particular words; this was then followed up with focus groups to discover why people found certain words offensive, and not others. In studying audiences, it is not unusual to combine a broad method such as questionnaire survey with a more textured one such as the focus group or the open-ended interview.

There will often be situations when your object of analysis does not fit neatly into the three categories of 'texts', 'audiences' and 'industries' I have used in this book. Sometimes you will be interested in the relationship between texts and readers, or between producers and their audiences. In such cases, it is sometimes appropriate to conduct two separate studies, using different methods, and compare the findings.

In Chapter 4, we will discuss interviewing people in the industry and in Chapter 5 interviewing audiences. Sometimes, though, it is valuable to interview producers and receivers of the same text, as Dorothy Hobson did in her study of the British soap opera, *Crossroads* (1982). Hobson interviewed staff at ATV, the production company behind *Crossroads*, including actors, casting directors and producers, as well as interviewing audiences for this popular but much denigrated television series. Hobson had more time, resources and access than most readers of this book.

The key to combining methods is to know why you are doing it. Don't make access your only criterion – always have a good rationale for why you are combining two methods, and think about what this adds to your study.

A word of warning, though. As a general principle, it is better to do one thing well than to do several things shoddily. I am not an advocate of the 'scattergun' approach to research which says that if you look at your subject from as many angles as possible you will get the fullest picture possible. It is more pragmatic to define exactly what you want to look at and think carefully about what you are doing and why. The thinking phase may be time-consuming, but it is cheap and it doesn't hurt anyone! When you have limited time and resources, as most people reading this book do, it is better to spend your time constructing a well-designed study of one aspect of the media or culture.

FIGURE 1.2

Designing a
Research
Question

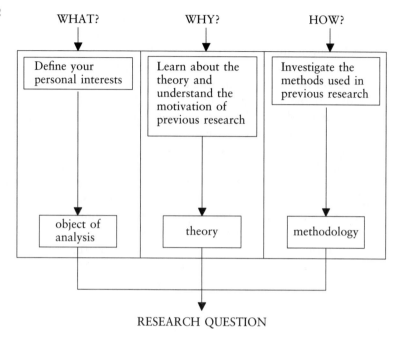

Phrasing your research question

Your research question, then, should include an indication of the object of analysis, the theoretical background and the method to be used. Each of these should complement the others, and your question should be phrased in such a way as to give an indication of what is involved in all three areas. Figure 1.2 presents a flow chart summarizing how these three elements relate to your research question.

Before you can determine the final wording of your research question, you will need to ensure that you can answer the following three questions:

1. What are you going to research?
2. Why is this a topic of interest?
3. How are you going to conduct your research?

The research question may or may not be the title of the project – you may want to give your project a more sexy and catchy title. If it is not the title, the research question should be clearly stated within the first paragraph in one concise sentence. Your research question should be on a topic which will sustain your interest for the duration of the study. Don't choose a subject which you know you will get bored of – make sure the topic is something you can commit yourself to working with.

If yours is a hypothesis-driven question, you must be able to express your project idea in the form of 'a statement which can be proved'. The task of conducting research must be directed towards proving something, preferably something which has not been proved before. It is a rhetorical requirement of writing academic essays that you must state what you intend to prove in the form of a hypothesis. This will be the product of your knowledge of the subject area derived from your studies to date, your reading and your own experience.

The use of hypotheses in media and cultural research is part of the adoption of scientific method. Scientific method is the standardized procedure by which scientists find answers to questions; it typically involves building on knowledge through replicable experiments. A clear hypothesis will help guide your research. Hypotheses can come in different forms. For example, they can be comparative: 'people like soap operas better than documentaries' or 'Internet dissemination is faster than video'. Alternatively, they can relate to a norm, as in the statement, 'Moving ITN news undermines the public service remit of commercial television'. Your hypothesis will set you off on a pattern of enquiry which will result in proving or disproving the statement to a greater or lesser degree.

Most research questions or hypotheses are *comparative* – comparing a text or set of texts with something. You can study a set of texts against a *hypothesis*, testing, for example, whether the news is biased in the way it represents a particular group, or whether Eminem's lyrics are misogynistic. You might study the themes against a *normative* ideal. For example, how sensitively do the social realistic themes of soap operas deal with topical issues? Or, should girls' magazines include sexualized images of boys?

If you are using people of any age as subjects, make sure that you are not exposing them to any harm, physical or psychological. If you have any doubt, consult your tutor and find out about the university's *human subjects policy*, or *ethical research policy*. It is not generally considered ethical to conduct research on children unless you are a very experienced researcher. There are serious ethical considerations involved in showing children media material they might not otherwise see, whether these are 'violent' videos or ordinary advertising messages. Children are not able to give informed consent to take part in a study because they don't understand what is involved.

Identifying sources and resources

What you decide to examine for your project will invariably be influenced by what you can access: it is impossible to research media texts audiences or institutions if you can't get hold of the relevant object of analysis. If you are interested in doing a textual analysis of some obscure films, for example, make sure you can get hold of viewing copies of them before your commit yourself to that subject. You will probably write a better project if you use films readily available for purchase or loan, if only because you won't spend so much time trying to get hold of them. If you are interested in researching audiences, why not use your friends, neighbours and family as resources? University students make good subjects (they are easy to get hold of and can easily be bribed). Your friends are probably interested in your work, and might well be flattered if you ask them to help out. Most social science research prides itself on its impartiality and considers that impartiality is not possible if their subjects are personally known to researchers, but it is impractical for students to take such an approach. As a student, you may have reservations about asking complete strangers to be respondents in your studies, and you should not be pressured into doing this if you don't want to. However, if you need lots of questionnaire responses, your fellow students are usually suitable to approach, even if you don't know them personally. Students in the canteen or bar may be willing to spend five or ten minutes answering your questionnaire. People who share your interests and lifestyle are often willing to help out, so think about asking neighbours or members of your church or fellow music fans if they are interested. One student of mine wrote an excellent project based on a survey of fellow members of the Beatles fan club. You will find that people with the same enthusiasms and interests are more than happy to talk about their obsession. If you have worked in a study group successfully during the rest of your academic career, encourage the rest of the group to keep meeting during the project: you will all benefit from discussing your ideas and progress with one another and it will help prevent you from feeling isolated. If you need to have interview subjects for your project, the study group is an ideal source.

Primary and secondary sources

Your sources; the material you are going to use (be it people, books, films or whatever), can be thought of as falling into two categories: *primary* and *secondary* sources. A primary source is the material which makes up your object of analysis; it comprises what you are actually going to study. While you are planning your study, you will read work by other people who have conducted their own primary analysis, but the work done by others comprises a secondary source for you. Thus, if you are writing about the films of Takeshi Kitano, the film *Hana-Bi* (1997), which he directed, wrote and starred in, would be a primary source: you would study the film and conduct your own analysis of it. As part of your research, though, you would want to see what other people thought of the film, and you would read books, articles and reviews about Takeshi Kitano and his films: these materials would all comprise secondary sources. It is quite possible that the same material might comprise a primary source in one study and a secondary source in another, depending on the object of analysis. If, for example, you wanted to analyse the responses from British film critics to Kitano's movies, you would use as your object of analysis the reviews in film magazines – these would now be the primary source. A television documentary about Steven Spielberg would be a primary source if you were studying how television constructs a particular view of film-makers, but if you were studying the films of Spielberg, it would be a secondary source, providing background information on the director. Where the object of analysis is audiences, the primary source will always be your subjects' responses. If you were interested in people's responses to the controversial campaign for the clothing company French Connection, which used the letters 'fcuk' in their campaign, your object of analysis (and your primary source) would be what your subjects actually say about these advertisements. You might use examples of the ads as prompts in focus groups or interviews, but the advertisements themselves would not comprise primary sources for your research.

In our field, it is sometimes difficult to draw the line between primary and secondary sources because we draw upon so many different media in our work. In general, whatever medium you are studying provides the primary source – thus, the soap operas themselves are the primary source for a study of *EastEnders* or *Coronation Street*, while television programmes about the soaps might provide secondary sources. If you are looking at the tabloid-ization of the press, the newspapers are the primary source and the books and articles which have been written about them (some of which may well appear in newspapers) comprise the secondary source. While you are doing original research, you are working with a primary source; when you are reading around your research, you are conducting secondary research. Your primary sources must be clearly explained and identified in your discussion of methods; if there are many of them, they should be listed in your appendix (see Chapter 6, page 63).

Reviewing the literature

Your research question should be addressing something new; you need to ensure that you are not reinventing the wheel by reading as much as you can get hold of about what has been written on your subject. You can begin with the documents used on your course: if you took a course on the subject area you are interested in, begin by looking at the reading list. Next, do a search of the library catalogue of your university to find out if there are any books on the subject. Get these out of the library and think about whether you want to get involved in this debate. Use the bibliography of books and articles to find more titles which may be relevant to you. If you find yourself reading a book from cover to cover, stop – you should be much more careful to read only what you have to read. You need to read widely and to think a lot about what you are reading. It is rarely necessary to read everything. It is a good idea to get in the habit of making decisions quickly about whether a book or article is going to be of relevance to you. In the first instance, you should aim to spend between three and five minutes deciding whether a book or article is going to be of any use to you. This is long enough to determine from the title and the chapter and section headings whether the book has any relevance to your topic. If it does, spend a further ten minutes scanning the contents of the relevant chapters or sections: look at the headings and the first sentence of each paragraph only. Make a note of the title, author and other details, and then put the book aside and write down the main topics covered and a couple of sentences about how it relates to your research question. Then move on to the next book or article. Aim to skim through several books and articles in this way, drawing up a list of from five to ten of the most useful texts. When you have made a list of the books, articles and websites which you have identified as being relevant, assess the importance of each one to you – you should not read the entire piece until and unless you have ascertained by skimming and speed reading that it is directly relevant to your subject. If you find four to ten books or articles that you will read and use in detail, you are doing very well. Most of the material you read will be relevant only as background reading, and you don't need to do more than scan it.

In writing your project, remember that you will not get your answers from books but from conducting your own research. The literature you read will usually provide you with secondary sources, which you must use to your own advantage. Be sure to get a balance between primary and secondary research: both are important parts of the project. Remember that one of the key criteria for assessing the project is usually that you can show that you can conduct original research. The requirement to show how your work fits into the field is usually less important, but remember that you are reading to demonstrate how your work fits in with previous literature. Don't waste time reading irrelevant things, however interesting they may be, and make sure that you don't get bogged down in reading more widely than is necessary. Your time is precious, and there will be lots of time for reading in more detail when you have graduated!

See Chapter 2 for more information on identifying sources and resources for your project.

Beginning to write your project

Now that you have read this chapter, I hope you are feeling more confident about how to conduct your project than you did at the beginning. You

TABLE 1.9	Your research question
Contents of a	A definition of your object of analysis
Project	A description of your primary sources
Proposal	An overview of the secondary sources you will consult
	A preliminary literature review indicating where your work fits into the field
	A timescale for your study
	Sample 'instrument' such as questionnaire or coding sheet
	What you hope to find
	Bibliography and indication of further reading

should have come up with a question for your research project and begun to look into the available literature on the topic. In the following section, we are going to look at how to conduct the first main piece of writing involved in the project: the proposal or outline.

Designing a proposal

Whether it is a requirement for completion of your project or not, it is highly recommended that you write a proposal or outline (see Table 1.9). You need to get down on paper exactly what you are planning to do, and you need to show it to your tutors and listen to what they say about it! Getting feedback on your proposal before you begin is essential.

Table 1.9 shows the main components of the proposal. Your proposal should include your research question: state very clearly what your object of analysis is going to be. Indicate how you are going to access it (for example, are you going to record episodes off air of television programmes, hire videos from the local store, or make photocopies of newspaper articles in your public library). Your proposal should include a schedule with sensible estimates of how long things should take. Draw up a detailed timetable of when you need to get things done by, starting with the submission date and working backwards. Plan your work carefully and realistically, allowing yourself lots of time to write up your findings – allow at least one-third of the available time just for writing, so if you have one twelve-week semester in which to conduct the entire project, make sure you leave the last four weeks just to write up the project. You should allow one-third of the time to do preliminary research, organization, writing your proposal and reviewing the literature.

Get going with any arrangements which involve other people as soon as possible – you don't want to rely on being able to interview people in March, only to find out that they take their annual vacation then. Make sure you can get access to any libraries or special collections, and book appointments as early as possible in your timetable.

Note taking

Make sure that you keep very good notes as you research your work. Write down the full bibliographic details of every book, article, newspaper or website that you even glance at – you never know whether you will need to go back to it later. Make sure that if you are going to quote from a television programme or other non-written source, you get the full details (see Chapter 6, 'Notes on references' pp. 165–70, for discussion of bibliographic conventions).

Take care not to confuse your *notes* and your *quotes*. A common cause of *plagiarism* is students accidentally copying as their own words someone else's work and not acknowledging it as a quotation. Deliberate plagiarism is a form of cheating and nearly always results in expulsion from university. Even if you reference the work, you should not copy directly except as a quotation (see Chapter 6 for further discussion). In your note-taking, be wary of using the words of others: when copying text or different pages in your notebook, use one colour of ink for actual words from texts and a different colour of ink for your own commentary. It is good to précis the work of others – but get into the habit of writing précis of ideas and concepts without having the original in front of you. In fact, whenever you are writing your own thoughts and ideas, you should not have anything in front of you except a blank piece of paper or computer screen. Do not use actual quotations until you get to the 'writing up' stage of the work and then go back to your sources again.

Working from an outline or proposal

Plan your work carefully and make sure that you know what you are doing and why! Use your proposal as a foundation for your subsequent work. Make a point-by-point account of what you want to say for each section of the project. Read to fill the gaps. Once you have started your project, you should not read any more 'background' material – everything has to be directly relevant to what you are working on.

Discussion

Getting started is one of the most difficult parts of writing your research project, as you have some very important decisions to make. You need to spend time thinking about the issues and deciding what is really interesting and relevant to you. You should settle on something which will sustain your interest through the duration of the assignment. Have a look at the questions

TABLE 1.10	1. Does your research question make sense?
Checklist for	2. Is the project feasible? (can you do it in the time available?)
Your Project	3. Do you have access to your primary material?
Design	4. Can you locate sufficient appropriate secondary sources?
	5. Have you discussed your idea with your supervisor?
	6. Is your question original?
	7. Does your question build on previous research?

in the checklist for your project design (Table 1.10). Can you answer every question honestly and fully? Don't go on with the project until you are able to address all the points raised.

Time management and the project

One of the main problems students have in general is managing their time efficiently. Today's students must often combine their studies with work, and many have family responsibilities which make it difficult to concentrate on their studies exclusively. Writing the project can sometimes present additional difficulties in terms of time management, as most people find working on an independent research project a challenge. Be warned that you have to exercise very strong self-discipline in undertaking the research project. Often the only deadline your university will give you is the final one – when that is several months away, it is sometimes tempting to get on with other things and put the project on the back burner. This is asking for trouble! When you are working on the project, you have to organize your own time. Get out your diary now and think about when you can spend time on your project. Ideally, you should try and do a little every day and set aside an hour each day to focus on the project. You might also try to think about how to integrate studying for the project into your everyday routine. For example, every time you go to the library, find some references for the project; every time you see a friend whom you like to talk to about ideas, have a chat about how your work is going; every time you pick up a book for another class, have a look and see if there is any information relevant to your project. Try to write something every day if you can, and give yourself regular time slots during the week when you can work on the project. A little bit regularly will get the job done more efficiently than leaving yourself a block of time at the end when there may well be other pressures which you are not able to foresee now. The extent to which students are left alone to conduct their project will differ according to what institution they are at and, sometimes, according to the personality of their supervisor. I would advise you to arrange several meetings with your supervisor and to make sure that you keep to them. Regular meetings to talk over how things are progressing (even if they are not going particularly well) are very important in helping to keep the project at the top of your agenda.

Many students write the project in their final year when there are several other important distractions which can make them forget to focus on their project. Remember that the project is one of the few opportunities you get to do your own research, and think about things which are of interest to you. Make the most of it. Enjoy!

2 Sources and Resources

Chapter overview

This chapter presents an overview of some of the sources and resources you can use in researching your project. The chapter is divided into two main parts: the first, *Media and academic sources*, examines the various ways in which you can identify and locate media resources and academic literature on your topic. Included here are some pointers on how to use indexes, catalogues, electronic databases and websites (Appendix 2 includes further discussion of websites and is handy to consult when you are using the Internet for your research). There are several different kinds of sources and resources available to the researcher in media and cultural studies, the number and availability of which are subject to constant change. The second part of the chapter attempts to pin down some *other sources of information* and discusses their relative usefulness for academic research. Various bodies, including trade organizations, production companies and government agencies, provide information about diverse aspects of the media and culture industries and consumers. This chapter discusses how we can use some of these sources in our own research.

Introduction

There is a vast array of sources available to you, and the range of material accessible to students has expanded phenomenally since the introduction of the Internet. The number of journals and books published in media and cultural studies has also grown, and students and lecturers alike often find it difficult to keep up. In any research project, it is important to ensure that you have access to the necessary resources in the planning stage. You should make sure that you can get research copies of any media artefact which constitutes your object of analysis: in other words, if you are writing about the changing representation of women in Quentin Tarantino's films, make sure you have access to copies of all his films before you finalize the topic. Don't make life more difficult than necessary by embarking on a project to investigate material that you might not be able to lay your hands on. Of course, more and more of the films and television programmes of the past are becoming available for domestic consumption through new technologies of distribution and reception, especially the DVD. This and other forms of digital technology have made much more media output accessible to scholars, albeit in an altered viewing situation from the original. The Internet is another technology which brings innumerable archives to a broader public, including the media student. The enormous changes in media technology in recent years have enhanced the availability and range of potential primary resources for us.

Secondary sources in the form of literature relating to the media and culture are also becoming more freely available. The information revolution brought about by increasing use of computer technology has led to some of this change. In addition, though, the expansion of publishing in academia, fuelled in Britain by new methods of funding, means that there are ever more books and journals published in our area.

Given the growth in the new technologies of media recording, distribution and storage, many of the suggestions in this chapter may well have been rendered obsolete or old-fashioned by the time you read this! You should thoroughly research the material available to you locally, as well as via the Internet, before you begin your project.

Media and academic resources

Locating media resources

Many formats of media are now readily available for purchase in the high street. Alongside the traditional music, you can find films, television programmes and radio broadcasts in your local HMV or Virgin. Bookshops often stock a range of media and can often order material for you. There are now multiple formats, and the back catalogues of film and broadcasting companies are providing their owners with lucrative second markets. These provide a wonderfully rich and varied resource for us and are fuelling a renaissance in film and television scholarship. Publishers are not always the friend of the scholar, though, and it is not certain how long these films will remain in print. Don't be caught out by finding that the films you wanted to research have suddenly gone 'out of print': research their availability early and realize that the shelf-life of media artefacts can be short.

Your local video/DVD store is a good source to try for things that are out of print, as is your university or local library. If the libraries locally are poor at maintaining their stock, it would be socially responsible of you to pressurize them into buying more in that area: use your university Board of Studies or Student Committee to put forward your case. In the meantime, the British Universities Film and Video Council (BUFVC) keeps an archive of material which is accessible to students under certain conditions – find out about them through the Internet or via your librarian (www.bufvc.ac.uk).

The British Film Institute (BFI) is another source for film and television programmes, but its archive, at the time of writing, is not very extensive nor very accessible to students. However, plans are afoot to improve this, so check with the library (address listed in Appendix 1) or with its website to find out about availability of material (www.bfi.org.uk). The BFI is a terrific source for books, periodicals and trade journals on all aspects of the film and television industries, however, and anyone researching these areas should find out about its collection.

If you are researching newspapers and magazines, you should first try to find out what your university or local public library keeps. You might be surprised at how much material librarians retain. The main repository for newspapers and magazines in Britain is the British Library Newspaper Library at Colindale (see Appendix 1 for details of the British Library's collections). This is a terrific resource for anyone researching the British press and publishing. The British Library is also home to the National Sound Archive, and there is a wealth of material for the musicologist and radio researcher here.

Today, of course, many archives are accessible electronically, and most have websites describing their collections and access policies. The best way to find out whether a media artefact is published or whether there is a collection relevant to your interests is to conduct preliminary research on the Internet by punching relevant search terms into your favourite search engine.

Using your university library

Despite advances in the provision of electronic information, libraries still provide the main resource for most kinds of research. Your own university or college library should be your first port of call in any research project. Ensure that you know what the library stocks in the way of media you may want to use for primary research. If a particular item is not held in the collection, ask what the procedure is for acquiring it; perhaps it can be ordered for you. This takes time, and that is another reason why you need to identify resources early in the project. Make sure that you are familiar with the range of *books* and *journals* available to you, but also ensure that you know what material is available via your university Intranet, library and/or information services department.

Find out if there are any special workshops on conducting independent research in the library; if there aren't any, ask your tutor or librarian if it is possible to organize one for your class. Most libraries these days are expanding their electronic provision at a very rapid pace, and although you might have had the university tour in your first year, there have probably been changes since then. Most students could benefit from a tour of the available resources once they reach the stage of conducting independent research.

Locating specialist libraries

There are numerous libraries and archives which are of direct interest to the media and cultural researcher. A list of some of these can be found in Appendix 1: 'Libraries and Archives of Interest'. Check out which ones are local to you and find out what resources are available in the local university and/or public libraries. Using a search engine to conduct a search on your subject might well turn up other physical or electronic libraries.

Academic journals

The most academically valid sources for you to consult are articles published in academic journals. Academic journals are where scholars publish their latest research. In current issues of the leading media and cultural studies journals, you will find the most cutting-edge research. Journals are usually edited by academics and are targeted at academics. If you are at the beginning of your research career, you may find that some of the articles are difficult to understand. This may be because they are very theoretical in approach, or because they use methods with which you are not very familiar. There are hundreds of journals in the area of media and cultural studies. Some of the most useful are listed below:

Convergence
Cultural Studies
Historical Journal of Film and Television
Journal of Popular Culture
Media, Culture and Society
Media History
New Formations
Screen
Television and New Media
Theory, Culture and Society.

You will need to use an index to find out what has been published of relevance to your project.

Using indexes and catalogues

In order to find what has been published, you need to be aware that there is a wealth of indexes, catalogues and databases at your disposal, with which you should familiarize yourself early in the research-planning stage. Your university library catalogue will be your first port of call to find out about relevant books and journals.

Book catalogues are the easiest and most direct way of finding literature on your chosen subject. You should be familiar with searching the book catalogue of your university or college library; if in doubt, pick up a leaflet or attend one of the sessions held by the library staff. Public libraries and academic libraries have their catalogues held on searchable databases, which you can use either in the library or remotely. The British Library catalogue is also available via most university library information services – this lists the holdings of the British Library. Unfortunately, the British Library is not accessible to undergraduate students, and postgraduate students need to get a letter from their course leader before they can use the facilities – check with the library itself before going there. The contents of the British Library are available via interlibrary loan, but this service can take time – if you need to use a book in the British Library you should order it via your library as early as possible.

Databases such as the *British Humanities Index* should be available to you via your university library. This indexes the literature published in hundreds of journals, magazines and newspapers. In order to find out what journal articles have been published on your topic, you will need to consult a relevant index such as the *Arts and Humanities Citation Index*. Indexes contain details of literature published in journals indexed by subject and/or author. They enable you to track down information published in the relevant academic journals. Journals provide the most up-to-date sources of literature about media and cultural studies, and you should consult the latest issues of these to find out what the latest research is. Indexes are increasingly available on-line, but are also published in book form. The *Film Literature Index* (State University of New York at Albany, quarterly), for example, gives bibliographic details of articles appearing in over 300 film periodicals from around the world. It has a comprehensive list of index terms, so you can look up topics relating to film and find where articles have been published. For example, if we want to find what has been written about films about sport, we could look up 'sport' or 'football' as a topic and find details of articles that have been written on that subject. If we look up 'boxing' in the latest available issue (vol. 28, no. 2), we find one entry:

> — BOXING IN FILM. [Prior to V26, 1998 use SPORTS IN FILM]
> "Farred, G. Feasting on Foreman: the problematics of postcolonial identification. Il port CAM OBS n39: 52–77 Sep 1996"

We can see from the cross-reference that in earlier volumes we would find articles about boxing in film under 'sports in film'. The main part of the entry tells us that only one article has been catalogued about boxing and film in this issue, and that it was published in *Camera Obscura* and written by G. Farred. It also gives us the issue number, pages of the article and date, so we can retrieve the article for ourselves. From the title, we know that it is about George Foreman, and the fact that the title includes the term 'postcolonial identification' leads us to think that it is about the fact that Foreman is an African-American. So we can quite readily tell whether it is likely to be relevant to our research topic and make an informed decision about whether we need to read it. There are similar indexes for literature of all kinds, and you will need to ask your librarian which ones are housed in your library in hard copy or electronic form.

Tracing information about journal articles on particular films is made easy by the SIFT database. This electronic database is published by the BFI and is available through libraries. It catalogues literature about film and television. It is searchable by:

1   titles (of films, television programmes, series, etc.)
2   personalities (performers, directors, scriptwriters and so on)
3   organizations (studios, publishers, production companies)
4   events (festivals, screenings and the like)
5   subjects (of articles in indexed periodicals)
6   periodical holdings in the BFI.

If you want to find out what has been written about a particular film, director or film genre, this is the place to start. The SIFT database also contains information about television, although this collection is more patchy.

Other sources of information

Sources of general information

Most public organizations and several private companies publish detailed information about their activities and are only too willing to provide these to students. If you are interested in the work of a particular organization, call or write and ask them to send you their press pack. The public relations or market research departments of most companies provide information of a general nature to people who want to know more about how they work. The Internet is also used by companies and organizations to publish details of their activities. Most organizations now find it convenient to have a 'web presence', and this provides a very valuable resource for the media researcher: several government organizations, industry bodies and private companies have excellent websites that are very useful for students doing research.

Often it is necessary to find general information such as who was the Prime Minister at a particular time or who produced a particular television programme. Encyclopaedias are the most obvious source for such background information, and your university or local public library will have hard copies of these. There are sources of general information available for such background research. The Internet makes many sources of general information readily available, so try looking here if you can't find what you need in the reference section of your library. Specialist encyclopaedias are published on various aspects of the media and culture industries; search your library catalogue by a relevant key word to find them.

Trade organizations

One of the advantages of the 'information revolution' is that there is abundant information available on all aspects of corporate and public life. Most companies, including media companies, publish information about their work on the Internet and in annual reports which are readily accessible to the researcher. At the same time, there is a plethora of organizations in support of the media industries, such as the Periodical Publishers Association (PPA), or the Independent Television Commission (ITC), which publish data about their industries. Several agencies function as 'independent' monitors of the media and culture industries. Most of the trade organizations publish information for commercial reasons, and not for the benefit of scholars. This does not mean that the information may not be useful to you, but you should be wary of what you read.

The publishing industry is well served by a number of well-established sources including *Willings Press Guide*, British Rate and Data (BRAD), and the Audit Bureau of Circulations (ABC). The ABC is the body responsible for collecting information on the circulation of magazines and newspapers. It was founded in 1931 to provide the advertising industry with reliable data about newspaper and magazine circulations. This information is vital to advertisers in determining in which periodicals to advertise. The ABC is governed by a council of representatives from the advertising and periodical publishing industries. It maintains records of the circulation of magazines and newspapers and is the accepted authority on how many copies are circulated of any publication in Britain. In 1996, the ABC added an electronic division, ABCE (www.abce.org.uk), to audit and report website activity. In 2002, the ABC began to work in alliance with the Association of Exhibition Organizers (www.aeo.org.uk). ABC information is considered highly reliable and is used extensively in the industry. The ABC has an excellent website which is easily searchable to obtain information on current circulations of newspapers and magazines in Britain (www.abc.org.uk). Most magazines and newspapers published in the UK are included in the ABC's data. You can use this site to find out the circulation of any magazine or newspaper audited by the ABC. ABC data is published in *Willings Press Guide*, a trade directory which contains useful information about the press and publishing industries. The other major source of data about circulations is BRAD, which publishes bulletins every three months with the latest figures on circulations. All of the trade sources mentioned above relate to magazines and newspapers and are aimed primarily at prospective advertisers.

If you want to know how many people watch *Brookside* relative to *EastEnders*, you don't need to do your own research. The information is readily available in trade journals such as *Television* or *Broadcast*. It is not difficult to find out *how many* in relation to audiences because the media industries make it their business to know; they need the data for their own internal purposes as well as for advertising and promotion. There is a wealth of published data already available to tell you how many people watch a particular programme. The Broadcasters' Audience Research Board (BARB) has one of the most comprehensive websites on audience statistics (www.intellagencia.com).

The radio industry, too, generates a great deal of data about itself that is publicly available. One particularly useful and informative website in presenting its methods is that of Radio Joint Audience Research Ltd (RAJAR) (www.rajar.co.uk). RAJAR provides the radio industry with audience ratings, and it has a good explanation on its website of how its data is collected. Here you can find out who owns which radio station, and how big the audience is for all British radio stations. This is very useful to students interested in conducting survey research of audiences.

Trade directories

The media industries are well served by various directories and handbooks, which typically include contact details of the companies and organizations involved in the industry. For example, *The Blue Book* (Mann, 2000), the standard guide to the British broadcasting industry, includes a directory of broadcasters and producers. The PACT Directory of Independent Producers (PACT, 2000) is the trade directory published by the producers' alliance for cinema and television, while the IVCA (International Visual Communication Association) publishes the *IVCA Business Media Handbook*. The film industry is well served by the *BFI Film and Television Handbook* (Dyja, 2001). BRAD, the standard directory for the publishing industry, contains a very comprehensive listing of magazines and newspapers and their advertising rates. In addition, BRAD includes detailed analysis of the latest developments in the industry, including which titles have folded and which are new.

Trade directories are valuable resources for finding the names and addresses of people in key positions in the industry and within particular companies. They are very useful if you want to find the names and addresses of potential subjects for a survey, for example. You should also use trade directories to find the contact details of potential employers and use the information provided to do some background research before attending an interview for work experience or employment.

Trade journals

One of the most widely used and readily available sources of information about media audiences is the trade journal. Every industry has its own trade journal to keep its readers up to date with the latest developments in the field. The media industry has several. Some of these are devoted to media in the advertising industry sense of 'companies which sell advertising space'. For example, *MediaWeek* is especially aimed at the advertising industry but contains news, information and statistics about all aspects of the media business. It has a good website with lots of industry information: www.mediaweek.co.uk. The leading trade journal for the creative side of the advertising industry is *Campaign*, which also has an informative website: www.campaignlive.com. These magazines are aimed at people in the various media industries who want to keep up to date. Trade journals carry lots of information about audiences for the commercial media – this is used by advertising executives to decide where to place advertisements for their products.

The broadcasting industry is well served by trade journals. *Broadcast* is 'the weekly newspaper for the television and radio industry' and contains news about all aspects of the broadcasting industries, including who signed deals with whom, the latest news on executive employment and new initiatives in the industry. It also lists ratings for the week two weeks prior to the publication date. Back issues of *Broadcast* can be used to find out what programmes attracted the highest number of viewers in any week. It also includes job listings and advertisements for production facilities.

The most important trade journal in the film business is probably *Variety* (www.variety.com). This is particularly strong on the Hollywood film industry, but includes features on the cinema around the world. The international editions carry details of US and International box-office receipts for the week before the publication date. Film reviews make up a large part of the copy, and these are written with the distributors and exhibitors as the primary audience. *Variety* covers all the major film festivals around the world and publishes feature articles on film companies. Originally aimed at the theatre world, *Variety* carries news, information and advertisements relevant to the stage, which it labels 'legit' theatre.

Trade journals frequently carry features which would be of value to students of the contemporary media scene, and previous issues are a valuable resource for researching the media and culture industries. You should find these trade journals in your university library in hard copy or in searchable CD-ROM form – ask whether your library can subscribe to them if it doesn't already.

Production companies

By far the most obvious form of media institution is the producer. Publishing houses, television production companies and film studios are all media institutions involved in media output. In general, there are two kinds of producers: those which exist to make a profit and those which do not aim to make a profit. Most media and cultural production falls into the former category: the main media industries of film-making, publishing and broadcasting are largely controlled by companies interested in making a profit.

Write to the relevant companies in the industry you are researching and ask them to send you a copy of their press pack: this contains information about the company for publicity purposes. It will include the names of people you should contact for further information and industry data on the company's performance. Most companies also have websites (sometimes these have replaced press packs), so use the websites to find out as much as you can about the structure and organization of a company. Public companies are also listed on the relevant stock exchange. Financial papers such as the *Financial Times* carry a lot of information about companies and their website – www.ft.com – is a very good source of information about the media industry in general as well as specific companies. The expansion in individual investors, especially Internet trading, has resulted in there being a great deal of information on the Internet about companies and businesses – some of it published by themselves and some of it by 'independents'. As with all information, think about the source, taking into account likely bias and considering source credibility. Do not automatically dismiss information about a company issued by its press office – but do not take it at face value, either. Think about why the press office is interested in putting that particular spin on the information. Why is this information furnished for public consumption and is there other information which is being withheld? Take this quesiton into account when evaluating the quality and usefulness of the information, but do not assume that, because it comes from a particular source, a piece of information is necessarily worthless – even if it is untrue, it may be worth investigating why a company would want to issue untrue statements.

The company reports of media companies contain much useful information for your dissertation. Most companies post these on their websites – see Appendix 2 for details of some of these. Companies House contains records of all publicly registered companies in the UK. British companies are obliged to keep accounts and to lodge these with the public records office.

Every industry from soap manufacture to soap opera conducts its own research. Commercial companies need to know who uses their products and what consumers like and don't like about their products. Manufacturers need to test new products and to develop images through research. The vast majority of research in industry (including the media and cultural sectors) is commissioned by private companies and used by them alone. The findings of such research is considered 'proprietary' and is not usually made available to the public – this research is conducted purely to help companies develop their corporate strategies, and making it public would mean that their competitors might get hold of it. As a consequence, research findings in corporations are not always accessible to scholars.

Companies sometimes allow researchers to investigate their historical or archived records, particularly if there is a new management or the business has changed so much that any findings would have no bearing on the current company. For example, the Rank archive of early film documents has been donated to the BFI in London and is available to scholars. There are other 'special collections' held by the ITC on the history of television, and the University of East Anglia is home to a collection of advertising archives (see Appendix 1 for discussion of these and other resources and special collections available). So there are lots of ways in which company information is available to the scholar.

Government sources and agencies

Governments of various levels take varying degrees of interest in the media at different times. UNESCO is one source of international information, which is disseminated through publications such as the *Communication and Information Thesaurus* (Aitchison, 1991). The European Union is also quite proactive in researching and publishing information about media and culture within its jurisdiction. In the USA, the Federal Communications Commission (FCC) regulates the media and communications industry. You can find out about its activities on its website: www.fcc.gov. British governments have had a variable record in terms of interest in media and culture. At the time of writing, the Labour government has been fairly proactive in encouraging greater participation in the arts. It also recognizes the culture industries as having a valuable role to play in the development of the social, cultural and economic life of the country. The Cabinet Office has its own website where you can find out details of government policy: www.cabinet-office.gov.uk. For more specific information about the media and culture industries, you should go to the website of the relevant government department, the Department for Culture, Media and Sport (DCMS), which provides a great deal of information about regulation and control of the industries within its rubric: www.culture.gov.uk. It has separate sections devoted to television and other media, arts, creative industries, film and music. Many of the most recent White Papers can be found here alongside relevant response papers. The site provides a user-friendly guide to government policy on issues of media and culture, and to the patterns and systems of regulation and control of the industries. If you want to research government policy on digital television or the growth of the arts sector, you will find lots of information here. You will also find lots of basic information about the organization and regulation of the media industries and excellent links to other UK organizations.

Regulators

In Britain and the USA, the media industries are regulated by governmental or quasi-governmental organizations. Many industries are controlled or regulated by organizations which are arms of the state or are non-profit-making organizations formed by the industry. At the time of writing, the Radio Authority, the government authority charged with allocating licences for radio broadcasting, has a terrific website with some excellent information about the industry: www.radioauthority.org.uk. The ITC does a similar job for broadcasting, and its excellent website contains very good information on all aspects of the television industry: www.itc.org.uk. These two agencies are to be merged into the Broadcasting Authority.

The ITC allocates licences to broadcast in the UK. The ITC is the current name given to the government watchdog of the television industry. In its various forms as the Independent Television Authority (ITA) or the Independent Broadcasting Authority (IBA), the government watchdog has surveyed attitudes to broadcasting in Britain since 1970.

The Broadcasting Standards Commission (BSC) is charged with ensuring that standards of decency and taste are upheld (www.bsc.org.uk). It produces codes of practice for terrestrial broadcasters as well as cable, satellite and digital television and radio. As part of its remit to monitor and investigate standards of taste and decency, the BSC funds academic research into issues of public concern. Research it has supported includes that by Andrea Millwood Hargrave into public attitudes towards offensive language in the media. This was published as *Delete Expletives* (2000), which is discussed in Chapter 5. Issues of public concern such as the consent given by children to participate in television have also been addressed by the BSC as in the research by Máire Messenger Davies and Nick Mosdell (2001). BSC-published research can provide good, reliable data on issues of public concern. The responsibilities of all of the above agencies is to be subsumed into a new Office of Communications (Offcom).

You should always bear in mind the source of information when considering the reliability and validity of data. Find out as much as you can about the methods of obtaining information. While you should always be wary of published information and think about its *source credibility*, you can usually assume that published data is reliable. The professionally gathered information reported in the sources above is a lot more reliable than you are likely to obtain for yourself, and professional researchers can be relied on to have anticipated and accounted for any bias.

Discussion

This chapter has provided an overview of the range of sources and resources you can use in your project. It should have given you some ideas on where to go in your search for primary and secondary material. Before you begin your project, you should find out who are the main players, what government bodies, regulators and organizations are involved in the area of media and culture that you are particularly interested in, and then spend some time researching the information they publish. The relevant websites are usually the best places to start, and here you will usually find contact names if you cannot find the information you need on the Internet. Make sure you are thorough about researching the available resources early in your research project. You may save yourself a lot of time and energy in trying to repeat what has already been done by someone else.

Analysing Media and Cultural Texts

3

Chapter overview

This is the first of three chapters in which the methods of analysis most suited to the student researcher are presented and discussed. This chapter focuses on analysing media and cultural *texts*. The chapter begins with a discussion of some of the advantages and disadvantages of using texts as your main *object of analysis*. It assumes that you have read Chapters 1 and 2, and have therefore got some idea of how to conduct your provisional research and are well on your way to writing your proposal. This chapter helps you with developing your research idea into a hypothesis in the section 'from hunches to hypotheses', and gives guidance on when it is appropriate to conduct textual analysis and when it is best avoided.

The chapter is divided into two halves: the first addresses the main methods of analysis in the media studies tradition and the second discusses methods derived from film studies but applicable to a range of other media and cultural forms. The second section is labelled 'typological methods' because the three methods considered here, genre analysis, auteur analysis and star studies, are all based on analysing texts which belong to a specific *type*.

The first main method of analysis covered in this chapter is *content analysis*, which, as we discussed in Chapter 1, is one of the most quantitative methods of analysis. The section opens with a discussion of what kinds of questions content analysis can address and looks at the advantages and disadvantages of content analysis. For our first case study, we have chosen the Glasgow Media News Group's key book, *Bad News* (1976), because it is one of the foundational books in British cultural studies and an excellent example of an early application of content analysis to television news. Throughout Chapters 3, 4 and 5 of the book, case studies will highlight key studies in the history of researching media and culture. This chapter presents a detailed section on the stages you should follow when conducting your own content analysis and some examples of the kinds of questions content analysis can address. We present a worked example of looking at the representations of race in fashion magazines for women. For people who are not well versed in manipulating numbers, the worked example is followed by a brief section on how to calculate percentages using the data gathered in our hypothetical study. Content analysis can be usefully combined with other methods of textual analysis, and some of these are discussed here. We present a second case study of a more recent piece of research by James Curran (2000b), which uses the interview in combination with content analysis to study the literary pages of the newspapers.

The second method of analysis is covered in less detail, largely because it is more difficult to be prescriptive about how it should be done. *Narrative analysis* is the name given to a host of different methods which examine the narrative structure of any text. We give special attention to Propp's form of functional analysis, and we give some advice on how to conduct your own narrative analysis, including the main stages you should follow.

Semiotics, which is concerned with the sign systems at play in texts, is the third method we consider in this chapter. The advantages and disadvantages of the various approaches included within this rubric are discussed. A classic case study is provided in the form of Roland Barthes's essay, 'Rhetoric of the Image' (see Case Study 3.3), and students are given guidance on how to conduct their own semiotic analysis. Semiotics is one of many methods which allow the scholar to investigate the ideological workings of the media, and we conclude the first half of this chapter with a discussion of the ways in which we can study media and culture to examine the ideological import of messages.

In the second half of the chapter, we examine the typological approaches which derive from film studies methods. We refer to these as 'typological' because they are all concerned with examining films according to shared characteristics of authorship, genre or performer. Most of the studies in these areas share common approaches, and since they all take films as their primary objects of analysis, the methods are best understood as being related, especially at the level we are working at in this book.

The first and best-recognized 'type' is *genre* – which of course means 'type'. Genre is the means by which Hollywood films have traditionally been produced and marketed, and readers will be familiar with the categories of Western, musical or thriller. As the case study for this section, we look at Jane Feuer's classic study of the Hollywood musical (1982), which is a comprehensive and theoretically rich examination of its subject. The musical has undergone several trans-formations since Feuer's study, but it is out of fashion at the time of writing. Readers are given some guidance on how to use genre analysis in their own research, whether it be in film studies or any other area of media analysis. A worked example of how one might use genre analysis to investigate a complex television text, *The Sopranos*, is presented.

One of the principal means by which films are classified, other than by genre, is by director. This form of classification is sometimes referred to as *auteur*, using the French word for 'author' because it was in France that the idea that films have 'auteurs' was first developed in a systematic way in the 1950s and 1960s, when such an idea was quite radical. Today, it is not untypical to classify films by their director, and we consider the search for the author as one of the key elements in auteur study. One of the ultimate 'auteurs' of contemporary cinema is Martin Scorsese, and we take as our case study Lawrence S. Friedman's analysis of his work (Friedman, 1999).

The star is another main means by which films have been classified and marketed under the classical Hollywood studio system and since. *Star* is more typically a popular than an academic classification, but star studies are well developed in film studies (see especially Dyer, 1982; 1987). In discussing how you might use star studies in your own research, this chapter debates the differences between primary and secondary sources for star studies and how to use the approach to look at stars, celebrities and performers in media other than film.

The chapter concludes with sections on how to combine methods of analysing texts and how to use textual analysis in conjunction with other approaches.

Introduction

Many of you will have chosen your degree subject because of your enjoyment of, and interest in, the products of the media. It is often our enthusiasm for particular films, television programmes or music that makes us want to learn more about our culture. When it comes to doing your own independent research, many of you will want to pursue your enthusiasm and investigate the products of the cultural industries. In the following sections of this chapter, we will consider some of the main methods you can use to conduct your own research into various media products, which we will refer to as media *texts*.

The study of texts makes up one of the most important areas of research in film, media and cultural studies. Most undergraduate and graduate courses include analysis of texts as a key part of the curriculum, and many of the discussions you have had in class will probably have centred around texts. In this chapter we will highlight some of the key studies which have influenced our understanding of how texts work. Textual analyses are often combined with other forms of analysis at both ends of the production/ reception continuum – you will find more discussion of these in Chapter 5, which addresses combining methods.

Researching media and cultural texts

The advantages and disadvantages of studying texts

There are several very good reasons for studying media texts. The texts themselves are readily *accessible*. Today many media artefacts are available for purchase in the form of videotapes, DVDs or CD-ROMs, making it much easier to gain access to a wide range of texts than ever before. The multiple forms also make texts easy to see and analyse. Media texts are part of our world: they are *social phenomena* and are often part of the debates about society going on in the world outside college or university. This makes them more topical and socially relevant, in turn giving a greater sense of relevance to our work. Studying texts can improve our understanding of cultural life – of how things mean – and meaning is one of the most important aspects of media use. Moreover, when writing your analysis of a film or television programme, you can expect your reader to have access to it, so you can assume a common frame of reference.

Most forms of textual analysis require you to have repeated access to your object of analysis, and that can be time-consuming. You need to be very careful about planning your study, and pay particular attention to the time management of your project. Many of the large-scale studies which we will address in this chapter, such as those of the Glasgow University Media Group, have been conducted by teams of several researchers and the methods employed can be rather labour-intensive. In this book we assume that you are doing your project alone and thus will not be able to conduct such expansive studies.

Some of the methods described in this chapter are also quite subjective, relying on the power of argument to make their case. Semiotic analysis, for example, is very interpretive, and different readers do not always share the same interpretation. While methods which are reliant on good analytical skills are well suited to strong writers, if you are not very confident of your rhetorical skills, maybe you should steer clear of these methods. A good textual analysis depends on the persuasiveness of the argument, and this in turn often depends on good writing skills. You can show off your writing skills in an analytical essay, but you will expose your weaknesses if you are not a good writer.

From hunches to hypotheses

One of the big problems with the interpretive approaches to textual analysis discussed in this chapter is that you need an argument before you begin analysing – but where do you get your argument from if you haven't yet analysed your text? It may seem that you are being asked a trick question: you need to know already what you are going to say before you find out what you are going to say. Before you begin, it is important to think about the preliminary stages of your analysis as opportunities to test hunches – analytical arguments are developed by having an idea about texts based on your normal use as a member of the audience. At first, all you have is a hunch. But don't write your project based on a hunch. Once you get a hunch (or maybe you have a couple of related ones about the same thing), get to work doing some preliminary testing. Begin your research now – read, think, write down your ideas on paper to see how they work; talk to your lecturers and classmates about your idea. A hunch is nothing more than a suspicion or feeling based on your knowledge of (in this case) media texts. Maybe you watch a lot of science fiction television and have a feeling that something interesting is going on in the representation of women. 'Is *Star Trek: the Next Generation* a feminist text?' you might ask yourself. This is a hunch. As we saw in Chapter 1, a hypothesis is a statement which can be proved or tested. In the early planning stage of your project, you will probably come up with several hunches before you can shape one of them into a workable hypothesis for your research question. In the analysis of texts, this will develop through your critical engagement with the texts you are most interested in.

If your hunch works out, then go with it. It is quite probable that your first idea won't work out and it will need to be refined and thought through again. Don't think of this as a failure – constant revision and review are necessary to the process of discovery. Few people are fortunate enough for their hunches to pan out first time. But by following your hunch in the first place, you have done some reading, looked at some more texts and done some thinking and some talking. Now you are better informed about the texts you are interested in, and you can develop a more informed working hypothesis. It might take two or three goes, but developing more and more precise hunches is the most effective way of getting yourself a good hypothesis.

When not to use textual analysis

Analysing texts can allow you to investigate a wide range of hypotheses about the nature of media and cultural artefacts. The methods discussed in this chapter can be used to draw out latent themes within texts and make connections between them. In studying media texts, you will be able to discuss an infinite number of themes and issues. However, there are limitations to what you can find out from studying media texts. If we have media texts as our only object of analysis, the conclusions we can make will be relevant only to those texts and not applicable to broader society. From textual analysis alone, it is not possible to make inferences about the state of mind of the author. Textual analysis does not give up the secrets of the creator's intention: to find out what the director of a film intended, it is usually necessary to ask them. Don't assume that you can garner the director's motivation from analysing the film: you are simply speculating. At the same time, textual analysis may give you a sophisticated understanding of your own responses to a film, but it will not help you in understanding how the film was received by other people. If we want to find out about the production of texts, or about their reception, it is necessary to use the methods discussed in Chapter 4 and Chapter 5. So think carefully about your research question and make sure that your primary object of analysis is the texts themselves before you embark on the methods discussed below.

Content analysis

One of the most direct methods of textual analysis, content analysis involves counting phenomena in texts (Bauer, 2000; Berger, 1998a; Krippendorff, 1980; Rosengren, 1981; Weber, 1985). Content analysis is typically called a 'quantitative' method because it involves counting and summing phenomena. However, it can be used to support studies of a more 'qualitative' nature. Content analysis is considered by one of its leading exponents, Klaus Krippendorff (1980), to be primarily a *symbolic* method because it is used to investigate symbolic material (media texts). Certainly, it is not as objective and starkly empirical as some critics suggest. In conducting content analysis there is much interpretive work to do, relying on a good knowledge of the texts under examination.

One of the advantages of content analysis is that it enables you to conduct your primary research and come up with your own facts and figures to use as evidence in your argument. You may count the number of stories, the number of images or the occurrences of mentions of a particular subject. You will use categories which you define in advance. Content analysis can be used to compare media content at different points in time to make an argument about historical change, to argue that there is more, or less, of something than there used to be. For example, you hypothesize that general fashion magazines carry more advertisements featuring black models than they used to, and think this is evidence of our living in a more multicultural society. You can get a definitive answer to the question of whether or not there are more black models if you compare the number of 'black', 'white' and 'Asian' models appearing in selected magazines during the 1980s and today. You select a representative number of issues of, for example, *Vogue* and *Cosmopolitan*, from both periods and count the number of models in each of the categories 'black', 'white' and 'Asian' (you will probably also want to include 'other'). You will then have factual evidence to support or refute that part of your hypothesis which claims that the representation of black and Asian models has increased. You will, however, have to conduct further analysis on the content of the texts to determine whether or not this may be a consequence of multiculturalism.

The kinds of questions content analysis can address

Content analysis is appropriate for studies of how much of a given phenomenon there is in a chosen set of texts. This method has been widely used in studies of the news, the press and television. Although it sounds highly rational, it has been used to study 'irrational' phenomena, too: Theodor W. Adorno studied the astrology column of the *Los Angeles Times* (Adorno, 1994) to investigate the philosophy of irrationality which he identified there. There are many different kinds of question content analysis can address, but it is best suited to comparative studies where some reliable facts would help. Think about the following two statements. Which one is more convincing?

Statement A: 'Old people are under-represented in television advertising.'
Statement B: 'Out of 826 people shown in prime-time television advertisements in the first week of May, only five per cent appeared to be over the age of 40 and less than one per cent over 65.'

Statement B has more force than Statement A. Your tutor would freely write '*evidence?*' against Statement A and would see from Statement B that you had done a thorough piece of research. Projects of all kinds can often benefit from a small-scale content analysis to support the overall argument.

The method is frequently used in studies focusing on the news agenda: some powerful studies have been conducted on the way that stories about AIDS first came to be covered; for example, Beharrell (1993). Previous researchers have looked at AIDS coverage and how it changes when a celebrity dies, for example. It can also be used in studies comparing what occurs in reality with a preferred norm. For example, Channel 4 was originally mandated to have more programmes catering to minorities than the other channels. To test whether this is true, a popular student assignment is to measure how many 'minority' programmes there are on each channel and see whether Channel 4 lives up to its brief. James Curran (2000b) uses content analysis to demonstrate that what literary editors *claimed* they were doing was at odds with what *actually* occurred in their columns. Although content analysis gives you evidence to support an argument, it does not provide you with an argument in itself; it is up to you to make sure that the powerfully persuasive description which content analysis provides is an adequate test of your hypothesis.

Advantages and disadvantages of content analysis

Some of the advantages of content analysis have been touched on above. It is a persuasive method which generates reliable, replicable facts. It is flexible, creative and easy for a beginner researcher to undertake. If you follow the steps laid out in the section below, conducting your own content analysis is very straightforward and requires only a basic level of mathematical skills. It is a very adaptable method, and most media and cultural texts are amenable to content analysis. The results can be readily presented in tables which are easily read, making it very accessible and comprehensible.

The disadvantages are that it can be insensitive; sometimes content analysis can be a bit of a blunt instrument. For example, in studies of violence on television, scholars have often simply counted acts of violence without distinguishing between vengeance, justice or acts committed by a mythical beast against a farm animal. If improperly operationalized or applied, it can generate meaningless data. The method is only as sophisticated as the categories which the researcher defines – so researchers have to be very careful to found their categories in theoretical research. Content analysis is often criticized for being too descriptive, and this is a weakness to which the beginner researcher is especially vulnerable: make sure that your hypothesis is well developed and that your categories operationalize it sufficiently to avoid this pitfall. Content analysis is sometimes criticized for lacking reliability; for instance, the way you categorize material does not cohere with how somebody else would do it. There are tests of 'intercoder reliability' which researchers use to try to eliminate the coder's bias. The most typical method is to ask two researchers to code the same data and then to compare the results – this is too time-consuming and expensive for most students (see Krippendorff, 1980, for more detailed discussion). I would advise students to show their categories to their supervisor before they begin coding the material and get their tutor's agreement on categories and definitions.

The main weakness of content analysis is that it can be laborious: coding hundreds of column inches of newspapers or hours of television programmes is very time-consuming. Make sure you can justify the inclusion of every single text you are going to study, and don't analyse more than you need in order to make your point. Computer-aided research is helpful in counting phenomena in written texts, but I would not recommend this for a researcher starting out, as it requires a level of computer sophistication and methodological ability which you may not have.

CASE STUDY 3.1. CONTENT ANALYSIS

The Glasgow University Media Group, 1976. *Bad News*. London: Routledge and Kegan Paul.

The Glasgow University Media Group's *Bad News* is one of the most important books in the history of British media studies. This book-length study applies content analysis to television news coverage of industrial relations in the 1970s. In conducting this groundbreaking study, the team used the most sophisticated research technologies available at the time, the video cassette recorder and the software system SPSS. Originally scheduled to gather data over one year, the study was cut to six months because the researchers underestimated the amount of material they would collect and the amount of time it would take to conduct the analysis.

The Glasgow University Media Group looked at the differences in media coverage of management and labour representatives in the reporting of industrial relations and found strong evidence of ideological bias at the heart of television news. The researchers categorized hundreds of hours of television, using story categories such as 'economics', 'city' and 'human interest'. The work was very labour-intensive, time-consuming and demanding of resources. During the 1970s, computers were still in their infancy and were considerably more cumbersome than now, and they had to use punchcards to enter the data. In addition to the content analysis, the team also interviewed some television news workers and carried out participant observation in newsrooms.

The project was particularly focused on the coverage of industrial action at a time when there were many strikes in Britain. In order to get a picture of the 'contours of coverage', the team categorized industrial news coverage for the period January to May 1975 according to various industrial sectors (for example, aerospace, textiles or mining). Using industrial data, they collated the number of strikes occurring in each of the industrial sectors and compared these figures with the number of stoppages reported in the news. They found that there was 'no consistent relationship' between the official records of stoppages and those covered on the television news. This, the study concluded, was accounted for by what it claimed to be a concentration on 'unscheduled interruptions to production and consumption patterns' (p. 204). It is the conclusions of the study which were the most controversial. The Glasgow University Media Group argue that television news lays the blame for industrial unrest at the feet of the workers. They argue that it is harmful and socially divisive for the media to focus on the people taking action as the villains of the piece while treating management as authoritative sources removed from the causes of the action.

The Glasgow Media Group continue to be involved in studying media content by a range of methods including content analysis (Eldrige, 1993; Philo, 1996; Philo, 1999). *Bad News* and the subsequent volumes *More Bad News* and *Really Bad News* are now considered foundational studies in the field, and any study of media content, especially if the primary concern is with news, should refer to these important texts. There is much to be learned from the experience of the Glasgow University Media Group in terms of the method of content analysis, including its strengths and its dangers. The methods employed by the group have grown increasingly diverse and more sophisticated since the publication of *Bad News*, but this research remains a key text in the history of media studies and an essential piece of background reading for anyone interested in conducting content analysis.

The Glasgow University Media Group comprises a group of British scholars who have been most consistently engaged in the analysis of media content, although the range of methods used extends far beyond content analysis (Glasgow University Media Group, 1980, 1982; Eldridge, 1993; Philo, 1996, 1999). Case Study 3.1 looks at the first major study to be published by the Glasgow University Media Group, *Bad News* (1976), a study of television news content. Other scholars have frequently studied broadcast television news by content analysis. Jackie Harrison's excellent study (Harrison, 2000) looks at the context of the production of broadcast television news. Harrison analysed one week's television news on the four terrestrial channels (BBC1, BBC2, ITV and Channel 4) during April 1993.

Good pedagogic descriptions of content analysis can be found in a number of textbooks aimed at students. Klaus Krippendorff's *Content Analysis* (1980) is still a standard in content analysis and a definitive guide to the method. Chapter 14, 'A Practical Guide', gives a step-by-step account of doing content analysis which differs from my own and is recommended for anyone thinking of doing more advanced content analysis. Daniel Riffe, Stephen Lacy and Frederick G. Fico's book *Analyzing Media Messages* provides a thorough grounding in the method aimed specifically at students of mass communications (Riffe, Lacy and Fico, 1998); Chapter 3 of Arthur Asa Berger's very useful textbook gives an example of how content analysis can be applied to the comics pages of newspapers (Berger, 1998a). Berger guides the reader through the technique of content analysis and provides a very good summary of the advantages and disadvantages of the method. Hansen et al. (1998) provide a good discussion of how to conduct content analysis and offer some interesting historical examples. My own study using content analysis to analyse teenage girls' magazines includes some further discussion of the method of content analysis (Stokes, 1999a).

Stages in a content analysis

Establish your hypothesis.   Make sure you have a clear hypothesis for your content analysis: be sure that you know what you want to find out. Your hypothesis should emanate from your reading, so be sure that you know how it fits in with the published literature.

Read widely.   Look at previous work focused on the medium in which you are interested. You should try to find previous content analyses focused on your object of analysis to discover how previous researchers have addressed your topic. But don't be shocked if you cannot find anything exactly on your theme. Your literature review should include books and articles on the medium as a whole. For example, if you are studying the celebrity magazine, you will find little on this precise topic, but there are several books and articles in the literature on magazines, popular publishing or literature for women which could provide valuable information and theoretical perspectives. You should also examine previous work using content analysis, whatever the medium, to find out more about how and why this method has been applied.

Define your object of analysis.   Isolate the material you are going to study and think about how your selection will help to test your hypothesis. State which texts you are going to study and why. You need to think about how many texts you are going to examine. It should be a large enough sample to be representative and yet small enough to be manageable. Six issues of a magazine provides plenty of material to code, and three half-hour episodes of a television programme should be sufficient if you are conducting a detailed content analysis. If in any doubt, go ahead and conduct a provisional analysis on *one* text using your provisional categories and then decide, first, how many you have time to analyse and, second, how many it is necessary to analyse to convince the reader of your case. You should always confirm with your supervisor that you have set yourself about the right amount of work to do according to the criteria laid down by your institution, so check with your tutor before you proceed.

Define your categories. Decide what categories of content you are going to be counting in your analysis and define them clearly. Ask yourself what you are going to be actually *counting* in your content analysis. If it is 'occurrences of black models in fashion magazines', decide how you are going to define 'black'? If it is 'mentions of Tony Blair in tabloid newspapers', should you include indirect references (for example, to the 'Prime Minister' or 'Tony'), or must his full name be used? Sometimes you will need to rely on your own cultural knowledge to determine whether particular items fit a category. Defining your categories as carefully as possible in advance will help; for example, if you are looking at representations of old and young people in television advertisements, define what you mean by 'old' (e.g. 'looks over 55 to me') and 'young' (e.g. 'looks under 25 to me'). Also, decide what you are going to do when the inevitable happens and the text you are analysing contains a phenomenon that you do not know how to categorize. For example, how do you code the age of the Jolly Green Giant? You will need a category of 'other' for most media and cultural texts, but in your test you should make sure that there aren't too many elements which fall outside your coding scheme.

Create a coding sheet to record your findings. Designing the coding sheet will help you to think about the categories themselves and is a useful exercise in making sure that you fully understand the texts you are studying. The coding sheet needs to be in the form of grid with the objects of analysis on one axis and the categories you are coding them into on the other. Make sure that you have all the information you will need. Make sure the categories reflect the variables you are going to discuss. For example, if necessary, you could put 'black' and 'Asian' in the same category if you are interested only in whether models are white or not. However, if you want to make a comparison between the representation of Asian and Afro-Caribbean women, you will need to code them as a separate category. As a general rule, be as specific as you can in the early phases, and when you want to make conclusions, you can aggregate the groups. If you have coded all non-white models as 'black', you will not have the opportunity later to disaggregate them into 'Asian' and 'Afro-Caribbean'. You will need to create a coding sheet which you can use for each separate text.

Test your coding categories. Try out your categories on a small sample to see if they works. You will save yourself a lot of work by testing your coding categories as early in the process as possible, and they may need to be revised in the light of what you find. If need be, don't be afraid to abandon your hypothesis and come up with a new one more suited to the actuality of the texts. You may find that you need to revise your hypothesis and/or your coding categories several times before you get them right. Keep a careful record of all these changes and ensure that you discuss them in your 'methods' section in the final essay – it is very important to show the reader how your ideas have developed.

Collect your data.   Once you have tested your categories and are confident that the coding sheet you have designed will get the information you need in order to answer your research question, you should go ahead and collect your data. Have a separate sheet for each of the texts you are analysing. Be very careful and methodical and make a note of any exceptions or particularly difficult decisions.

Sum your findings.   Use a second version of your log sheet to enter the summed figures you have collected. Add up how many occurrences of each category there are. It is easier to convert these to percentages for comparison's sake. In the case of the black model hypothesis, you need to be able to compare the 1980s sample with the contemporary one.

Interpret your data.   Once you have collated the information, you will be able to observe whether the relationships and patterns are confirming your hypothesis or not. What do the figures you have generated tell you about the content of the text you have been studying? Have an open mind at this stage. Do not be concerned if your original hypothesis is not confirmed. Think about why this might be so and allow the data to lead you to a new hypothesis if necessary.

Relate back to your question.   Now you can begin to make conclusions about whether or not your hypothesis is borne out by the data. Be honest with yourself. It is not a worse project if your hypothesis turns out not to be true: remember that the way you execute your study is more important than the conclusions you are able to draw at this stage. Perhaps you have proven your hypothesis unreservedly – if so, great. It is more likely that you will have not completely found what you were looking for – even better. You learn more (and so does the reader) when you reflect on how and why things did not go according to plan. Reflect on what you could have done otherwise and how you would have done things differently with the benefit of hindsight. Have you answered the question – partially or wholly?

Present your findings.   Whether your hypothesis is proven or not, you need to present your findings neatly, using appropriate tables and charts. Show how you conducted the content analysis by including discussion of how you carried out each of the above stages. Use published studies as models of how to present your own work.

TABLE 3.1

Coding Sheet for
a Hypothetical
Content
Analysis

Models in fashion magazines:

Use one sheet for each separate magazine.

Title:	Date:	Issue number:			
Kinds of content	No's of separate models	Race/ethnicity	Gender	Couples	Totals
Advertisements					
Fashion spreads					
Features					
Totals					

Discussion. Finish your study by discussing the strengths and weaknesses of content analysis as applied to this question. Seriously discuss how you might have conducted the study otherwise. Show that you have learned from the experience.

In Table 3.1 we provide an example of a coding sheet for a study looking at the race of models used in women's magazines. In this example we would note the occurrences of models according to predefined categories.

Calculating percentages

You need to convert your raw data to percentages in order to be able to compare across your sample. In our example, for instance, the number of pages in each magazine is different and the number of pages devoted to fashion differs, too. We first need to decide whether we want to find out about the number of models per issue, in which case we need to express the number as a percentage of the total content. If we want to consider the number of models of each race in the fashion pages alone, we need to express our data as a percentage of the number of models in these sections of the magazine. In order to calculate the percentage of models of each category as a total of the number appearing in the fashion pages, we need to make the following sum:

Number of models of each category divided by the total number of models in the fashion pages multiplied by 100

If there are 23 models featured in the fashion pages, 11 of whom are 'black' and 5 of whom are 'white' we could calculate the percentage like this:

Black models = 11; total in fashion pages = 23;
percentage = 11/23 × 100 = 47%

White models = 5; total in fashion pages = 23;
percentage = 5/23 × 100 = 21.7%

We can now compare occurrences of 'black' and 'white' models across all the magazines in our sample, independent of how many there are.

Combining content analysis with other methods

Content analysis can also be used to very good effect in conjunction with other, more interpretive methods, such as semiotics (discussed later in this chapter) or interviews (considered in subsequent chapters). Peter Beharrell's analysis of how the British papers covered HIV and AIDS is illustrative of the way *semiotics* and *content analysis* can be combined to create a nuanced and sophisticated account of news coverage of a particular issue (Beharrell, 1993). A powerfully persuasive example of how *content analysis* can be combined with *interviews* is James Curran's insightful study of literary editors (Curran, 2000b).

CASE STUDY 3.2. CONTENT ANALYSIS AND INTERVIEW

James Curran, 2000b. Literary editors, social networks and cultural tradition. In James Curran (ed.), *Media Organizations in Society*. London: Arnold, pp. 215–39.

James Curran's essay in a volume he edited uses content analysis and interviews to investigate the working patterns of editors of the book review sections of newspapers. Key gatekeepers in the publishing industry, literary editors determine what books get reviewed, and by whom. They thus have a strong influence in shaping the coverage garnered by books. Curran aimed to investigate 'how the literary editors do their job, and how their judgements reflect and influence the hierarchy of knowledge in our society' (p. 215).

Twenty-two interviews were conducted in total: 11 in 1986 and another 11 in 1999. When editors were asked about the process of selection, Curran found that two alternative explanations were offered. On the one hand, the editors claimed that books 'select' themselves for coverage and that the editors are merely responding to the events in the publishing industry. On the other hand, they also claimed that the editors' decisions are determined quite instinctively.

Using content analysis on the books sections of the newspapers allowed Curran to contrast what the editors claim they are doing with what actually gets into print in their newspapers. Thus, for example, the editors see their job as alerting the public to books that are important, yet when Curran analysed the range of books reviewed, he found that science and technology books were seriously under-represented. Less than 2% of the space was devoted to books in these categories. Social science and politics were also under-represented.

Content analysis revealed that the most frequently reviewed books were in the categories of biography, literary fiction, history and general humanities. Curran presents detailed tables showing the distribution of book review space in national newspapers (p. 219) and in weekly magazines (p. 220).

Curran argues that the bias he reveals is the product of the education and background of the editors themselves. He found that the vast majority of editors interviewed had degrees from Oxford or Cambridge (55% in 1986 and 64% in 1999), and that of these, virtually all had degrees in the arts or humanities (94% in 1986 and 100% in 1999), mostly in English or history. The editors choose to commission reviews of books of interest to them and select in the areas about which they are most knowledgeable.

By using content analysis as a means of garnering statistical information and interviews about the subjective nature of the decision-making process, Curran is able to draw attention to contradictions between the claims made by these particular cultural workers about their work and their actual output. As he says, 'Subjective impression, however informed, is not as reliable as systematic analysis based on careful measurement using social-science procedures' (p. 218).

Content analysis is a method which is deceptively easy: in the weakest studies, it does not amount to much more than counting phenomena, but the best work uses the reliable empirical data content analysis can generate to make important and valuable contributions to our understanding of media texts. The strongest use of content analysis is to provide reliable data to support interpretive analyses.

Concluding comments on content analysis

Content analysis is the ideal method to use when you want to make an argument about quantities of things. There is no better way to demonstrate that there is a lack of something or a surfeit of something else than by actually counting: the number of black people on television, proportion of domestic news devoted to health issues, the ratio of female to male performers featured in music magazines – all are topics which are quantifiable. What does it mean if there are hardly any female performers featured in music magazines? It is not worth knowing that only 15 per cent of acts featured are female unless that is part of a discussion about how and why that situation prevails. Content analysis is fine for getting evidence, but you always need to ensure that it is evidence in support of a sustained argument. Content analysis is a powerful method for making explicit facts about content which may not be immediately obvious. As Krippendorff and others have observed, content analysis is a method which deals with symbolic phenomena and is therefore necessarily interpretive (Krippendorff, 1980).

Narrative analysis

We saw in the above section how some kinds of cultural artefacts can be quantified by content analysis. In this section we are going to look at some of the methods we can use to examine the overall pattern of the *stories* or *narratives* of texts. In *narrative analysis*, we take as our object of analysis the entire text, focusing on the structure of the story or narrative.

It seems a basic human characteristic to tell stories about ourselves, about our world and about the people and phenomena we encounter. Some of the most ancient forms of culture are in the form of stories, and the foundations of the world's major religions are conveyed from one generation to the next in narrative form. Stories are fundamental to the oldest known cultural forms: myths, ballads and poetry are all driven by narration. So, too, are contemporary media structured around narrative: this is what hooks us into a good film, an exciting television series or a compulsive computer game.

There are some cultural forms which do not necessarily have a strong narrative: abstract painting or sculpture, for example. But it is impossible to exclude the possibility that people will look at even a plain white canvas and narrativize – create a story in their minds based on what the artist was doing. Martin Creed, winner of the Turner Prize for Modern Art in 2001, had a light going on and off every five seconds in his exhibit at Tate Britain. This minimal piece had no 'story', but the press attempted to interpret it as a product of Creed's philosophy of art. Even when we think, 'What the hell was the artist up to?' we are still narrativizing, trying to make up a story to explain the picture.

It is not just fiction and art which convey narrative. Factual media are also creating narratives (van Dijk, 1988; Nichols, 1991; Garrett and Bell, 1998). The news is structured around 'stories' and story elements as much as any theatrical performance (Bell, 1991; Bell and Garrett, 1998). Narrative is a component of just about every media and cultural form to a greater or lesser extent. The drive to narrativize is present in human responses to the world – we can't help ourselves; we interpret the world through narrativization. Narrative also conveys the ideology of a culture, and it is one of the means by which values and ideals are reproduced culturally. Thus, narrative analysis is often used to unpack the ideological intent of a piece of work (for more discussion of ideological analysis, see pages 76–8 below in this chapter).

In general, narrative analysis requires us to uncover the structure of cultural artefacts. Paying attention to the narrative requires that we do not get 'carried away' by the story, but resist the temptation to suspend disbelief. We interrupt the story in order to analyse and dissect it. A good story always hides its mechanism, so we need to prevent the text from doing its job of making us forget it is a narrative. In analysis, we need to adopt a critical distance in order that we can better understand how the story is structured. There are various tools which we can use to do this, and in the next sections we discuss functional analysis.

Functional analysis

The analysis of narrative is a powerful and useful way to explore media texts, and a relatively neglected one of late. One of the key approaches to narrative analysis derives from Vladimir Propp's *Morphology of the Folk Tale* (1968). Propp, an anthropologist who studied the history of the folk tale in Russia in the late nineteenth and early twentieth centuries, found remarkable similarities in structure across a wide variety of stories. Propp explored the fundamental elements in folk tales and found that there was enormous commonality across them. All folk tales, according to Propp, have common elements, which he labelled 'functions'. Each character performs a function within the narrative and can be defined according to this role. Thus, the 'hero' is the person who is set a task – whether it is the suitor who wishes to marry the beautiful princess in the fairy story, or the cop who has to solve a crime in the police drama. The *'donor'* is the character who gives the hero something to help him in his task, according to Propp. Thus, the elf who gives the suitor a magic cloak is a donor, but so, too, is the informer who tells the detective where to find a suspect.

Propp's model of analysis can be applied to any story – it requires the identification of key characters and the classification of those characters according to Propp's schema. A good in-class exercise is to analyse folk stories from different countries or cultures to see whether they share common properties. Working in small groups, students should tell a story from their culture (in outline) to the group. The group can then see if they can identify the functional roles which Propp claims are present in all stories. The universality of Propp's claims can then be tested.

Functional analysis is also suitable for investigating stories in forms other than folk stories. The classical Hollywood Western, for example, has been subject to a detailed and insightful functional analysis by Will Wright in his influential book, *Six-Guns and Society* (1979). There has been some work investigating the properties of classical Hollywood film as containing Proppian elements and Arthur Asa Berger shows how useful Propp's method is in his analysis of the cult television series, *The Prisoner* (1982).

Discourse analysis is founded on the analysis of story structures; for example, the story is what is at stake in Bell's analysis of news discourse (Bell, 1991). News and current affairs programmes make good objects of analysis for narrative analysis. Despite their claims to 'objectivity' they are in fact highly coded and conventional texts, as Bill Nichols makes clear in his work (Nichols, 1991). But any form of product with a story could be analysed by discourse analysis.

Conducting your own narrative analysis

The texts most frequently subject to narrative analysis in our field are films and television programmes. However, we have seen how Propp, one of the pioneers of this approach, developed the method to investigate folk litera- ture. Narrative analysis still forms the basis for much analysis of traditional forms such as the novel, poetry and drama. There is no reason why you could not conduct a narrative analysis of any form. What you will be looking at is the underlying message of the text: 'good overcomes evil'; 'boy meets girl'; 'the little guy triumphs over big business'. The precise nature of your analysis will depend on the object of analysis.

Conducting your own narrative analysis can be a useful way of dissect- ing a text and finding out the ideology of the structure. What is the underlying message about heroes? You need to get an overview of the text in a very abstract way and should follow similar steps whether you are analysing a film, song lyrics or a television documentary. As we said above ('from hunches to hypotheses', page 55), you will have an idea that you want to investigate – you can conduct a narrative analysis only when you have developed your hunch into a hypothesis.

Stages in conducting a narrative analysis

Select your text(s) carefully. Narrative analysis involves very close reading and is best conducted on a limited number of texts to begin with. Choose one feature film or television drama episode or the coverage of one news item in not more than five days' newspapers.

Become very familiar with the text. View/read/listen several times. Think about the explicit themes of the text. What is it about? Why is it interesting?

Define your hypothesis. What do you want to say about the text? You need to work from your first interest in the text and work towards a *hunch* about the text. When you have an idea about what you think is interesting about the texts, work out if you can prove *why*. Then try to make a statement regarding what you intend to prove or disprove by your analysis – this is a hypothesis.

Write out the skeleton of the plot as it happens in the text. Pay attention to the characters and the order of events as they are told.

Using the plot outline, write down the story as it happens chronologically. What is the 'back story'? Identify how the plot differs from the chronological order of events.

Identify the 'equilibrium' at the beginning and at the end of the text. Has the world of the text changed before and after the story, or has the old order been restored? If there has been a change in the equilibrium, list the ways in which the world has changed *before* and *after* the story. What is given as the 'agent of change'?

Define characters according to their 'function' in the plot. Don't get too fixed; be prepared to change your mind. Who is the 'hero'? the 'villain'? the 'donor'? Whoever gives something to the hero is a 'donor'; whoever is in need of rescuing is 'the princess'. A character may begin as a hero and end as a villain.

Relate your findings to your hypothesis. Does your analysis endorse or contradict the hypothesis you first had? What evidence have you mustered to support or refute your idea? Has your idea changed in the light of the evidence you have collected?

One of the strengths of functional analysis is that it allows you to identify common properties across a series of texts. It is very useful in the typographic studies discussed later in this chapter. For example, if you want to show how much texts of one genre have in common, despite having diverse visual schema, you could use the structural analysis unearthed by narrative analysis to make your point. The underlying ideology can be elicited.

Narrative analysis of moving images is further discussed by Hansen et al. (1998: Chapter 6).

Semiotics

Semiotics (literally 'the science of signs') is useful when you want to analyse the meaning of texts. It is derived from the work of Ferdinand de Saussure, who investigated the properties of language in his *Course in General Linguistics* (Saussure, 1983). Saussure believed that semiotics could be used to analyse a large number of 'sign systems', and there is no reason why it could not be applied to any media or cultural form. Semiotics is a form of *hermeneutics* – that is the classical name for the study of the interpretation of literature. So, if it is the *meaning* of something that you want to study, especially visual media, semiotics may provide the best approach for you. In practice, media and cultural researchers use semiotics quite narrowly, and it seems to have fallen from fashion.

One of the key theorists of semiotics, Roland Barthes, developed the ideas of Saussure and tried to apply the study of signs more broadly (1967). Through a productive and exciting career engaging with the many facets of culture, Barthes included fashion (1990), photography (1984), literature (1987), magazines and music among his many interests (1973; 1984). One of his central preoccupations, discussed in Case Study 3.3, is 'How does meaning get into the image?' (Barthes, 1984: 32). And that is the key to semiotics: it is about how the producer of an image makes it *mean* something and how we, as readers, *get meaning out*. It is not always the case that the reader gets the same meaning out of something that the producer put in. Semiotics is one of the most interpretive of methods for analysing texts, and its success or failure as a method relies on how well researchers are able to articulate their case.

CASE STUDY 3.3. SEMIOTICS

Barthes, Roland, 1984. Rhetoric of the image. In *Image, Music, Text.* Translated by Stephen Heath. London: Fontana, pp. 32–51.

This key text in the history of semiotics is one which anyone interested in analysing visual images, especially advertisements, should study in detail. Barthes's short essay applies the theory of semiotic analysis developed by Saussure for the study of language to the study of images. Barthes chooses to analyse an advertisement because of the purposeful, deliberate nature of the message advertisements contain. The advertisement chosen is from a French magazine for a brand of Italian foods (pasta, sauce and cheeses) trading as 'Panzani'. The advertisement shows a string shopping basket with packets of Panzani pasta, sauce and Parmesan cheese as well as fresh produce (tomatoes, green peppers, onions and mushrooms).

Barthes pulls apart the various meanings of the advertisement looking first at the literal meaning, or denotation, and secondly at the connotations. The Panzani advertisement connotes 'italianicity' to Barthes – the pasta and produce to make a sauce; the Italian-sounding name of the company; the red, yellow and green of the produce reiterating the idea of *Italy* through reference to the Italian national flag. Barthes examines the relationship between the linguistic code – the words written in the copy and on the produce – and the images. For Barthes, images are *polysemic* – they have multiple meanings and are open to diverse interpretations. But Barthes also maintains that images are rarely presented to us without words of some kind accompanying them and that this accompanying linguistic code serves to limit the potential meanings of the text. Barthes shows that the language used, the words, narrow the potential meanings of the image.

This essay demonstrates the relationship between the denotative and connotative codes of analysis between what is *shown* and what is *implied*.

Semiotics breaks down the content of texts into their component parts and relates them to broader discourses. A semiotic analysis provides a way of relating specific texts to the system of messages in which they operate. It provides the intellectual context to the content: it addresses the ways in which the various elements of the text work together and interact with our cultural knowledge to generate meaning. Semiotics has the advantage of generating what Clifford Geertz (1973) refers to as 'thick descriptions', meaning textured and complex analyses. Because it is so subjective, semiotics is not reliable in the traditional social science sense – another analyst who studied the same texts may well elicit a different meaning! But this does not devalue semiotics, because it is about enriching our understanding of the texts. As a method, semiotics is interpretive and, consequently, necessarily subjective.

Semiotic analysis is usually applied to images or visual texts (Berger, 1987; 1998a). This method involves putting into words how images work by relating them to the ideological structure which organizes meaning. Semiotics has been applied to the study of photography (Ramamurthy, 1997), advertising (Williamson, 1978), shopping (Miller, 1998), and fashion (Barthes, 1990; Garber, 1992). The main theorists who have contributed to our knowledge of semiotics are Roland Barthes and Umberto Eco. But most of their most important work was done several years ago. Within our field, there has been a move away from the study of texts and towards the study of audiences and reception (see Chapter 5). This is regrettable, not least because in popular discussion, the content of media and cultural texts and its meaning remain interesting and important.

Advantages and disadvantages of semiotics

One of the key advantages of semiotic analysis is that it demands relatively few resources. It is possible to conduct a semiotic analysis of only one text or image (although this is not necessarily recommended). Because the method is interpretive, it does not have to be reliable in the sense of being applied to a large number of texts. The generalizability of semiotics is not always relevant, making this method appropriate for studying a limited number of texts. The essential factor in semiotic analysis is that you have to have a high level of knowledge about your chosen object of analysis. For example, if you are not into rave culture, do not attempt a semiotic analysis of flyers because you will not know what the various codes mean. You need to be part of the interpretive community using the relevant media to be able fully to understand the conventions in operation.

Conducting your own semiotic analysis

Advertisements are today made by people well versed in semiotics – 'Semiotic Solutions' even is the name given to one advertising company. A knowledge of visual and linguistic codes is essential to developing any advertising strategy. Judith Williamson's groundbreaking study of the semiotics of advertising analyses several advertisements culled fairly randomly from women's magazines (Williamson, 1978). Williamson makes no apologies for her selection being quite subjective. Her work is frequently assigned in undergraduate and postgraduate classes because it is one of the earliest studies to analyse advertisements so closely. Williamson's analysis is informed by an ideological position critical of capitalism, and very much a product of its time; yet the semiotic approach she takes contributes to the development of semiotics today. Semiotics is now part of the creative process of advertising. It provides a good vocabulary for talking about what advertisements have always been about: giving value to products by making them meaningful to potential purchasers. It is not surprising that advertisements lend themselves so well to semiotic analysis. Advertisements make excellent subjects for semiotic analysis – although sometimes you may feel that you are simply unpicking the work of the creative directors of any campaign you are studying. Focus on a campaign or the semiotic strategies used in marketing a particular product category, such as alcohol or perfume, to get the richest raw data. Benetton is a company whose advertising strategy has been well researched and analysed, and the fashion industry in general makes a good subject for semiotic analysis. Some ideas for semiotic analysis are listed below:

- the image of the boy band – themes of masculinity and youth
- the semiotics of music videos by a particular artist or within a particular genre
- signs of 'hip' and 'youth' in fashion advertising today and in the 1960s
- semiotics of the bad boy: Eminem's star persona.

Stages in a semiotic analysis

Let us look at the stages involved in conducting a semiotic analysis of fashion spreads in women's magazines. We are interested in comparing the codes surrounding the fashion spreads for older and younger women. Our hypothetical hypothesis is as follows: 'Codes of sex and sexuality are more commonly used in fashion spreads aimed at the mature woman than the younger woman.' There are no rules about which precise texts one should focus on or how many texts are necessary. Roland Barthes, in the case study above, wrote a very stimulating essay based on the analysis of just one advertising image, whereas Judith Williamson (1978) discussed dozens. It is up to the judgement of the analyst to determine how many are enough to make the case.

Define your object of analysis. Before we begin, we need to decide what our object of analysis is. Ideally, this should be related to our hypothesis – the object of analysis should be one which permits us to test the hypothesis. Taking our example of fashion spreads in women's magazines, we need to select our sample for analysis according to our hypothesis. Our hypothesis above suggests that we need to compare magazines with a young and an older audience. We define our object of analysis as the fashion pages of a magazine for younger woman, *Cosmopolitan*, compared with one aimed at older women, *Vogue*. We know that these have different classes of readers, but they are both high-profile magazines with a strong interest in fashion.

Gather the texts. First, you need to decide what images you are going to look at. In our example, we would have to go to the shop to buy the relevant issues or order them directly from the magazine's marketing department. Whether it is magazines, television programmes or films, gather together all the texts you are going to study before you begin your analysis. The exact number depends on the depth and breadth of your research and the import-ance of the semiotic analysis for the rest of your project. (Is semiotics the only method you are going to use, or are you using it as one among a few methods?)

Describe the texts. The first stage of your analysis is to describe the content of the texts or images very carefully. Carefully identify all of the elements or *semes* of the image. In our example, you will be looking speci-fically for connotations of sexuality, but in the first instance focus on the denotation – where is the setting? – is it urban or exotic? Domestic interior or wild countryside? How many models are there? Describe their pose. Separate out the linguistic message (the words) from the visual imagery and describe each as precisely as possible. You need to identify exactly what is included: discuss text and its relationship to image; is colour used? how? Try to stick to description of the literal image and text, or what is *denoted* by the images.

Interpret the texts. The next stage allows you to begin to discuss the meanings and implications of each separate sign individually and then collectively. Here you are considering the connotations of the texts. What is the relationship between the linguistic signs and the images? How do the two codes of signification work in relation to one another? Does reading the words give you a different interpretation of the images than just looking at the images alone, or are the words reinforcing the images? In our example of fashion photography, if the images did not have the prices and stockists of the clothing on them, indicating their status as fashion images, what would the images alone signify? Pornography or knitting pattern? Think about ambiguity – could they mean different things to different people?

Draw out the cultural codes. What kinds of cultural knowledge do you need to know to understand the text? How are the images drawing on our cultural knowledge to help us to create particular kinds of meaning? Are the cultural codes those one would expect from readers of this particular publication?

Make generalizations. What can you say about how the texts you have studied *mean*? To paraphrase Barthes, how has meaning got into your sample? How can you compare the ways the codes are being used in this sample? Are there different kinds of codes being used? How could you categorize these codes?

Make conclusions. Does your analysis confirm or refute your hypothesis? In our example, are fashion images in magazines aimed at older women more or less sexual than those aimed at younger women? Why/not? What other codes and conventions do they draw on that we had not anticipated before we began?

Combining semiotics with other methods of analysis

Semiotics can very usefully be combined with other methods of analysis. It is particularly fruitful to combine semiotic analysis with content analysis. You could use content analysis to determine how many of a certain kind of image exist in a given set of texts and then use semiotics to analyse a smaller selection in more detail. This combination would give you some breadth (looking at a range of images) and depth (analysing a small sample closely). For example, you might conduct a content analysis of the genres of music broadcast on MTV across peak weekday evenings to ascertain what kind of music gets the most coverage in terms of number of plays. Then you could use this data to determine which is the most popular genre (let's say it is rap) and then conduct a semiotic analysis of one or two of the most frequently played videos of this kind.

Semiotics could also be combined with participant observation or interviews with magazine editors, fashion photographers or publicists (both methods are discussed in Chapter 4). It is also possible to conduct your own semiotic analysis and then to have this confirmed by presenting your ideas to a focus group (discussed in Chapter 5). Semiotic analysis should be used to focus on the underlying meanings of texts, while other methods can be used to provide the context in which the texts are published, produced or received.

Reading more about semiotics

There are several useful overviews of semiotics aimed at students. One of the best is Jonathan Bignell's *Media Semiotics* (1997), which has a good discussion of Roland Barthes and sections on applying semiotics to advertising, women's magazines, newspapers, television news and drama, and cinema. John Storey also considers semiotics in the chapter 'Structuralism and Post-Structuralism' in his *Introductory Guide to Cultural Theory and Popular Culture* (1993). In *Researching Communications* (Deacon et al., 1999), the chapter 'Analysing Texts' has some useful examples and discussion. I would recommend anyone interested in finding out about the range of work which can be done with semiotics to dip into Barthes's *Mythologies* (1973) as a starting-off point. One scholar who has applied Barthes's insights to contemporary cultural artefacts with tremendous grace and style is Dick Hebdige – see, in particular, his essays 'Object as Image: The Italian Scooter Cycle' and 'The Bottom Line on Planet One: Squaring up to *The Face*' (both in Hebdige, 1988).

Ideological approaches

An ideology is a system of ideas or beliefs, and all media artefacts are the products of an ideology. The ideological position being put forward may be explicitly spelled out, as it is in religious tracts or political manifestos. But more often the ideology is *implicit* and one has to read into the text in order to find the ideology at work. When the Glasgow University Media Group investigated the news, as, for example, in Case Study 3.1 above, they found that a genre of television which works hard to present itself as non-political, was, they argued, highly biased. By identifying a particular ideology at work in a text which its producers claimed was not ideological, the Glasgow Group helped draw the attention of media scholars to the fact that all media artefacts are ideological in a way.

The purpose of discovering the 'ideology' or 'system of belief' under-lying a message is at the root of most forms of textual analysis: the purpose is usually to find the hidden meanings and values which may not be explicit at a first reading. Thus, most methods of analysis, like all methods of pro-duction, are 'ideological' in that they are informed by systems of ideas and thinking whether the analysts are explicit about it or not. It is impossible to do any kind of research without having an ideology. Ideology is to analysis what accent is to speech: you cannot be understood unless you have one, but if you make it too obvious or strident, no one except your closest allies is going to understand you.

There are often cases where the ideology of a piece of research is explicitly spelled out, usually in the case of oppositional or critical research. There isn't a method called 'ideological analysis' – but any method can be used as part of an ideological project. Your own ideology or point of view will be part of the theory informing your hypothesis. You will have a position that you want to prove embedded in an ideology whether you are using content analysis or focus groups. Some scholars insist that there are particular 'feminist' or 'Marxist' methods, but my own opinion is that the ideologies of feminism or Marxism are best served by studying topics of relevance by the methods most appropriate to the task. For example, a feminist investigation of television might look at the 'glass ceiling' in tele-vision management, or at the number of women in traditional housewife roles in situation comedy. The methods employed would be the same as for any other topic: but the choice of topic and the theoretical grounding would reflect the political interests of the investigator.

Perhaps the most renowned scholars of ideology in the media are Max Horkheimer and Theodor Adorno, whose essay on the 'Culture Industries' has been frequently republished (Adorno and Horkheimer, 1993). Hork-heimer and Adorno argue that the American media convey a particular ideology in support of the status quo. The culture industries, they maintain, squash any potential for radical change by offering individual solutions to social problems. Horkheimer and Adorno's anti-capitalist ideology compels them to affirm that the media should be fulfilling a role more uplifting of the human spirit by encouraging people to rebel against the system. But, because of the industrial nature of artistic production under capitalism, it is not possible for the artefacts produced to have the liberating potential Adorno and Horkheimer believe they should.

The work of Noam Chomsky on the news attempts to demonstrate that there is a pro-American agenda in reportage of Third World countries (Herman and Chomsky, 2002). Theodor Adorno's study of horoscopes shows how the apparently politically neutral astrology columns of the *Los Angeles Times* are, according to Adorno, vehicles of a particular capitalist ideology (Adorno, 1994). The Marxist scholars Dorfman and Mattelart (1975) argue that Donald Duck cartoons are conduits of individualism and anti-Marxist ideology.

The analysis of ideological content does not always have to be from a Marxist perspective: there are several studies from a feminist perspective or which simply highlight the ideological import of particular texts. In my view, it is possible to use almost any method in conducting an ideological analysis. It is perfectly possible for you to conduct ideological analyses of media texts, and you could do so using content analysis, narrative analysis, semiotics or any of the methods we will discuss in the next section. The interpretation of the underlying philosophy at work in a text provides the mainstay of much textual analysis. However, researchers interested in ideology are also often interested in power and economics. Marx's most valuable contribution to the study of society was in raising the level of interest in the material world or economics. Researchers interested in power and economics are more likely to be found studying the way the media industries work. In Chapter 4, we discuss some Marxist approaches to the study of media power and ownership (see pages 103–5).

Typological approaches

In this section we look at various methods used to think about media texts as belonging to a set or type. We have labelled these various approaches *typological* because the similarities in approach between the methods are so great. The methods focused on here (genre studies, star studies and auteur) all derive from film studies, but they all can, and should, be applied to other areas of media and cultural studies. If you are interested in the work of a particular author – whether songwriter, film director, television producer or advertising creative – you can learn a lot from thinking about that person as an 'auteur'.

Using film studies methods

One danger of methods of analysis derived from film studies is that they can be too descriptive. This is often exacerbated by the fact that, because we want to study things we admire, we can sometimes praise the work more along the lines of a supportive review than a critical piece of analysis. One way to avoid this is to make sure that you have a clear hypothesis (see Chapter 1 for more discussion of forming a hypothesis). As part of the process of developing critical distance you need to develop a way of watching which is detached and dispassionate. You need to make sure that the texts you are discussing are being used as *evidence* to support an *argument*. Try to get the balance about equal between your use of examples from the films (or other texts) as evidence and the argument which you are making to justify including the examples. The examples need to be carefully chosen as supporting your argument most closely. You can't say anything without evidence and you shouldn't use evidence without its being part of an argument. Film studies methods, like the others we discuss in this book, need not have a hypothesis in the exact sense of the word, but they certainly need to have an *argument* or *thesis*. You have to be saying something. It is not acceptable to embark on a project to study a film or set of films without knowing why or what you are looking for (see the earlier section, 'From hunches to hypotheses', page 55).

Methods of analysis and 'types'

A key element in our understanding and analysis of cultural products is the notion of *type*. The organization of literature into types has precedents dating back to the ancient Greek and Roman classifications of comedy, tragedy, satire and so on. Usually, people are well aware of the type of work they are making; most people who use media and cultural products do so fully aware of what *type* of product they are using. Classifying media texts according to type is not difficult. Types are convenient categories for creators and consumers of media and cultural texts, and they are used to label and classify material across the entire range of media output. In most circumstances, it is not terribly interesting to classify cultural products because they are usually true to type: we all know the difference between a soap opera and a game show, for example, and would think it banal to define *EastEnders* as a soap opera – typically, types are not controversial.

Things get interesting when new forms develop or are identified, or when established types have to be rethought. For example, *Big Brother* has several elements of a game show from the point of view of the contestants, but the pleasure we get in watching is more like soap opera. Is *Big Brother* a game show or soap opera? This is more interesting than asking whether *Coronation Street* is a soap opera. But exactly how interesting depends in large part on how you tell it. An interesting piece could be written using the hypothesis: '*Big Brother* is more soap opera than game show.' Just how interesting depends on the authors and how creative they are. Any kind of typological research is at the far end of our scale of interpretive methods. It is highly interpretive and not remotely reliable: a second researcher might have a completely different view and be able to demonstrate his or her argument with equal rigour. The proof of studies of typology is in the strength of the argument made and reference to the texts under examination.

Types are rhetorical terms which exist to help our understanding; they are not absolutes. New types are developed by producers and new labels generated by researchers and commentators on the media. Typological analyses are based on categorization and classification of texts. In this section we will be examining how texts can be analysed using various *typologies* derived from film studies. Genre, auteur and star studies are all methods of textual analysis which have their antecedents in the study of cinema but which are applicable to many other media and cultural products. In this chapter we will discuss the origination of these methods in film studies but will also give examples and sample hypotheses using other media. The categories *genre*, *auteur* and *star* are very familiar to us from popular literature about the cinema. But within media and cultural research, each of these terms refers to a very specific method of analysis, requiring the researcher to study a set of texts linked by a set of common characteristics (of genre, author or star) and to make original claims about the relationship of one or more texts to that type. All methods have a great deal in common with one another, and that is why I link them together in this chapter as typological studies: they are all studies of types and as such have several similarities in execution.

Strengths and weaknesses of typological studies

If you are very familiar with a certain type of text, typological studies allow you to exploit your own knowledge and permit you to indulge yourself in your own interest. Any study of typology requires a very detailed knowledge of the texts, and I would recommend that you undertake such studies only if you are already very familiar with the texts and want to theorize your interest. As with all textual analyses, you need to have a very high level of rhetorical skill and be able to use the media texts you are looking at as evidence in your work. If you are not already a fan of the subject matter, you could quickly become bored by it. All of these forms of study are very time-consuming, and you should not attempt to undertake these approaches unless you are prepared to put in a lot of time working with them. You cannot do typological analysis of films based on a single viewing, and I would recommend that at least three are necessary. You should watch each film in your set once as a 'naive' viewer; after thinking about all the films for a while, you should watch them again a second time in order to analyse your hunches and a third time to confirm your ideas and to select specific examples. You may need to change your mind at any time in this process, rethink your research question and view the whole lot again. Make sure you allow sufficient time to view the whole set of material several times when planning your time.

You need to have a high level of rhetorical skill to undertake these methods, you will be required to display a high level of analytical ability and you should not undertake these methods unless you are a confident writer.

The relationship between textual analysis and archive research

It is very important that any form of typographic analysis includes a significant element of archive research. It is absolutely vital that you research what has been written on your chosen topic, and that you show that your reading has informed the way you think about the topic. However, archive research is no substitute for looking at the media: textual analyses of the kind addressed in this chapter all require close and detailed study of your chosen texts. Reading what other people have written is no substitute for your own research and ideas, although their work should supplement yours. However, you cannot find out what to do by researching in the library. The answers to your question won't be found in the pages of the academic journals. You do need to do some library work – find out what others have said and make sure you don't go over old territory. Research should always *add* to our knowledge – not regurgitate it! Use the archive for background research. Get your facts straight. Find out about the field. Do not think the film analysis (textual) can be done in the library. If you are doing a film analysis, most of your research time should be spent looking at and thinking about the films. But this should be done from an informed perspective which can be obtained only by doing library research.

Most typological studies are based on a few very basic structures:

- how far a particular text fits (or does not fit) a given type
- whether a text is of one type or another (for example, is it a thriller or a comedy?)
- whether a text is one category of type or another (for example, is it the product of its star or its auteur?)
- how an existing classification of a type needs to be redefined in the light of recent developments in the medium.

The structure of the essay is to come up with the means by which it would or would not fit the classification in your hypothesis and then provide evidence for and against the relevant criteria.

Genre study

One of the key ways in which films have been developed and marketed is along lines of genre. The classic Hollywood films are frequently classified generically: musical, Western, romantic comedy, film noir – all these are terms which describe a genre (Schatz, 1981). Genres come and go in fashion:

Westerns and musicals are currently out of fashion while war movies are undergoing something of a resurgence, and the gangster film has survived many a twist in its fortunes. The only genre which never seems to go out of style is the comedy, although that is because it is so flexible (Neale and Krutnik, 1990). The Western is an archetypical genre, perhaps because of the strong iconography and close relationship with the myth-making function of the West in the American imagination. Several key essays on the Western are collected in Ian Cameron and Douglas Pye's book (1996), although perhaps the most important book on the Western is Will Wright's *Six-Guns and Society* (1979).

The idea that films are more commonly the product of their genre than of their author developed in film theory in the 1960s. Hollywood studios have been mass-producing films with specific types for marketing purposes from the earliest days. *The Great Train Robbery* (directed by Edwin S. Porter in 1903), for example, is one of the first studio films, and it was produced and marketed as a Western. The Western grew out of the comics and dime novels of the nineteenth century, which were themselves marketed according to genres popular at the time (Wright, 1979). The term *genre* also has origins in art history, where it is used to refer to popular paintings (as opposed to literary or highbrow ones), a fact which gives *genre* the connotation of being lowbrow. It is a term still used in the publishing industry to distinguish mass market books from *literary* ones.

Within film studies, genre research investigates films by relating them to other films of the same genre. Films are often studied according to their genre: the musical, the Western and the romantic comedy are all categories which we know well, and there is a great deal published on specific genres, most of it at the popular rather than academic end of the spectrum. Genres are largely the product of the studio system. The studios in the classical Hollywood era (approximately 1930–60 [Bordwell, Thompson and Staiger, 1985; Neale and Smith, 1998]) made films of each genre – Westerns, comedies, musicals, etc. – to ensure maximum audiences in their cinemas overall. Some studios specialized in particular genres; for example, MGM was known for the musical and Warner Brothers for the gangster movie.

What kind of typology is genre?

You must excuse the tautology in talking about types of type (as we are here). Genre is one of the most easily identifiable means of classifying films because it is so readily used by the film industry, especially the Hollywood film industry, for marketing purposes. The style and iconography of advertising for the cinema play on the audience's knowledge of genre. Films are marketed according to genre so that we know what we are going to see when we buy a ticket – the horror film is clearly identified as such by trailers, posters and other advance publicity. Genres also set up a relationship between the film-maker and the audience; when we choose to see a thriller, for example, we enter the cinema expecting to be excited. Films play on these expectations in the credit sequences, getting us into the mood rapidly. The genre classifications let us know what we can expect from the films; the films themselves will also use 'in' jokes and references which only the audience members familiar with the genre will get. Such devices flatter the audience, making them think that they are part of the cognoscenti, and encourage a greater sense of identification between the audience and the genre. This builds a community of familiarity with the conventions which is reinforcing.

Genre is also a *semiotic* category in that there are codes and conventions which films of a genre share. For example, elements such as location, style and *mise en scène* are all part of a coded system which one can identify through semiotic analysis. For example, gangster movies include key iconographic elements such as fast cars, images of urban decay and Italian American restaurants – these are all *signifiers* of the gangster genre.

Genre is also a *narrative* category: the boy-meets-girl structure of the romance is an invariable deep structure of any movie of the genre. 'If you've seen one, you've seen 'em all', we may hear people say of horror films, or action movies. The gangster movie has to have: the stake-out, the chase scene, the 'execution', the betrayal – all are narrative conventions which have grown up over the years, and which are developed and worked on by subsequent film-makers. Altman (1999) says: 'The pleasure of genre film spectatorship thus derives more from reaffirmation than from novelty. People go to genre films to participate in events that somehow seem familiar' (Altman, 1999: 25). Another pleasure of the genre film is in seeing how each key element is reinterpreted or reinvented for contemporary mores and values, as genres do change over time. One of the most widely studied of genres, the Western, had its origins in some of the first films ever made at the beginning of the twentieth century such as Edwin S. Porter's 1903 movie, *The Great Train Robbery*. The Western came to maturity during the 1940s and 1950s with films such as *Shane* (1953) and the great Westerns directed by John Ford, including *Rio Grande* (1950) and *The Searchers* (1956). The Western was also a television genre during the 1950s and 1960s, and television drama became the more typical vehicle for stories about the West as the cinema declined in cultural significance. In the 'post-Hollywood' era, the Western has become more parodied. *Unforgiven* (1992) is an example of a very late Western which is highly critical of the basic tenets of the cowboy ethos – *Unforgiven* takes as a key theme, the settlement of the West and deromanticizes it.

There have been many different theories put forward to explain the changing pattern of genres. But, in general, genres do go through trans-formations. Martin Rubin (1999) argues that the thriller has gone through three distinct phases: *formative*, *classical* and *modern*. These three broad categories might be applied to any number of genres. Hansen et al. (1998: 179) cut the cake a slightly different way when they argue that there are five stages in the history of a genre:

Five stages of genre development. Source: Hansen et al (1998): 179
1. experimental
2. classical
3. parody
4. deconstruction
5. postmodernism

Whether there are three or twenty-three stages is a matter of personal interpretation. It is up to you, the researcher, to determine where the work you have chosen for your object of analysis fits along the trajectory of the genre in question.

Steve Neale (1992) explores the revival in romance films in the early 1990s. He identifies specific features of the 'new romance' genre through a textual analysis of the characters and themes of some key films from the late 1980s and early 1990s. Neale provides a typography of what he labels 'the new romance' through comparing key elements of classical and new romantic films such as *Splash!*, *Something Wild* and *Roxanne*.

According to Jane Feuer (1982), the musical genre has a cycle: it begins as an outcrop of the musical stage. It develops as a means of showcasing performers – the stage element is present in early musicals of the 1930s to justify the signing and dancing. During the 1950s, it develops into a genre where the singing and dancing can just occur as part of ordinary life, and no one notices that it isn't normal. But eventually the genre becomes about making a film about putting on a show, and then a film about films about putting on a show, before finally becoming a self-referential joke.

The classic gangster film is usually about the downfall of a hood. The themes are betrayal and self-destruction. The genre was developed during the 1930s by Warner Brothers – a studio which was very much concerned with themes of social justice. *The Public Enemy* (1931) starred James Cagney, who was cast as the archetypal gangster in films such as *White Heat* (1959), *Little Caesar* or *Scarface*. The gangster film is usually set in the city; it is a truly urban genre, concerned with how people struggle to survive and the moral choices people have to make to survive. The gangster film glorifies the gangster, even if he is killed off in the end. The bravado and wit of the man taking a stand against the law are admired in the genre. Ideologically, it celebrates the individual hero. It shows groups as providing solidarity and companionship, but, ultimately, proves that no one can live outside the law for long. The genre was significantly rewritten by *The Godfather* series, in which the family was seen as crucially important. Individual psychological analysis is still a feature of the gangster film after *The Godfather* but it is played out against the backdrop of the family.

While auteur criticism (discussed below) links films to the psychology of the director, in genre criticism it is more likely that the film will be seen as a product of its time. For example, the British gangster film of the 1990s is read as an allegory of Thatcherism by Claire Monk (1999a). British gangster movies have different sets of preoccupations and themes than their Hollywood counterparts, in large part because of the different cultural location of the villain in the two societies (Chibnall and Murphy, 1999).

CASE STUDY 3.4. GENRE STUDY

Jane Feuer, 1982. *The Hollywood Musical*. London: Macmillan.

This analysis of the Hollywood musical charts the history of the genre starting with its origins in the music hall and popular theatre. Various recurrent themes are identified and analysed with careful and detailed illustration from over one hundred musical films. Feuer argues that the musical has much in common with 'folk art' of a preindustrial era, yet it is a mechanical medium in which the relationship between the audience and performers is temporally and spatially remote. According to Feuer, the musical works to reconstruct the sense of community we have lost in the industrial age by recreating that lost spirit of camaraderie on the screen. She claims: 'The Hollywood musical becomes a mass art which aspires to the condition of a folk art, produced and consumed by the same integrated community' (p. 3). Feuer presents the case that the musical genre has changed and adapted through time – she creates a roughly chronological categorization of the main subgenres of the musical.

Conducting your own genre research

In using genre study as your method, you are going to be conducting a rhetorical analysis of a text or set of texts. The kinds of hypotheses you can use are based on the extent to which one or more texts do or do not adhere to the conventions of the genre. Those conventions may be semiotic, narrative or representational.

Type 1. How far does a particular text conform to a genre? There has to be a surprise here. It is pretty boring to say that *The Godfather* is a typical gangster movie. The twist could be that it goes against intuition (*The Godfather* is a typical rites-of-passage movie, for example). But you need to be proving something that we wouldn't have thought of, or have some original insight. Rhetorically, you need to establish clearly what the typical conventions are of both the genre that one would assume the text belongs to and the one that you are going to demonstrate that it actually does belong to. Then you have to demonstrate that the text is not so familiar after all.

Type 2. Is a new genre developing? Developing a *neologism* for a new genre is a good take on genre research. If you think that there is a set of films which have something in common which has not been identified before, you could make a case for a new genre. For example, let's take the hypothesis 'John Woo's films are a reinterpretation of the classic gangster film.' You would have to look at the classic gangster film and determine the main codes and conventions. Then you would have to compare these to the codes and conventions of a number of Woo's films, such as *Hard Boiled* or *Face Off*.

Of course, there is no reason why genre study should be confined to the cinema. There are generic conventions available for being investigation and interrogation in every medium. Perhaps one of the most interesting is television. After decades of relative stability in genre programming from approximately 1955 to 1984, the television industry in Britain is in a state of flux. Looking for new ways to package old ideas, television producers are among the most assiduous in stealing genre conventions. There have been many hybrids in recent years.

The most egregious mixing of forms is probably the costume drama and news. It has become commonplace to have actors perform scenes from high-profile crime stories, even in mainstream news programmes such as *Newsnight*. In the area of documentary this is even more pronounced. *Victorians Uncovered: Virgin Trade* (Channel 4, 27 March 2001), for example, used reconstructions of notorious nineteenth-century scandals involving procurement of young girls for the sex industry. If you took this as your object of analysis, you might use as your research question: 'How far is documentary film becoming more like costume drama?'

This question would require you to conduct a comparative analysis of both genres before subjecting the text in question to analysis. If you were to ask, '*Big Brother*: only a game show?', you would have to investigate the extent to which *Big Brother* is typical of a game show and whether it is something more. If you thought there was more to it than a game show, you would have to determine what. In either case, you would need a good knowledge of the various television genres being investigated.

A worked example: applying genre analysis to The Sopranos

If we take as our object of analysis, the television series *The Sopranos*, we can immediately perceive that this series has many of the hallmarks of a gangster movie. *The Sopranos* is written and directed by David Chase. Commissioned by American cable network HBO, it had its first airing on US television. The series stars James Gandolfini as Tony Soprano, the boss of a Cosa Nostra family in New Jersey. Ostensibly a 'waste management consultant', Tony is identified early on as a contradictory character, at once ruthless and magnanimous. The characters of Tony and his gang pay homage to *The Godfather* as well as traditional gangster movies such as *Little Caesar* and *Scarface*. Tony's world of New Jersey and the mob owes much to Martin Scorsese's *GoodFellas* (1990), in which the home life of the gang is carefully drawn, and the actions of the protagonists are shown in parallel with their often complicated family lives. Tony is a family man in the Mafia sense and the demographic sense – and the family drama makes up a great deal of the action. His wife, Carmela (Edie Falco), runs the home and raises their two children, Meadow and Anthony Junior. The twist on the traditional gangster trope is borrowed from a 1990s gangster movie, *Analyze This*, in which the mob boss is referred for therapy. When translated into a television series, this idea includes the family background, and we are introduced to the boss as head of household. *The Sopranos* has much in common with the American situation comedy. It is a series revolving around the exploits of home and work, the figure of Tony linking both environments. *The Sopranos* is made for television, of course, and has several features in common with television programmes which also focus on the family and the workplace, such as *Murphy Brown*.

If we wanted to take these ideas further, we could analyse the features that *The Sopranos* shares with the gangster movie and with the situation comedy. We might hypothesize: '*The Sopranos* has more in common with the situation comedy than with the gangster movie.' Table 3.2 lists the conventions of the gangster movie and those of the situation comedy. To test our hypothesis, we first need to establish the codes and conventions of the relevant genres, by reference to the literature and to a wide range of texts. Next we need to analyse how far the text under investigation (in this case, *The Sopranos*) is typical of the genres in question. In analysing *The Sopranos*, we would probably find that the text mixes elements of various genres liberally and knowingly. It has the format of a soap opera, being centred around the work and family of a single larger-than-life character – in this respect, Tony Soprano has lots in common with Murphy Brown. But in terms of content, it has many of the hallmarks of a postmodern gangster film. *The Sopranos* is a very sophisticated text which successfully mixes genres in a delightful and exciting way.

In conducting your own genre analysis, you could apply a similar approach to a different text. If you want to investigate the extent to which a text (or set of texts) belongs to two different genres, you could follow the method laid out above. Identify the main characteristics of the relevant

	Gangster Movies	Situation Comedy
Setting	The city Harsh social background	The city Middle-class USA
Location	The mob hangout Glamorous clubs Lavish mansions	The home The workplace
Iconography	Flash clothes Guns	Everyday clothes
Narrative events	Heists Hits Double-crossing	Dating Social events Barbecues
Characters	Gang leader Gangsters Rival gangsters	Family members Workmates
Plot structure	Closure Sometimes dies Sometimes is reformed Sometimes is redeemed	Open-ended Maintain equilibrium Endless

TABLE 3.2 Comparison of Some Conventions of Gangster Films and Television Situation Comedy

genres from the literature and from your own knowledge. Then you need to analyse carefully the texts to see to what extent they have features in common with one or another genres.

Auteur study

Kristin Thompson and David Bordwell argue that 'one of the most influential ideas in cinema history is the belief that a director is most centrally responsible for a film's form, style and meanings' (1994: 492). They go on:

> To a great extent, the academic study of film in the English-speaking countries arose from auteurism. The premise of individual artistic expression proved congenial to scholars trained in art, literature, and theater. Moreover, auteurism's emphasis on the interpretation of film called on skills already cultivated by literary education. (Thompson and Bordwell, 1994: 514)

The idea (myth?) of the 'author' of mass media is advanced everywhere: the search for authors is one which happens at every level of criticism and appreciation. We need to personalize media production, and the idea of the author allows us to do this. But it is a myth – there is no single organizing intelligence in a film, and any decent director will tell you that his or her work is reliant on cinematographers, editors, art directors, actors and writers.

We use the French term 'auteur' to describe the study of the role of an author in the creation of a media text because of the importance of the French scholars writing in the magazine *Cahiers du Cinéma*. The writers in this journal of the 1950s and 1960s explored the power of the Hollywood film. They were among the first people to classify these films according to director, to screen a director's films together, and to think about the relationship between films of various genres as if they were made by the same director. For example, they studied the work of John Ford, a director who worked in various genres but whose work nonetheless displayed a 'single organizing intelligence'. If we wished to apply these methods, Spike Lee would make a good case study because he makes films in so many different genres and with such diverse subject matter. Is there a 'single organizing intelligence' in his work? Examples include studies of Hollywood directors from the classical Hollywood period, such as Howard Hawks (Wood, 1981), Alfred Hitchcock or John Ford. More recent directors to be given similar treatment include Joel and Ethan Coen (Mottram, 2000) and Steven Spielberg. Case Study 3.5 presents an example of a recent book about Martin Scorsese which deliberately puts the case that Scorsese is an auteur.

CASE STUDY 3.5. AUTEUR ANALYSIS

Lawrence S. Friedman, 1999. *The Cinema of Martin Scorsese*. Oxford: Roundhouse Publishing.

Friedman's study of the cinema of Martin Scorsese begins by acknowledging that the idea of the auteur seems a little out of date in the modern world. François Truffaut is credited with developing the theory of the auteur, an approach which, Friedman acknowledges, seems rather old-fashioned and elitist given that the boundaries of high and popular culture have been significantly blurred. Yet, for Friedman, the idea of auteur 'finally boils down to . . . personal vision' (p. 10), and there is no other director who has 'created an intensely personal cinema on the order of Martin Scorsese's' (p. 10).

The Cinema of Martin Scorsese charts Scorsese' film-making career, beginning with his student films of the late 1960s and continuing to his 1996 film, *Kundun*. Scorsese's output has been phenomenal and he is a leading light in the American cinema. Among his most critically acclaimed films are *Taxi Driver* (1976), *Raging Bull* (1980) and *GoodFellas* (1990). Scorsese's films span the range of genres, including musicals (*New York, New York* [1977]), costume dramas (*The Age of Innocence* [1993]), thrillers (*Cape Fear* [1991]) and, most famously, gangster movies. Despite these diverse interests,

Friedman argues that Scorsese remains the ultimate auteur because of his continuing interest in the underlying moral conflicts of all his characters.

In parallel with the discussion of the films Martin Scorsese has made, Friedman discusses details of Scorsese's private life. This is a classic study in auteurism because of the way Friedman strives to make connections between Martin Scorsese's personal interests and preoccupations and the films he has made. Thus, Scorsese's strict Catholic upbringing is considered to be the source of the theme of guilt which, argues Friedman, is 'a recurrent motif, perhaps *the* recurrent motif in Scorsese's life and art alike' (p. 11). The conclusion that Friedman reaches after analysing Scorsese's biography and films is that Scorsese's vision is ultimately religious: 'How to live a Christian life in a fallen world is the recurring theme of his major films' (p. 186).

Friedman has written an unashamedly auteurist study of Martin Scorsese's films. *The Cinema of Martin Scorsese* is an example of the clear application of auteur theory: it makes parallels between the *biography* and *filmography* of its subject and analyses the films by focusing on the common themes in the life and work of the artist.

Other studies in a more popular vein do not directly acknowledge their roots in auteurism, nonetheless, it is not uncommon in journalism and film literature to find parallels being made between a film and its creator.

Books about auteurs are very often biographical, and it is not uncommon for research on films made by an auteur to focus on the psychology of the film-maker. During World War II, there had been no Hollywood films shown in France, and after the war they began to see them again – suddenly, there were hundreds of films available and the French appreciation of American cinema was very high. Many critics wanted to demonstrate that these films were worthy of serious critical appreciation and set about studying and analysing them according to the methods of art and literature – these methods ascribe agency to the author – whether painter, writer or other creator. The *Cahiers du Cinéma* writers did not rule out that anyone could, theoretically, be an auteur, but focused most of their attention on the director as auteur. Its writers argued that the director of a film was the person most in control and thus able to stamp his or her own ideas and thoughts on the film. These critics developed the theory of the *politiques des auteurs*, or auteur theory, in which they maintained that the auteur (usually the director) was the 'single organizing intelligence' behind a work. The political impetus behind auteur theory was a reaction against attempts by the French establishment to dismiss American culture in general and Hollywood cinema in particular as ephemeral, junk culture, or simply entertainment. The *Cahiers du Cinéma* writers were intent on proving that the cinema had to be taken seriously as 'art'. Most people now accept that popular culture should be studied seriously (especially within media and cultural studies), so this contention is not very controversial today, but in the 1950s this was quite a radical statement.

The promotion of the idea of the auteur occurred at a formative stage in the development of film theory and media studies. A lot of popular criticism is still derived from auteur criticism – reviews and interviews with directors in newspapers and magazines reinforce this idea that the director of a film is the key creative person, although we know that it takes hundreds of people to make a film, and that the person who puts together that group of people (usually the producer) actually has as much input. Peter Wollen argues that the auteur theory is enormously productive for the study of film, but that there is much that needs to be done:

> We need to investigate and define, to construct critically the work of enormous numbers of directors who until now have only been incompletely comprehended. We need to begin the task of comparing author with author. . . . Moreover, there is no reason why the auteur theory should not be applied to the English cinema which is still utterly amorphous, unclassified, unperceived. (Wollen, 1998: 78)

There is plenty of scope for students to make the case that particular filmmakers are indeed 'auteurs' in the classic sense of the word.

Auteurs are everywhere

Auteur analysis has not only been applied to the cinema, of course. The idea of the auteur originates in English literature where the author has long been the primary means of categorizing and studying literature. The questioning of the 'great man' theory of literature and of the canon came about in the 1960s at the same time that the film critics were applying notions of authorship to the movies. The idea of the auteur is not unique to high cultural forms, but can be applied to other forms, too. Auteur analysis has been applied to the study of advertising, for example it has been argued that Tony Kaye, the advertiser turned artist who directed *American History X* was a brilliant advertising creative who shaped the Benetton campaigns in the 1990s.

Auteur analysis has been applied to the study of television, where sometimes the auteur is the *writer* of the drama, like Dennis Potter (*The Singing Detective*; *Pennies From Heaven*; *Karaoke*) or Jimmy McGovern (*Cracker*). In other instances, it is the *producer* who is selected for the accolade, as is Steven Bochco, the producer of *Hill Street Blues* (1981–87). This famous American police series shows the humanity of police officers in what is arguably the first of *modern* police dramas. *Hill Street Blues* paved the way for contemporary television police dramas such as *NYPD Blue* (also a Bochco show). Evidence of Bochco's authorial control can be seen in the fact that, when he and Michael Kozoll were asked by NBC to do a police series, they agreed only on condition that they could have complete artistic control.

David Marc and Robert J. Thompson examine the role of the television producer, including Steven Bochco, in *Prime Time, Prime Movers. From 'I Love Lucy' to 'L.A. Law' – America's Greatest TV Shows and the People Who Created Them* (Marc and Thompson, 1995). Marc and Thompson place their enquiry firmly in the realm of the auteur when they pose the question: 'Who is the author of television?' Marc and Thompson argue that, despite the highly industrial nature of modern media production, 'the artistic act still thoroughly depends on the conscious effort of the individual creator' (1995: 4). The *individual creator* in the case of television is the producer, and *Prime Time, Prime Movers* presents brief biographies of over two dozen producers of American television. The selection is based on a subjective measure of the 'greatest' American television shows; the importance of the producer is based on the implicit claim that this role is the single most important one in the production of a television programme. They include in their list the producers of the most important situation comedies, dramas and soaps. The historical producers are Norman Lear (*All in the Family*; *The Jeffersons*; *Archie Bunker's Place*); Sherwood Schwartz (*Gilligan's Island*; *The Brady Bunch*) and Jack Webb (*Dragnet*). Among the more recent producers, they discuss the documentary maker Ken Burns (*The Civil War*; *The Story of Jazz*), the situation comedy producer Diane English (*Murphy Brown*) and, of course, Steve Bochco, whose *Hill Street Blues* reinvented the television police series, and who also created *L.A. Law, Doogie Howser, M.D.* and *NYPD Blue*. This study contrasts significantly in approach with Jeremy Tunstall's study (1993) of British television producers discussed in Chapter 4 (Case Study 4.2, pp. 115–17).

Where you think that a set of texts (films, radio programmes, songs) have been shaped by the influence of a single author (despite being mass-produced), you could use auteur analysis. You need to show that the common characteristics are the product of the single authorial voice (and not of some other shared characteristic such as production company or star vehicle). Typically, auteur study involves an element of psychological attribution: asserting a link between the psyche of the auteur in question and the themes of her or his work. This is a fruitful and interesting approach for you to take to work which would not typically be considered to have an 'author'.

Star study

One of the key ways that films are made and marketed is via the vehicle of the *star*. The film industry has made and promoted celebrity performers throughout its history (Balio, 1976a). The key work on star studies has been done by Richard Dyer (1982; 1987), who uses a range of sources and methods to analyse the phenomenon of stars. The study of movie stars is a recurrent, if intermittent, topic within film studies. The Canadian journal *CineAction* devoted its 55th issue (2001) to the study of stars, including essays on Ethan Hawke (Wood, 2001), Anthony Hopkins (Johnson, 2001) and Hugh Grant (Sweeney, 2001).

The star system grew up as part of the Hollywood cinema. Stars are featured players or principal performers in a film. But they are more than that – there is a whole paraphernalia of literature and publicity devoted to building a star image. Stars attend gala awards, premieres and openings; they appear on chat shows and games shows; they give interviews to magazines and television programmes – all of these activities contribute to the construction of the star image. It is this public persona of the star that you would access in your analysis. Star studies are not concerned with the real Tom Hanks or Julia Roberts – they are concerned with the image of 'Tom Hanks' and 'Julia Roberts' as saleable, realizable commodities. The way to research stars is through the paraphernalia surrounding them as well as the film roles they take. Star studies are a form of discourse analysis exploring how the star is developed in divergent sources. The primary analysis for such work involves looking at the many places where stars are figured. The primary sources for star studies including the following:

- films in which star appears
- posters and advertising for films
- interviews and appearances on television
- press coverage and stories in the print media
- official and unofficial fan literature.

Most scholars working in this area today owe a great deal to Dyer's work, a debt acknowledged by Susan Holmes in her study of film stars on British television (2001). This essay is an analysis of the star image of Joan Crawford in the British television programme *Film Fanfare*, which ran on ABC television in the UK from 1956 to 1957. She also uses as a primary source contemporary magazines, especially the popular general interest magazine, *Picture Post*. She shows how major movie stars, such as Crawford, engaged in a renegotiation of their star identity by appearing on *Film Fanfare*. Holmes discusses the shifting relationship between film and television at the time and shows how Crawford's star persona was also changing at this time. Her secondary research, then, would have involved an investigation of the status of the two signifying industries and the state of Crawford's career at the time. Holmes finds that 'While the central paradox of stardom, that of being constituted as ordinary yet extraordinary, was partly modelled on conventions established by other media, television reshaped it within the specificity of its textual form' (Holmes, 2001: 186).

The star is an abiding phenomenon and one that continues to be investigated and studied. There are stars who have become inalienably associated with particular genres. Later in their careers, they can trade on this; for example, when Bruce Willis appears in *Sixth Sense* as a jaded child psychologist, the casting plays on the fact that he is an action hero no more.

Star studies in non-film media

So far, we have mainly discussed the construction of film stars. A much neglected area of research is that of stars of other media. What, for example, makes a television star? Cilla Black, Michael Barrymore and Graham Norton all are great television performers. Many people would argue that they are stars, but is this so? In the field of music, there are several performers who regularly are labelled stars, but their images are rarely subjected to detailed analysis as stars. Madonna, George Michael and Elton John have all had long careers at the top of their profession and are every bit as well known as the movie stars of Hollywood's heyday. There is every reason to subject these 'stars' to the same kind of analysis that other theorists have applied to James Cagney or Bette Davis.

Your star study could focus on stars you particularly admire (or hate – but it is a good idea to have some strong feeling). Think about their career and what stage they are in. Select three to six different elements – a performance on television, an interview in a magazine, an album – and analyse what they are saying about themselves and their public personae.

Star study involves archive research, textual analysis and semiotic analysis to be fully successful.

Combining methods of analysing texts

Combining typologies

It has become an orthodoxy within film studies to consider the kinds of typological analysis discussed in the section above to be quite separate, and scholars typically conduct work which focuses on the auteur *or* the genre *or* star studies. There are very good institutional reasons for this specialization of method and approach that are not always beneficial to improving our knowledge and understanding of the media. If you want to study texts as the total product of genre, auteur and star, by all means go ahead. You could combine typologies to unpack which elements of a text are the product of its creator, which are attributable to its genre and which are attributable to its performer. This would provide a strong basis for an interesting study of texts from any area of media and culture, including dance, music, television or film. Just because the methodologies discussed here have not been applied to a particular form in which you are interested doesn't mean they cannot or should not be. The methods discussed in this section were all developed by scholars of film, but they are readily applicable to any other medium.

There are times when you might want to get a general overview of a set of texts and then focus on more detailed aspects. One might use content analysis to give a quantitative account of how many of something occurs and follow this up with a more textured semiotic or ideological analysis of the meanings. For example, Peter Beharrell's study (1993) combines content analysis of press coverage of HIV and AIDS with careful ideological analysis of the news. First of all, he charts the history of how much coverage of HIV/AIDS there has been in the press, measuring stories in column inches. Subsequently, he investigates the more nuanced changes in attitudes towards AIDS and HIV. This research unravels the different ideological positions of the press and investigates shifts in their various agendas. Beharrell's extremely comprehensive and wide-ranging study is much too complex for researchers just starting out to emulate in terms of scale. Nonetheless, the study of the relationship between changes in the amount of coverage of an issue and the cultural location of that phenomenon is something which could be undertaken.

My own book, *On Screen Rivals* (Stokes, 1999c), looks at the historical relationship between the film industry and the television industry. The later chapters comprise a textual analysis of films from 1927 to 1990 which are 'about' television; they examine the changing depiction of television in films in Britain and the USA. The textual analysis is thus grounded in an historical survey of the economic relationship between the two industries. The attempt is made to examine the relationship between the film and television industries and to situate the films about television within this. Thus, the cultural construction of television can be seen to be partly shaped by the relationship of the real-world phenomenon of the television industry to the medium, representing television symbolically.

Using textual analysis in conjunction with other approaches

One of the criticisms levelled against methods which focus on texts is that they ignore the contexts of production and consumption. Sometimes the relationship between the text and its producers is of interest. In such a case, it may be appropriate to investigate how the production influenced the final text, as, for example, by interviewing a director about his or her film. Your research might well take you on to combine methods of textual research with methods of industry analysis. Likewise with audiences: you may find that your interest in a particular television programme leads you to ask what people get out of their viewing – in this case, you could combine textual analysis of the programme with in-depth interviews or focus groups with people who watch the programme.

Methods of analysing texts are frequently combined with other methods in published research. We may frequently want to conduct some kind of textual analysis in combination with some other method, such as interviews with producers or audiences. If we want to compare what people do with what they say they do, we may take as an example James Curran's study of literary editors. Curran's study has two parts: he conducts a content analysis of what books literary editors have reviewed, and then he compares this with what literary editors say they are doing in interviews with him. Combining content analysis of what gets into print with interviews eliciting the editors' beliefs about their decision-making processes proves very illuminating. Curran's study identifies some interesting discrepancies between what the editors say they do and what they actually do. Here content analysis provides an interesting real-world measure to compare with interviewees' perceptions. 'What it seeks to understand is how literary editors do their job, and how their judgements reflect and influence the hierarchy of knowledge in society' (Curran, 2000b: 215).

Curran's work has often focused on the real-world working activities of professionals in the media. His theoretical interest is to show how pro-fessional norms and values inflect media production. His work could be extended by students interested in exploring the relationship between what producers of media artefacts claim they do and what they actually do.

Discussion

There are many methods for studying media texts, and this chapter has highlighted the necessity of matching your method carefully to your object of analysis. You must bear in mind the relationship between your object of analysis and your method throughout your study. I hope this chapter has given you lots of ideas as to how you might approach your research project when analysing media texts. But there are limitations to what you can study using the methods discussed in this chapter. No amount of textual analysis will tell you what the motivation of the director was, nor whether the text was a success or not. You can do content analysis until you are blue in the face, but you won't learn anything about the way audiences respond to media products. In the next two chapters, we will look at the way in which you can study media institutions and media audiences.

4 Researching Media Institutions and the Culture Industries

Chapter overview

In this chapter we look at some of the ways that the beginner researcher can investigate the media and culture industries and organizations. We begin by defining what we mean by 'culture industries' and discuss the range of media and cultural artefacts students can research. As with any other industry, a great deal of research into media and culture is conducted or commissioned by companies and organizations involved in the production, distribution and dissemination of the media. This research typically has what we can call an 'administrative' goal – this research is primarily aimed at helping the organizations and companies concerned reach their own goals. This chapter begins by considering how we can assess the value of work done by institutions and industries which research the media. The government also has an important role to play in determining the shape of the media and culture industries through legislation, subsidy and regulation.

A number of scholars in our field have addressed the relationship between theories of culture and the practice of the media and culture industries. Much of this work is heavily indebted to the work of the philosopher Karl Marx. Marx's impact on the social sciences and humanities has been immeasurable; here we discuss briefly some of his legacy for the study of the media and culture industries. Students are encouraged to think about the importance of the material reality of the media and culture industries in their own work.

Another key area in which the relationship between theory and industry has been well investigated in our field is that of technology, especially theories of new technology. In this chapter we look at the ways in which we can investigate how technological change can influence the culture industries. This chapter also considers what particular problems and opportunities are afforded to the researcher of the media industries.

The first method discussed in this chapter is *archive research*, which largely involves research of published material, either in the library or via the Internet. This form of research is well suited to investigating the past, and we discuss the applications of this form of historical research to our field. We focus on film history as one area where some particularly interesting work has been conducted. Our case study in this area is Paddy Scannell and David Cardiff's thoroughly researched and engaging social history of early broadcasting (1991). We take the reader through the stages of archive research and discuss the uses and application of this kind of work.

While archive research uses documents as its primary source for investigation, the second method we discuss in this chapter, the *interview*, uses people as its main focus. Jeremy Tunstall has been a prolific investigator of the media industries with this technique, and we have selected as a case study his book, *Television Producers* (Tunstall, 1993). We offer some advice on how to arrange and conduct interviews and some examples of the kind of issues one can address by this particular method.

Participant observation, the third method discussed in this chapter, is an ideal method to use for studying behaviour among workers if you have access to relevant workplaces. It is recommended that this method be used by students who have work experience including close access to people who make significant decisions in a company. The case study we discuss here is Philip Schlesinger's important study of BBC newsrooms, *Putting Reality Together* (1987). This book presents a well-argued case for participant observation and demonstrates how rich theoretical work can be generated using this direct method of observation. The stages in a participant observation are presented and discussed.

The method of studying the recollections of ordinary people, either in individual interviews or groups, is known as *oral history*, and we briefly discuss this method here. If you have access to people who were working in the culture industries at interesting or important periods in their history, this method may provide you with some good information. It is more likely that oral history will be used by students to research audiences, and so this method is discussed in more detail in the following chapter, which looks at Shaun Moores's study of early radio use (see pages 151–2). The final case study in this chapter is Kembrew McLeod's study of discourses of authenticity in hip-hop, which combines interviews with textual analysis to generate rich data about the music industry (McLeod, 1999). This chapter concludes with a discussion of the kinds of research students can undertake using their own contacts, interests and aspirations.

Introduction

One of the key issues fuelling debate within media studies education currently is the relationship between 'theory' and 'practice'. Both of these terms are highly complex, but at stake is the way that theorists and prac-titioners interact: frequently, this is cast in terms of the 'academy' versus the 'industry'. One of the most important conclusions to be drawn from this debate is that academics and students of the media need to have a much more detailed understanding of the activities of the 'culture industries'. There has been insufficient attention in our fields to matters of *production*; on how and why media and cultural products are made – on the material reality of the cultural industries. People who work in the media and culture industries justifiably criticize academics for ignoring the industrial and commercial imperatives under which they operate. In the history of media and cultural studies, the investigation of institutions and organizations has often been overlooked while academic attention has focused on the media products and their users (Curran, 2000a). One of the hurdles we have to overcome in researching culture industries is the scepticism of people in the industry regarding media and cultural studies. You may have read newspaper articles which criticize media studies without showing much understanding of what we do. People who work in the industry will often tell you that the texts are made for institutional reasons alone and that scholars read too much into them. Often industrial insiders don't want to theorize their work and prefer to focus on doing the job at hand. This is not unusual – all industries tend to *naturalize* their processes of production. However, as students of the media, we know that it is precisely when something is *naturalized*, made to seem normal and ordinary, that we most need to study it. It is our role to question the norms and values of the industry and to subject the workings of the media to serious analysis.

Researching the media and culture industries

There are a large number of industries which come within the rubric of 'media and culture' (Stokes and Reading, 1999; Childs and Storry, 1999), but relatively few are studied in our field. In your university library, you will probably be able to find several books and journal articles about newspapers, television and cinema, but the shelves will be more sparse if you want to read up on publishing, radio or theatre. Furthermore, within these well-researched areas such as television, you will find that some topics are more thoroughly studied than others: news and soap operas are two genres which have generated quite a lot of academic attention, while light entertainment and music programming, for example, have been less frequently studied. In settling on a topic for research in this area, students should try to focus on the industries in which they are personally interested, and not those on which there has been a lot of work published. If there is already a large literature on a topic, there may not be much new you can say about it.

What are 'culture industries'?

Throughout this chapter we will be using the term 'culture industries' to refer to media and culture producers. For our current purposes, we are going to define this term as follows:

> *A culture industry is one which has as its main function the production or distribution of art, entertainment or information.*

We need a term which embraces the BBC, an independent magazine publisher or a musician struggling to get gigs; all should be included among the 'culture industries', and all are equally valid objects of analysis for our studies. An *organization* could be a single-person company or a multi-national corporation. The point is that it is formed with the purpose of producing cultural *artefacts* or *events*, which may be in the form of art, entertainment or information. These could be products in the traditional sense of a book or a music CD, or events such as a performance, dance or multimedia presentation. Any of the organizations or their employees could form the focus of your study of cultural industries. A useful summary of the main theoretical paradigms within which media industries have been studied is provided by James Curran (Curran, 2000a). The following sections provide an overview of the main approaches to the topic.

Administrative research and the culture industries

As scholars of the media and culture, we spend a lot of our time thinking about a range of ideas relating to the role of the various industries in society. We sometimes forget that the vast majority of people who work in the business of making cultural artefacts do so in order to make money. The profit motive is a strong determinant of why particular decisions are made in the culture industries, as in any other industry. When studying the culture industries, it is important to bear in mind that market forces and economics are the most significant forces determining what is done. The culture industries are involved in the production of artefacts which need to compete in the market place. Even the most charitable arts organization needs money to survive, and acquiring funding is a major part of the activities of private companies and non-profit-making organizations alike. Students of the media and culture industries need to have some understanding of the balance book even if they are not studying a profit-making organization. The economics of the market place applies to everybody these days, and there are no culture industries which operate entirely outside these forces. The drive to survive is what spurs on most organizations, whether they be profit-making or charitable concerns, and in the real world that means making money. Whatever culture industry you are going to study, you must make sure that you understand the economics of the industry and how organizations make their bread and butter.

The vast majority of research into the culture and media industries has no explicit political perspective, but rather is intended to be *instrumental* (see Chapter 1, pages 21–2). That is to say, most research is conducted by and for particular industries or companies, with the purpose of advancing the aims and objectives of the organizations commissioning the research. Most media organizations subscribe to services which collect reliable information about their sector. For example, information is collected by the Broadcasters' Audience Research Board (BARB) on television-viewing figures, and this is used widely by the television industry to monitor programmes and to develop programming strategy. Public companies are obliged by law to publish their accounts, and most companies issue an annual report which contains information on their activities for the year. In addition, companies conduct research into their own market position and that of their competitors. This kind of *administrative research* is produced solely for business purposes, but it can have value to academics as a source of information which would otherwise be impossible to find. Administrative data can be used by academics as a secondary source in their research, especially where it can provide facts and figures which would otherwise be too expensive to collect. Information on some of these sources can be found in Chapter 2 of this book. Most research into the culture industries, then, unlike academic research, does not have the growth of knowledge as its goal, and the information is not gathered to advance a theory of any kind. The vast majority of research into the media and culture industries is *administrative* and *functional*, having practical uses and applications for the relevant industries.

Some of the research which is conducted in the private and public sectors is not available to the general public because it is considered *proprietary*; that is to say, it is the property of the company which commissioned it. Often research costs a lot of money to support, and the funders do not want to share the knowledge they have acquired, because they have obtained it in order to improve their status in the market place. It is very unlikely that you would gain access to such information, and you should be sensitive when asking companies for information that they may not want to release. However, a great deal of information is freely available via the Internet.

The regulatory environment for the culture industries

In most countries in the West, including Britain and the USA, governments take an active interest in the media and culture industries. Broadcasting is one of the most heavily legislated media industries in Britain, with each successive broadcasting institution established by an Act of Parliament. The BBC, for example, funded by licence fee, was established during the 1920s in Britain at a time when many other industries were nationalized or being brought under state control. The director-general of the BBC is appointed by the board of governors, who are in turn selected by the government of the day. Successive governments have left their mark on the development of the BBC and the media system in Britain. During the Thatcher period, the philosophy of laissez-faire which instructed Conservative economic policy fed into media and cultural policy (Goodwin, 1999). Whether or not state funding exists for a particular culture industry is clearly dependent on prevailing governmental attitudes. At various times, support for media and culture industries has been justified on the grounds that cultural products can help to forge national identities or push political agendas. At other times, they have been supported on the same grounds that other industries might be: to provide employment and economic opportunities.

National governments clearly have the strongest influence on the shape of media industries in their own countries, but the European Union has increasing powers to influence the shape of the media in its member states (Collins, 1999). The significance of legislation and the regulatory environment on the culture industries provides an interesting research area. The impact of changes in regulation on particular industries and their operation could provide an interesting focus for your work. Whatever your topic, it will help you to understand the way the culture industries work if you find out about current legislation and follow the debates about pending changes in regulation. The relationship between politics and the media is particularly valuable for anyone interested in the power of the media (Wheeler, 1997).

Marxist approaches

Although Karl Marx himself had relatively little to say directly about media and culture, many subsequent scholars have applied his writings to our field. Marx was a *materialist*; that is to say, he considered the economics of a society to be crucial to understanding how society functions at all levels, including the ideological (Marx and Engels, 1964; 1974). Marx's work has been most influential in studies of how the social structure of a society is reflected in its culture. Marx and Engels affirmed that 'The ideas of the ruling class are in every epoch the ruling ideas, i.e. the class which is the ruling *material* force of a society, is at the same time its ruling *intellectual* force' (Marx and Engels, 1974: 64). The strong relationship between the structure of society, and the cultural products of that society is clearly evident in the above quotation from *The German Ideology*. The writings of Karl Marx and Friedrich Engels on the subject of how members of a society understand the world and their place in it has been influential on subsequent researchers.

The culture industries are the main purveyors of such ideological work and their influence has been taken up by subsequent Marxist scholars. One of the most influential among these was Antonio Gramsci, whose *Prison Notebooks* discusses the importance of culture for maintaining the political power of a ruling elite (Gramsci, 1971; 1985). Another key interlocutor in the debate about ideology is Louis Althusser, whose work has been extremely influential on the early formation of cultural studies in Britain. Althusser sees culture as one aspect of the 'ideological state apparatus' that contributes to the control of the ideas of a society by the people in power (Althusser, 1979; 1984).

Perhaps the most important inheritors of the Marxist tradition in studying the culture industries are two German scholars who emigrated to the USA during the 1930s, Theodor Adorno and Max Horkheimer (see Held, 1980). It was in the book *The Dialectic of Enlightenment* that they put forward the notion that contemporary culture was a 'culture industry'. The work of Adorno and Horkheimer on the 'culture industry' has been reprinted in several textbooks and readers, and has come to represent the key work in the Marxist approach to the study of culture (see, for example, During, 1993). As committed Marxists, Adorno and Horkheimer believed that the big businesses that controlled the content of media messages were operating towards ideological ends. Within the Marxist paradigm, the media are studied by materialist/historical methods, usually to show the power of the ruling class economically and ideologically. One of the leading scholars in this tradition today is Jürgen Habermas. Although he is a sociologist primarily, Habermas's work on the *public sphere* has led him to investigate the role of the media in shaping the political and social life of a society (Habermas, 1989).

The idea that one should 'look to the money' to understand the workings of the media underlies the project of material analysis which is at the heart of the work of media scholars such as Nicholas Garnham (1990), Colin Sparks (1986; 1999) and James Curran (2000a) (see also Garnham, 1997; Murdock, 1997; Hall, 1986; Goldsmiths Media Group, 2000). Much of the work applying Marxist theory to the culture industries is highly theoretical, and the scholars working in this area have a sophisticated knowledge of Marxist writings. When you come to conduct your own research, you could think about Marxism as a way of informing your own ideas, if you wish, but you would be well advised not to attempt to make a contribution to the field yourself.

One of the key theoretical underpinnings of our research, which is derived from Marxism, relates to the power of the media. The idea of the media as having 'power without responsibility' is one that you may well be familiar with through reading James Curran and Jean Seaton's important book on the subject (Curran and Seaton, 1991). The idea that the press and broadcasting industries operate on a par with major political institutions such as the government or the monarchy is investigated by Curran and Seaton. There are several post-Marxist theoretical paradigms for studying the media and culture which come in and out of fashion. If you are familiar with the work of a major cultural theorist, if you have studied their work thoroughly earlier in your course, then applying their ideas to an examination of some area of the industry can provide a fruitful approach. However, you should beware taking on a whole new theoretical approach at this stage.

It is likely that students reading this book are near the beginning of their academic careers and will therefore not yet be in a position to build new theories of the media. You cannot be expected to make a meaningful contribution to the theory of the field in your undergraduate or even postgraduate work. That is not to say that you should ignore questions of theory altogether. On the contrary, I think that the theory section of your dissertation should be the driving force behind your ideas and thinking (see Chapter 6, 'Reviewing the Literature').

Theories of technology

The culture industries have also been widely studied as technologies. The history of technology and the impact of technological change on industry have provided some useful approaches. Some key theorists in our field have addressed this theme, including Marshall McLuhan (1995) and Langdon Winner (1977). The industrial application of technologies new and old is discussed in two excellent collections, one edited by Donald MacKenzie and Judy Wajcman (1999) and the other by Hugh Mackay and Tim O'Sullivan (1999). Here you will find examples of the practical application of theories of new technology. The theorist who has made the biggest contribution to our understanding of the impact of new technologies on contemporary society is probably Manuel Castells (1996; 1997; 1998; 1999). Castells's *Network Society* is an elegantly written and comprehensively researched treatise on the social significance of computer technology. Brian Winston's work has thoroughly and coherently explored the relationship between media technology and society (1986; 1998). There is, then, no shortage of theoretical background on the role of new technology in relation to the media.

The use of theories of technology in your own research should serve as background or in helping you to design your research project. You cannot be expected to contribute to the theory of new technology, but you could reasonably expect to conduct a small-scale study of the impact of a particular new technology (for example, digital editing) on one company or industry.

How we can research the culture industries

In Chapter 1, we discussed the importance of isolating the precise aspect of the media or culture that you wish to investigate: first of all, you need to focus on your object of analysis. Table 1.7 (page 25) shows the main paradigms for researching industries. In order to find which suits your project best, narrow your area as much as possible. Decide which industry you want to research first, and then think about what aspect of that industry you want to investigate. Is it a particular company, period or set of workers? If you have the access or connections, perhaps through work experience or personal networks, you may be able to study a company from the inside. Table 4.1 shows some of the general topic areas you could think about if considering research in this area. You might be interested in analysing the *history* of the media industries, and you would certainly find plenty of information about this in the various archives available to you (see Appendix 1 for further details of some of these). If you are interested in examining this history from a more personal perspective, you might think about conducting interviews with people who were present, either face to face or by e-mail, telephone or letter. It is, of course, possible to combine methods of analysis to get a variety of perspectives on the same subject. Some days observing the activities of people in their workplace supplemented by face-to-face interviews with selected personnel would be a good combination of approaches for the beginner researcher to use in conducting a small participant observation study.

Table 4.1 gives some examples of objects of analysis; you could probably think of many more. The precise method we are going to use will depend on how we operationalize our object of analysis – that is to say, it depends on the exact nature of our question. If, for example, we are interested in doing some research on Channel 4, there are a number of different approaches we could take, depending on the nature of our question. Table 4.2 presents a

TABLE 4.1	1.	The history of a particular channel/newspaper/magazine
Examples of	2.	The response of a company or industry to changes in market conditions
Objects of		
Analysis for	3.	The response of a company or industry to new legislation
	4.	The response of a company or industry to new technology
Studying	5.	The reasons behind the introduction of a particular media phenomenon such as cable television or text messaging
Culture		
Industries	6.	The industrial rationale for an expansion of a new genre or a revival of an old one such as magazines for children or game shows
	7.	Demographics of the media industries; for example, the ethnic composition of the workforce
	8.	The influence of a change of personnel on a company or industry, such as the impact of a new Director General on the BBC
	9.	How patterns of work and professional practice influence media output. For example: How do newsrooms work? How do new magazines get launched? How do programmes get commissioned and made?

range of question areas we could investigate, and shows how our methods and sources would vary depending on which precise area we wish to investigate. In each case, our precise object of analysis varies and, consequently, a different method is called for. The five questions posed in Table 4.2 all refer to the history of the channel, but each calls for a different approach. Thus, if our primary interest was in the history of the channel and when and why it was launched, we would look at information in various archive sources, including newspapers and trade journals as in Question 1. If, however, we were more interested in what people thought about Channel 4 at the time, we would be more likely to use the oral history method, perhaps employing focus groups or one-to-one interviews as in Question 5 on Table 4.2.

Access to evidence

In researching the culture industries, a key question is *access*. It is often very difficult for university students to get direct access to organizations. You may be interested in learning how EMI markets new bands, but if you have no way of getting anyone to answer your enquiries, you are not going to be able to investigate the decision-making process from the inside. One reason that so much media research focuses on texts is that the cultural artefacts themselves *are* publicly available. If you took a different slant on the above topic, you could look at how EMI markets new bands by studying the campaigns in the form of billboard and print advertisements and promotional articles in the music press. Access to media industry insiders can be difficult to obtain, but it is still possible to research this area using the available evidence.

There are two general kinds of evidence: *documentary* evidence (such as written sources) and *people*. Any research that you do will use one or both of

TABLE 4.2

Methods for
Addressing
Different
Aspects of
Researching
Channel 4

Question	Method	Object of analysis
1. Why was Channel 4 launched?	Archive research	Newspaper reports Trade journals Government acts Government committee reports Channel 4 publicity and website Books about history of television
2. Why was the channel controversial?	Archive research	Newspaper reports Trade journals
	Interviews	People involved in decision making
3. How did Channel 4's output differ from other channels?	Content analysis	Output in comparison with other channels
	Participant observation	Observing how decisions about output are made
4. What was the media's response to Channel 4?	Archive research	Newspaper reports Trade journals
5. How did viewers respond?	Oral history Focus group	Audiences to Channel 4 programming

these forms of evidence. Research methods based on *documents* constitute the main forms of *archive research*, which we will discuss later in the chapter. Those which use *people* as their evidence include the *interview*, *participant observation* and *oral history*.

Using documents

Brendan Duffy writes about using documents for research and argues that there are broadly two different kinds of research: 'source-oriented' and 'problem-oriented'. *Source-oriented* document research is undertaken when the investigation of the source material motivates the research. In this kind of research, one would begin from the position of having access to an archive or set of resources which one wishes to investigate. For example, a student at the University of East Anglia might have access to the advertising library held there; alternatively, students at the University of Kent can access the archive of the British Centre for the Study of Cartoon and Caricature (see Appendix 1 for further details). In the course of your initial investigation, you may find that there is an archive or collection local to where you work or study on which you could base your research. The research question you developed would depend on your own interest in the particular collection, but source-oriented research uses the documents available as the impetus for the research.

The *problem-oriented* approach to document research takes as its starting point a problem which one has developed out of reading other accounts or secondary sources (see Chapter 1, pages 31–2, for further discussion of primary and secondary sources). Here the documents are the object of analysis, but the research question has been generated as a result of reading secondary sources, and not the documents themselves. The problem-oriented approach 'involves formulating questions by reading *secondary sources*, reading what has already been discovered about the subject and establishing the focus of the study before going to the relevant *primary sources*' (Duffy, 1999: 107). One might thus develop a question about the formation of a particular media company or of a piece of media legislation from reading around the subject. The archives of that company or relevant trade journals may then form the primary source.

Archive research

One of the most frequently used of all methods of media research, including cultural and film history, is archive research. Archive research involves accessing original documents and using these as the basis of your research or object of analysis. Some of the key texts in our field were based on research carried out in archives, such as Asa Briggs's *History of Broadcasting in the United Kingdom* (Briggs, 1961–1995). An archive is a place where records are kept, usually public records, although archives are commonly held by private and public organizations of all kinds. The BBC's Written Archives Centre in Caversham provided the source material for much of Briggs's work and for many other scholars. In the area of British television, this archive is an invaluable resource. The Independent Television Commission keeps a comprehensive archive of resources of interest to students of television in general. Film scholars are well served by the British Film Institute (BFI) library, which has a good collection of literature from Britain and overseas on all aspects of film and television. Most of these libraries are accessible to students, although conditions do apply (see Appendix 1 for more details of archives of interest).

Several university libraries have specialist archives which you may be able to access for your dissertation. For example, the University of Kent is home to the Centre for the Study of Cartoons and Caricature, and the University of Stirling houses the John Grierson Archive. See Appendix 1 for details of other relevant archives, and find out whether a library local to you has any special collections which you could study.

Historical research

Archive research is one of the main methods used in all forms of historical research, including those based on texts and audiences. Film, television and advertising archives are used to gain access to the actual texts as well as documents about them. Here we are concerned with the use of archives for historical research of the *industrial* aspects of culture. The culture industries have been widely researched by historians of all political persuasions, and the main object of analysis for historical research is the archive (see next section for oral history). The relationship between the media and modernity is a key area of enquiry (see, for example, Thompson, 1995), as is the development of media technologies (see, for example, Winston, 1998) and the importance of computers in particular (Castells, 1996; 1997; 1998). The newspaper and television industries are among those which have been most thoroughly researched (Curran and Seaton, 1991; Seymour-Ure, 1996; Williams, 1998). Case study 4.1 presents the work of media scholars Paddy Scannell and David Cardiff (1991).

CASE STUDY 4.1. ARCHIVE RESEARCH

Paddy Scannell and David Cardiff, 1991. *A Social History of Broadcasting. Volume 1. Serving the Nation*. Oxford: Basil Blackwell.

Scannell and Cardiff's *A Social History of Broadcasting* (1991) is an exploration of the social and cultural meaning of British broadcasting, focusing on the years 1922–39. During this period, broadcasting became coterminous with the British Broadcasting Corporation (BBC). Although Scannell and Cardiff necessarily discuss the BBC, they insist that their book is not a history of the corporation. Instead, they make a larger claim for their project, arguing that it 'attempts to account, historically, for the impact and effect of broadcasting on modern life in Britain' (p. x). This is planned as the first volume in a series and concentrates on the early days of broadcasting in the pre-World War II period. This is when broadcasting became 'a state-regulated national service in the public interest' (p. x).

The primary sources for Scannell and Cardiff's research were the archives of the BBC Written Archives Centre (WAC) at Caversham. At the WAC, the authors were able to consult minutes of BBC management boards and departmental meetings, policy files, production files, transcripts of broadcasts, press cuttings and other documents to piece together an account of the *routine* work of broadcasting. They also researched various BBC documents and publications, including *The Radio Times* and *The Listener*. In their desire to investigate the public understanding of the BBC, Scannell and Cardiff also conducted archive research elsewhere. The legislative context was gained through their research into various official sources, including the reports of various government committees and Hansard. The social understanding of broadcasting was researched through analysing periodicals of the day, including *Radio Pictorial* and *Radio Magazine*, as well as the music press, including *Melody Maker* and *Musical Times*.

Scannell and Cardiff concentrate on the social relationships of broadcasting and focus on broadcasting at the level of production in terms of programme planning and programme making. Key to the social history of British broadcasting is the idea of public service broadcasting, which is explored in the introductory chapter. *A Social History of Broadcasting* concentrates in Part 1 on broadcasting and politics, looking at how controversial subjects are dealt with by the BBC, at the management of news and political debate, and at broadcasting and two key issues of the day: unemployment and foreign affairs. Part 2 looks at the production of information, in the BBC departments responsible for news, features and talks. Part 3 looks at music and variety, with chapters on various aspects of music policy, taste, entertainment and variety. The final part looks at how broadcasting relates to its audiences and concentrates on the relationship between the national and the regional. There is a case study on Manchester and its programmes. The last chapter of the book examines the importance of the listener to radio.

Scannell and Cardiff have written a vital resource for anyone interested in researching British culture in the 1920s and 1930s. Scannell and Cardiff's work takes an engaging and interesting approach to the history of broadcasting and is an excellent model of how to incorporate various sources into the research of media history.

Researching film history

One of the most thoroughly researched media industries is that of the Hollywood cinema. The history of the cinema produces a large number of popular and academic books each year. The five-volume *History of the American Cinema* is a comprehensive survey of the American film industry as impressive in its scope as Briggs's *History of Broadcasting in the United Kingdom* (Balio, 1993). The methodology of film history is well discussed by Kristin Thompson and David Bordwell (1994). Tino Balio, one of the leading historians of Hollywood cinema, uses archives as a fundamental part of much of his research (1976a; b; c; 1993). The book he wrote about a major Hollywood studio, *United Artists* (1976b), for example, was based on the archive acquired in the 1970s by the University of Wisconsin–Madison. The directors of United Artists gave the university all of the company's documentation up to 1951 (Balio, 1976b). Balio's study is based largely on these files supplemented with interviews with some key players including Charlie Chaplin and other directors of the company. Later work by the same historian tends to focus on contemporaneous newspapers and trade journals as the primary resource. For example, Balio's 1998 essay on the globalization of Hollywood in the 1990s uses the trade paper *Variety* (discussed in Chapter 2), and *The New York Times* as its main sources (*Variety* is cited 28 times and *The New York Times* 16 times in this essay) (Balio, 1998).

Archive research is one of the most widely used methods of investigating the cinema, and any textual analysis can benefit from reference to the literature which has been published on the cinema. Yet there is a wide range of other methods for studying film from a historical perspective, many of which are discussed in Robert C. Allen and Douglas Gomery's interesting book on the topic, *Film History* (1985). The Hollywood film industry is one of the most carefully studied of all the culture industries. Industry studies tend to focus on studios, and company and studio profiles are a mainstay of the field.

Conducting your own archive research

Most projects will require you to do a certain amount of archive research. You will need to visit a library or look at websites to find out what other people have said about your topic or your method of research. If you are using the archive as a secondary resource or as background material, you will be focusing on getting specific pieces of information out of your research. When using the archive for background material, you should get the best out of each visit by ensuring that you know what you are looking for in advance.

The following is a guide to conducting research which uses the archive as your primary resource.

Stages in archive research

Archive research requires careful planning before, during and after you visit the archive. You need to make sure you know what you are going to look at and why.

Define your object of analysis carefully. Make sure that your object of analysis is one which can be accessed – if not, redefine it.

Define your research question. Ensure that your question relates to the literature in the area. What paradigms are you building on or contributing to? Make sure you have a clear, concise research question.

Identify the archive sources. Visit the archive early during the design process. Find out the scope of the material available on your topic: is there so much you will never get through it? If so, redefine your object of analysis or conduct an analysis of a *sample*. Either way, you will probably have to rephrase your question. You have to *be flexible* in conducting this kind of research, as the material is not always there exactly as you expect it to be! Initially, you should spend one or two sessions just getting to know what is held in the archive before finally settling on what you are going to look at.

Define the range of work you are going to study. Make sure you get any necessary permission and that you allow yourself sufficient time with the material. Determine how many items you are going to be able to study in the time available.

Gather your data. Study the archive material selected carefully to get the required data. You need to begin looking in detail at the contents only when you have surveyed the whole range of material available. Take careful notes of the items you investigate.

Collate the information. Gather together the notes and information you have collected from the archive visit and start to categorize your material.

Refer back to your initial theory. Think about why you wanted to do this in the first place! Does the evidence you have gathered wholly support your initial hypothesis? Have you changed your mind in the light of what you have found? Were there any surprises? Think through these questions honestly and organize your ideas along themes which you initially proposed and any new ones that have arisen since you began the research. Can you reach a conclusion?

Write up your findings. Relate what you have found to your initial research question. Include in your discussion any false paths you followed.

Uses of archive research

Researching an archive collection, whether it be of films, ephemera or written material, can be immensely rewarding. If you are researching a collection which has not been previously studied, it is exciting to uncover something which no one has looked at from a scholarly perspective before. Using an archive of original material allows you to generate data first-hand from primary sources. However, what you find in the archive is not always what you expect, so be prepared to be flexible and to shift your focus in the light of what you find.

You may have to travel to visit an archive. There is a list of archives and contact details in Appendix 1 of this book. Make sure you contact the archive before you visit to find out what the conditions of access are and whether it has the sort of material you need to look at. It is usually necessary to go to the archive itself, even though more and more information is available on the Internet. Archive research typically requires you to consult original historical documents.

The interview

Whereas archive research focuses on what has been written or recorded, in *documentary sources*, interviews are the primary means by which we use *people* as sources of evidence in our research. The interview as a method in media and cultural research enables us to find out about people's ideas, opinions and attitudes. As with the other methods discussed in this chapter, the interview might be your primary method or it may be used to gain background information. You may find that your study will be enhanced if you include just one interview with a person who is an expert in that area and can give you key information. If your study uses interviews as its primary source, you will probably need to interview several people to ensure that your subjects are representative. In this section we will be focusing on using media and culture industry workers as subjects, while in Chapter 5 we look at the interview in the context of *audience* research. The discussion in Chapter 5 includes more detail on matters of questionnaire design, which are important when you are planning to administer the same set of questions to a large sample of subjects (see pages 141–8). When discussing interviews in the context of the media industry, as we are in this section, I assume that readers will be looking to conduct one or two interviews with industry personnel and are more interested in garnering complex, *interpretive* data from their subjects.

One of the pioneers of using interview research to investigate the culture industries is Dorothy Hobson. Hobson's 1982 investigation of the early evening soap opera *Crossroads* used both producers and audiences as subjects. Hobson's work is typically cited within media and cultural studies as a foundational piece of audience research. Her investigation of the audience for *Crossroads* was one of the first pieces of major research in Britain to look at the way the viewers of such a devalued television programme enjoyed, appreciated and used the television text. *Crossroads: The Drama of a Soap Opera* was instrumental in bringing greater emphasis to the audience's role in interpreting the text. It was especially timely in raising the level of debate about women's genres and is now a classic of feminist television studies. But this ignores the large part of the book that is devoted to the analysis of the attitudes and opinions of the people who made *Crossroads*. Hobson investigated the processes of production of *Crossroads* and interviewed the producers, editors, writers and performers of the programme. She found that, despite the fact that the show was perceived as depressing and downbeat by many critics, the producers felt they were making an uplifting programme in which characters overcame adversity with a spirit of hope and optimism. It is interesting that Hobson also interviewed the performers and found that in several cases their real-life character bore a resemblance to their on-screen personae – an observation which, for Hobson, explains the high level of 'realism' of the performances.

Interviews have been used more recently to study British soap operas. The research of Lesley Henderson (1999), for example, elicits some interesting insights into how and why soap operas address serious social issues such as breast cancer or domestic violence. Henderson interviewed personnel who worked on the leading television soaps in Britain, including *Coronation Street, Brookside* and *EastEnders*. People at various levels of the production process were interviewed, including writers, producers and script editors. One scholar whose work has tended to use a large sample of employees in the media industries is Jeremy Tunstall (1993; 1996). Interviews are a useful way of researching the ideas and attitudes of industry workers, not least because it is a method which is familiar to media workers, as it is widely used in documentary products and in media research generally.

CASE STUDY 4.2. CONDUCTING INTERVIEWS

Jeremy Tunstall, 1993. *Television Producers*. London: Routledge.

In writing *Television Producers* (1993), Jeremy Tunstall and his research assistants, Mark Dunford and David Wood, interviewed 254 producers working in British television. Tunstall focused on the role of 'series producer' or 'series editor', the person he considered 'the highest level of person who is in regular daily editorial or "hands-on" control of the content of a series or programme' (p. 5). The book discusses the management role of the producer and whether or not the producer can be seen as an 'auteur'.

The role of television producer was in a state of flux at the time of the interviews. Between 1955 and 1982, there had been only two large organizations, the BBC and ITV, running television and there was a very stable pattern of employment and career paths for producers. The era of the mature duopoly, in which the BBC and the ITV networks pretty well controlled British television history, was coming to a close by the early 1990s. Moreover, the full impact of the launch of Channel 4 and the Thatcher revolution was taking effect on the British television industry, so there were many factors influencing the role of the television worker.

Subjects for the study were identified by looking through trade publications and at credits listed in *The Radio Times* or at the end of broadcast television programmes. Tunstall insists that no particular attempt was made to make the interviewees representative of the industry as a whole, beyond the fact that they were selected from across the main programme genres, including documentary, sport and comedy. Letters were written requesting interviews and were followed up by telephone calls. Interviews were arranged to take place in the offices of the subjects during the period March 1990 to July 1992, and the standard length of an interview was about 70 minutes. The interviewers followed a prepared list of questions, administering the same open-ended questions to each producer, although these did change slightly as the study progressed. The interviewees were given assurances of anonymity at the time of the interviews, and although some gave permission for their names to be used, most of the subjects are quoted anonymously.

Subjects were interviewed about their careers and the changes in the role of producer during their time working in television. Tunstall found that the producers were aware of their employment becoming more casualized. Jobs which had once been seen as secure for life were now more typically offered as short-term contracts. At the same time, the research found that producers were becoming more autonomous and had greater freedom in their work. Tunstall concludes that, although producers are key players in television, they cannot be said to operate as *auteurs*. Instead, he finds that the *genres* according to which television programmes are made are the most important determinants of professional mores and values. In British television, it seems that departments operate along fairly fixed generic conventions which shape the working patterns within the industry.

This wide-ranging interview method is typical of Tunstall's work. He and his researchers have conducted a similar study of the newspaper industry (Tunstall, 1996). This kind of work relies on sound knowledge of the industry and an ability to synthesize a large amount of information into a coherent argument.

Case Study 4.2 shows that Jeremy Tunstall interviewed a large number of producers, some 254 in all – it would be beyond the resources of anyone reading this book to be able to have so many subjects. It is quite possible to conduct excellent research using a smaller number of interviewees. James Curran (2000b) interviewed eleven literary editors of the major newspapers in his study of book reviews in the press. Because the population he is targeting is quite small (there aren't that many literary editors of national newspapers), these eleven comprise a large percentage of the total. Curran is making generalizations about a relatively small group of people, whereas Tunstall makes conclusions about the television production industry as a whole (see Case Study 3.2, p. 65, for further discussion of James Curran's method).

Tunstall and Curran both conducted face-to-face interviews, but it is not always necessary to do that. In Chapter 5, we discuss designing surveys and focus groups: although these methods are typically used to investigate audiences, it is possible to use them in industry research also. One interesting way of conducting interviews is via the Internet. It is often easier to administer a survey questionnaire by e-mail and to use the electronic responses of your subjects as your raw data: after all, the e-mail response needs no transcribing and interviewees are more likely to respond when they can do so in their own time. Some interesting work has been done in the area of media production and identity, especially in research conducted from a feminist or queer perspective. For example, Frances Cresser, Lesley Gunn and Helen Balme (2001) investigated 'women's experience of publishing on-line and how they perceive the construction of on-line identities and the politics of their publications' (p. 458). They interviewed thirty-nine female authors published in e-zines during August and September 1998. The interviews were structured at first, and followed up by more informal exchanges which solicited more textured and in-depth responses.

The telephone also provides a good means of interviewing people. Use it to find out who in an organization you should speak to. You may find that your study will be improved if you include just one interview with someone who is an expert in a key area. If your study uses interviews as its primary means of eliciting data, you should follow the steps below in conducting your study.

Conducting interviews

To interview or not? Interviews are very time-consuming and can be wasteful of people's time. So before you plan to conduct interviews at all, ask yourself if they are really necessary. The interview is not the appropriate method to use for background material on a company, for example. You might find that the information you need is readily available from the public relations or marketing department of a company – always try these sources before you approach the chief executive. There are alternative sources (see Chapter 2: Sources and Resources). Contact the company and ask to be sent a press pack if you need general information. Interviews should be used, as we said in Chapter 1, only for eliciting personal attitudes and opinions. So you should embark on an interview study only if your primary object of analysis is the words of your interviewees: make sure that the interviews are necessary to confirming the hypothesis.

Remember that the people you are talking to are professionals and are unlikely to want to criticize their company or industry. Don't expect anyone to 'spill the beans' – most industry people will not be willing to talk about the negative side of the business to an outsider. It is quite likely that students will be given the official line on any controversial events from most employees within the media, or any other, industry. So, when you are designing your study, try to anticipate what the likely response is going to be and whether this is going to be helpful in answering your research question. Before you begin your interviews you should always discuss with your supervisor what form the interviews should take.

Select your interviewees carefully. You must target the right people – and get permission to interview early in the project. Don't assume that people will talk to you – some people get lots of requests to give interviews to undergraduates and are too busy to do so. Interview as few people as is necessary to conduct your study; interviews are very time-consuming for both interviewer and interviewee, so make sure that you don't waste people's time. Never assume that you will get an interview – people are not ashamed about letting students down. Be very grateful if you do. Aim for the right level of person: if you are interested in the adoption of new technology, you will want to speak to a person in the company interested in that area; if you want to find out about employment policies, you should interview someone in human resources. Don't assume that you have to interview the chief executive officer of a company to get reliable information. If you are using personal contacts, ask them what procedure you should follow to request an interview.

Decide how you are going to conduct the interviews. You could conduct interviews face to face, by telephone, fax, e-mail, letter or survey. Try to match the means with the subjects: if you think this industry sector is more comfortable with e-mail than the telephone, go with that, but if you think the letter is better, why not write to your subjects? It is often a good idea to write a letter first, informing the potential subjects about your project and inviting them to take part. In many studies, this would then be followed up with a telephone call to arrange a face-to-face interview. However, people may be reluctant to give face-to-face interviews to undergraduates and five minutes on the telephone may be the best you can hope for. If you need only a five-minute conversation, why do more? Be parsimonious with other people's time and select the easiest and least time-consuming method for your interviewees.

Conduct background research. Find out as much as you can about the structure of the industry and the company and about the roles of the people you will be interviewing well in advance.

Planning the interview. Draw up a list of questions or topic areas. Be ready to go with the flow, but make sure you know precisely what information you want and what questions are likely to elicit this. Practise the questions in advance so that you don't read them, or, better still, be prepared to speak from bullet points listing topic areas.

Conducting the interview. Be prepared and look prepared. The interview is the method to get the opinions and attitudes of your subjects, and they are unlikely to be free with these if they are not relaxed, so try to establish rapport with the subject. Be friendly and courteous; shake hands with the interviewee and smile; thank the interviewee for agreeing to talk to you at the beginning and end of the interview. Never use academic jargon in an interview. If subjects use a term that you don't understand, apologize and ask them to explain. Make sure you record your interview – practise at home with friends at using a tape recorder if you have not used one before, and make sure you have spare batteries and tapes with you! It can be very embarrassing if your equipment breaks down during the interview. You should always get permission before you record an interview and before you turn the recorder on, and you should explain why you need to record the interview. Refer to your list of questions or topic areas, but don't read from it. Listen carefully to the responses and try to conduct a natural conversation – this will elicit more interesting and spontaneous conversation from your interviewee.

Take notes. Even though you are recording the interview, you should still take brief notes during the interview. It will help if you tick off the topic areas as they are covered or jot down a question while the person is talking so you don't interrupt.

Transcribe the interview. A transcript of an interview is very helpful if you are going to analyse it in detail. But it is very time-consuming to type up an entire interview – professional researchers would employ an administrator to do this. If you do transcribe the interview, the transcript should be included as an appendix and would not contribute toward the final word count (see Chapter 6 for notes on the appendix). It is quite legitimate to submit tape recordings of interviews with your project and to quote from them as appropriate in the essay. Clearly identify the date and subject of any recording submitted.

Reflect. Does the interviewee support or refute your research question? Does he/she say anything surprising or unexpected? Does he/she endorse what you were thinking or give you some new ideas? The basis of all analysis is comparison, so compare the actuality with your expectations. Also, compare the various interviews with one another. Think about what areas the subjects are agreed on and where they differ. Think about what accounts for these similarities and differences.

The interview will help you elicit what people want you to know about them. In the short time your interview takes, the interviewees are pretty much in control of how they want to be seen. This is often seen as a weakness of the interview method: the subject may well not tell the truth for various reasons, and the interviewer is unlikely to have any checks on this. While the interview is a valuable means of gaining information about what people think they should say about their roles, if you want to find out what they actually do, you will have to spend some time observing them. The method suited to studying people's behaviour in the workplace is *participant observation*, which will be discussed in the next section.

Participant observation

Studying behaviour in the workplace

One of the hurdles we have to overcome in researching media industries is the scepticism of people in the industry towards media studies. You may have read newspaper articles which criticize degrees in media studies without seeming to realize what we do. It is not unusual for people in the professions to be wary of academics. As mentioned above, people who work in any industry think that their practices are normal and ordinary and not subject to question – they take for granted that what they do and say at work are routine and normal. One of the methods of understanding the routines is through participating in these routines oneself. Participant observation is a method which derives from anthropology and is used by scholars conducting *fieldwork*, usually living among distant peoples to understand their way of life. Anthropologists may spend several years befriending and learning about their subjects. In our area, most participant observation is done in industries by people who already work there or who have very good contacts, and the fieldwork is conducted over several months.

While asking people about their work may give you certain insights, observing their behaviour gives a different perspective. If one wishes to study what people actually *do* in the workplace, participant observation is an ideal method. Scholars have used this method in the past to examine the decision-making process at work, the professional norms and values of media workers, and how the ideology behind their work gets translated into media content. It has the advantage over interviews that you are observing first-hand, and not relying on your subjects' reports of their behaviour. Some of the most influential participant observation studies have been based on the news industry. Case study 4.3 presents a summary of Philip Schlesinger's foundational study of the BBC news conducted in the 1970s.

CASE STUDY 4.3. PARTICIPANT OBSERVATION

Philip Schlesinger, 1987. *Putting Reality Together: BBC News* (2nd edn). London: Methuen.

Philip Schlesinger's 1978 study into the workings of the BBC newsrooms (reissued with a new introduction in 1987) was based on research completed in 1977. Schlesinger investigates the journalistic culture of the newsroom by examining the routines and practices which are employed. He places his work within the tradition of *ethnography*, an approach which is based on 'theoretically informed observation of the social practices of cultural production' (p. xxxii). Schlesinger uses theories of news production and observes the extent to which these are reflected in the behaviour of his subjects. The main driving force behind his research is the desire to understand how the newsroom operates. Schlesinger looks at this from a practical perspective of how the day is organized and so on, but also from a theoretical perspective. What are the ideological frameworks within which the news is produced?

The fieldwork for this study took place in the national newsrooms at Broadcasting House and Television Centre in London and examined both radio and television news services. Two methods were used to gather data about the locations: one he calls *direct observation* and the other *interview*. (Both of these would be necessary if you were conducting participant observation yourself.) The direct observation involved over 90 full days in the newsroom over a period of four years. Schlesinger calculates that he spent some 1,260 hours observing the activities of the BBC employees. He also interviewed 95 members of staff. The fieldwork allowed Schlesinger to immerse himself in the culture of the newsroom as he tried to find out first hand what it was like to work there. After each period of observation, it was necessary to reflect on what he had observed. Schlesinger shows that an important part of the method of participant observation is thinking about the data according to pre-established theoretical perspectives. Schlesinger is able to demonstrate the importance of a corporate ideology in the way that the news is managed on a day-to-day basis.

Putting Reality Together is one of the first studies to take a theoretical perspective on the activities of media workers. Schlesinger is working in a highly politicized environment, but one where those politics are routinely denied. This is a key study in the history of media studies because of its bold method and its insightful analysis of the way in which cultural artefacts (in this case, the news) are produced.

It is possible for students who wish to study the patterns of behaviour and activities in the workplace to conduct a small-scale study, especially if they can use contacts that they already have.

Using your work experience for participant observation

A significant obstacle in undertaking this kind of research is *access*: it is very unlikely that a major media company would allow you to observe anything very controversial. However, if you have good contacts in the media, you could use these to get inside an interesting organization. If you are doing work experience or have a part-time job in the media, you may be able to use this to generate research. In a small business, you are more likely to have personal contact with the boss, and, if this is appropriate, ask whether you could spend some of your own time observing the work process of the business. For example, if you are working in a small independent music company, your employer might be sympathetic to your studying the norms by which a new band is signed.

Stages in participant observation

Participant observation requires a high level of cooperation on the part of your object organization, so you need to make absolutely sure that you get the full permission of all the people involved. This includes your line manager and all the people you are going to be observing. Take care and show full respect for everyone – how would you like it if some researcher wanted to watch you and ask you questions while you were trying to work? You need to be well prepared before you begin your fieldwork in order to get the best out of your research.

Before fieldwork begins.   Read as much as you can about the industry your company is involved in and find out about its status within the industry. Write a description of the industry showing how your target company fits in. Draw an organizational plan of the company (use their annual reports to help you) and think about how the section you are going to study fits in with the whole. Design your study carefully, writing a detailed plan and a schedule. Make sure that your research question can be appropriately answered by the fieldwork (if not, either rewrite the question or use a different method). Get permission, in writing, to conduct fieldwork from the relevant people in the organization well in advance. Arrange exactly what days you are going to be observing. I would suggest that undergraduates aim to spend approximately ten full days in observation, although obviously this will vary from project to project. Because your time is limited, it is unlikely that you will get a very full picture of what is going on purely by watching. You should therefore organize in advance to conduct background interviews with key personnel to ask them about their roles.

During fieldwork.   Always be prompt and efficient during fieldwork. Take your cues on how to dress and behave from everyone else, as it is important not to stand out too much and distract people from their work. Introduce yourself to everyone on the first day, and schedule a time with all subjects individually, at their convenience, to talk to you about their work. Try to find out what people are doing by asking questions politely when your subjects are not busy. Try to engage people in conversation in quiet periods or away from the work environment, as, for example, around the coffee machine.

Take notes as you go along. Make your writing as unobtrusive as possible – if possible, leave the room to write your notes. Keep them brief and frequent. At the end of each day, make notes in your diary about what happened. Spend time after each period of fieldwork relating your observations to your research question. Before you go back to the field again, look through your notes from the previous visit and try to fill in any gaps. Make provisional analyses and sort your notes as you go along – you may need to redefine your research question as you go along, so be flexible and open-minded about what you find and don't be too concerned if you don't find what you were looking for.

After fieldwork.   Spend some time reading through your notes and diary, and think carefully about what you have found. Reflect on your experience and write up the stages in your thinking during the observation period. After you have carefully reflected on your experience, you can begin to write down your findings. Include what you found as well as what you *did not* find. Write down your mistakes – it is better to reflect on them than to pretend they never happened. You will learn more from this experience if you think seriously about where you went wrong. Go back to the literature which formed your research question and see if you have different ideas about the theory after having done your fieldwork. Reflect also on the method you undertook – could you have found out more if you had behaved differently? Maybe if you had looked at a different department or been given different access, you could have made some more interesting observations – these are the kind of things which are worth commenting on. When you come to write up your essay, you may want to include a diary or log of your visits as an appendix, but the bulk of what you write will be your interpretation and analysis of what was going on, not a simple chronology of what happened. As with all projects, write it up with reference to the theories and writings which informed your original research question (see Chapter 6 for further details of writing up your project).

Oral history

Oral history involves interviewing people about their past experiences and memories. The most typical use of oral history in our field is in researching audiences, and we discuss the subject in more depth in Chapter 5. Shaun Moores's investigation of radio use is discussed in Case Study 5.4 p. 152. In keeping with much oral history, Shaun Moores's study falls within the rubric of social history, as he is studying the responses of ordinary people to developments in new technology (Moores, 1988). He is focusing on the audiences for radio in the 1930s. However, it is possible to conduct an oral history study of the culture industries if you have access to people who witnessed significant developments in the history of the media. Mark Williams, for example, interviewed Monty Margetts, the presenter of an early television cookery programme, using many of the techniques of oral history (Williams, 1999). The biggest difficulty is in getting access to people in the industry to interview about the past. As a beginner researcher, you may not be able to entice people who played key roles in the industry to talk about their past careers. However, if you are personally acquainted with such people and they are willing to talk to you, it is possible to conduct some interesting original research by this method. For example, one of my students wrote a fascinating study of pirate radio in the 1960s based on interviews with her father and some of his colleagues from that period. If you have family or friends with interesting pasts, interviewing them in an oral history study could provide some valuable insights.

Your subjects in oral history do not need to be very high profile to have interesting things to say. If you do know people who were working in the industry at the time that you are interested in (and remember that history could include the recent past), then, by all means, consider using oral history as a method. You do need to be well prepared before the interview, so make sure that you read around the subject and understand the main debates and issues from the perspective of the media historian. As with any fieldwork, make sure you have a well-developed research question *before* you conduct the interview. It is most unprofessional to waste people's time unless your interviews have a clear focus. Draw up a list of questions or main points that you want to cover in advance, and, if possible, give your subjects notice of the kinds of things you are going to ask them so that they also can be prepared. Even if you are interviewing people who are well known to you, such as a close relative, they will realize that you are serious and will, in turn, take your project seriously if they can see that you have done your home-work. When you treat your interviewees with respect and consideration, they are more likely to treat you in the same manner.

Begin the interview by asking your subjects to clarify relevant facts – their job title, periods of employment and so on. Don't expect them to know government legislation or the specific dates of historical events. Don't argue with or contradict them. In oral history, you give absolute respect to the person recounting the past. Make sure you tape-record your interview, and keep to the subject. Try to let your interviewees do most of the talking – you should only chip in for clarification or to keep them on the subject.

Combining methods of researching industries

It is a very good idea to conduct some research into the industry of relevance to your research project, whether or not the industry is your primary focus of analysis. In most cases, it will be beneficial to combine the methods discussed in this chapter with those for analysing audiences or texts. Most published research these days will ground its discussion of audiences or texts in a consideration of the economics of media and cultural production. One of the leading researchers of media industries is James Curran, whose study of literary editors we used as a case study in Chapter 3. Curran has worked widely on the media industries, using archive methods among others (Curran, 2000a;b; Curran and Seaton, 1991).

A researcher working in a less traditional medium than James Curran is Kembrew McLeod (1999). Like Curran, McLeod explores the relationship between media output and the goals of media producers. But while Curran is working with the establishment media, McLeod is examining a subculture which identifies itself outside and against the mainstream.

CASE STUDY 4.4. MCLEOD/RAP

Kembrew McLeod, 1999. Authenticity within hip-hop and other cultures threatened with assimilation. *Journal of Communication*, 49, Autumn: 134–50.

Kembrew McLeod is interested to understand what is meant by the expression, 'keepin' it real' and other claims of *authenticity* which he hears hip-hoppers and their fans make. McLeod examines the discourses of 'authenticity' in the hip-hop community he collected from four different sources: hip-hop magazines, Internet discussion groups, press releases sent to hip-hop music critics and hip-hop song lyrics. From these various texts, McLeod collected and classified 800 separate claims of authenticity and analysed their context to identify what is meant by 'keepin' it real'. By subjecting these expressions to discourse analysis, McLeod was able to categorize them into six different 'dimensions' (see Table 4.3). The second phase of his study involved McLeod in interviewing twenty-three hip-hop artists to find out if the ideas of authenticity he had elicited from the literature was supported by them. The interviews followed a standard format in which McLeod asked his subjects the following five open-ended questions:

> What does the phrase 'keepin' it real' mean to you?
> Who, in hip-hop, isn't keepin' it real?
> What makes someone real in hip-hop?
> What makes someone fake in hip-hop?
> How do you feel about the way the phrase 'keepin' it real' is used in hip-hop?
> (p. 138)

McLeod is sympathetic to the community he is studying and is interested in investigating how the idea of 'authenticity' is used as a means of protecting a culture which sees itself under siege. McLeod unpacks the meaning of 'keepin' it real' for the hip-hop community (see Table 4.3). He believes that these particular semantic dimensions would not necessarily be found in other subcultures, but he does conclude that his method is applicable to other groups:

TABLE 4.3
McLeod's Dimensions of Authenticity in the Hip-Hop Community

	Support Claims of Authenticity	
Semantic dimensions	Real	Fake
Social-psychological	staying true to yourself	following mass trends
Racial	Black	White
Political-economic	the underground	commercial
Gender-sexual	hard	soft
Social locational	the street	the suburbs
Cultural	the old school	the mainstream

Source: McLeod, 1999: 139.

The specific semantic dimensions developed in this paper cannot be gener-
alized beyond hip-hop. However, the method used to derive this information
can be used to study other cultures and subcultures threatened with
erasure, assimilation, or both, to understand how these cultures similarly
employ authenticity to maintain their identity. (McLeod, 1999: 148)

The combination of (text-based) discourse analysis and interview enabled
McLeod to analyse the nuances of a phrase which is used in nebulous and
shifting ways by the hip-hop community. 'Keepin' it real' may be unique to the
hip-hoppers he was studying, but other expressions of authenticity are
frequently made by subcultures – unpacking a term which has resonance and
significance for a particular group can be a very useful form of cultural analysis
and one which most readers of this book could undertake given access to
members of the in-group.

McLeod's industry contacts were clearly invaluable in securing access to
so many high-profile artist in the hip-hop community; it is unlikely that
many readers of this book would be able to get access to as many leading
artists in their chosen field. But you don't need to interview 'experts' or
'professionals' to conduct your own research along these lines. One or two
interviews with key players in the field can provide valuable insights into the
mechanisms of the industry.

Discussion

There are several ways of approaching research into the media and culture
industries, and I hope that this chapter has given you the confidence to try
some of them. We have discussed the methods of archive research, interview
and participant observation in most detail and have also considered oral
history as a method. All of these are well suited to undergraduate or postgraduate research projects.

Even if you don't base your study on the industry, almost any research
project can benefit from having a section which investigates the economic,
regulatory and cultural environment of the industry producing the texts or
addressing the audiences you are investigating. It is always a good idea to
include discussion of the industry, as this demonstrates an understanding of
context. The media and cultural industries provide rich and varied sources
for analysis.

5 Methods of Analysing Audiences

Chapter overview

In this chapter, we examine some of the ways in which we can analyse media audiences. We begin by considering what is meant by 'audiences' and discuss some of the rationales for studying them. We next consider some of the main paradigms for thinking about audiences, including *media effects* and the focus on the audience as '*reader*'. We then briefly consider the ethics of audience research before going on to look at the first of our main methods. One of the main ways in which audiences are studied is through observation, and we consider the history of the observation of audiences by *experimental methods*. The use of ethnography is much more prevalent in contemporary audience research, and we present, as our first case study, Liebes and Katz' investigation of television audiences.

This chapter also looks at the ways in which audiences can be studied by asking them about their behaviour. We look at some of the issues raised in *questionnaire design* through a detailed analysis of the ITC survey. The issues of types of question, constructing scales and sampling are touched upon before we discuss some of the more common problems in questionnaire design.

One method of studying audiences which is much debated in the press and elsewhere is the *focus group* – we begin our section on this topic by discussing the advantages and disadvantages of the method. Case study 5.3, *Delete Expletives?* (Millwood Hargrave, 2000), uses the questionnaire and focus group to examine audience attitudes towards swearing in the media. This section concludes with some pointers on organizing your own focus group. Focus groups can also be used as parts of oral history projects, which is the next main method discussed in this chapter. Oral history is a useful method for studying the social history of the media, as Shaun Moores does in the last case study of this chapter.

Researching audiences for media and culture

Who, or what, are audiences?

In previous chapters, we have discussed how we can study texts and industries. Now we turn our attention to the third major area of analysis: *audiences*. In media and cultural studies, the term 'audience' is used in the everyday sense to refer to the people who attend a particular performance or who view a film or programme on television. But we also use the term to refer in a broader sense to people who are exposed to, or who respond to, media culture. Indeed, in its broadest sense, the term 'audience' is almost interchangeable with 'society', for it is used to refer to the many ways in which the media relate to the broader social world. In this sense, all people in a society constitute a potential audience for any media product. In the following discussion, we will be considering audiences in this inclusive sense and thinking about methods of researching people's relationships with the media.

Several kinds of research are undertaken into audiences by organizations, institutions and individuals. People who produce media artefacts, government regulatory bodies, lobby groups and politicians are just some of the many people who study audiences. Governments need to know if people are being informed about issues; programme makers need to know whether people like their programmes; advertisers need to know what magazines their target audience read and regulators need to keep up to date with public manners and mores. All kinds of agencies, public and private, make it their business to find out what kinds of media are used, when, where and how. Some of these are discussed in Chapter 2. Here we look in detail at those methods which are most suitable to students beginning their research careers. The first set of methods we discuss are those which involve *observing audiences*, focusing especially on *ethnography*. Secondly, we look at ways of *asking questions*, and here we discuss *interviews*, *focus groups* and *surveys*. These are all used mainly to research contemporary media use, but we also consider how these same methods can be used as a means of researching the past use of media and culture within *oral history*.

In Chapter 4, we looked at the people who produce the media, and we considered some of the methods we could use to study them. Here we will find that there is some overlap; after all, we are still talking about researching *people*, and some of the same ground rules apply whether the people we are investigating are *producers* or *consumers*. The methods of *interview* and *survey*, for example, can both be used effectively to research media production or consumption. However, conceptually, the ways we think about *producers* and *consumers* of media artefacts differ in important ways. Mediated

FIGURE 5.1

The Sender/
Receiver Model
of Communication

Sender $\longrightarrow$ Message $\longrightarrow$ Receiver

communication makes a distinction between the *source* and the *receiver*, meaning that producers of the media and culture are fulfilling a different function from the people who consume the artefacts and events. The earliest models of mass communication theory placed producers and consumers at different ends of the communication process.

Figure 5.1 shows the simple sender/receiver model of communication. This process has historically been considered as a linear one, originating with the message being sent by the sender and ending with its being received. This model has been built on and developed by scholars who say that feedback is important and that receivers have ways of telling producers what they want. Despite claims that we now live in a fragmented world, the media are still largely mass and the basic principles of the model remain fundamentally sound. The implication for the present discussion is that because messages originate with one group of people and are received by a different (albeit overlapping) group, conceptually they have very different relationships to the message. This necessarily suggests that different theoretical paradigms for understanding their relative roles and that different methods of investigation are required. Thus, although the interview, for example, is a perfectly legitimate method of interviewing both producers and viewers, the exact way to go about interviewing each different group may well differ. We use different methods for studying producers and consumers because they constitute different analytical objects and they have distinct relationships with the media. Asking what producers think of a particular television programme, for example, will elicit different kinds of answers than asking viewers.

Why study audiences?

We live in an increasingly mediated society and the rate of change in the media environment is unprecedented. In these days of globalization, we also are increasingly conscious of the rapid changes in media services in the twentieth and twenty-first centuries. This awareness inevitably leads us to ask about the impact of the communication revolution on our lives. Questions about the impacts and influences of the media have driven research for the past century.

Audience research puts human experience at the centre of our enquiry. Researching audiences for media and culture allows us to investigate the social uses of the media. By looking at how texts are *received*, we are able to understand the impacts, influences and effects of the media. Audience research also allows us to examine what people get out of the media, what people like (and don't like) and why.

Researching media effects

One of the most controversial ideas in media studies, and one of the most widely debated themes, is the notion that the media have 'effects' (Moores, 1993; Gauntlett, 1995; Barker and Petley, 1997). Many people are attracted to studying the media because they have read or heard arguments that the media are powerful influences on our lives. In many newspapers, especially the tabloids, criminal behaviour is often linked with certain kinds of media habits. Sometimes – for example, in rape cases – it might be reported that the defendant had a large collection of pornographic images on his computer and the reader could easily infer that this was in some sense a cause of the perpetrator's behaviour. Sometimes, defendants try to use the media as a defence, arguing that their actions were caused by media viewing. The film *A Clockwork Orange* was withdrawn by its director Stanley Kubrick because criminals said they had been influenced by it. In other cases where apparently senseless behaviour is difficult to understand, people may attribute the cause of such actions to violent media. Often in the past, violent videos have been seen as the 'cause' of aberrant social behaviour – for example, in the reporting of the trial of the two children convicted of killing James Bulger, spurious links with the film *Child's Play III* were made. There are many reasons why it would be convenient to blame the media for things which we don't or don't want to, understand.

The media are often blamed for social ills to the detriment of identifying the real causes of the problem. In the past, politicians in the USA and the UK have found it more convenient to blame various sectors of the media for social ills than their own policies and actions. It is easier to pass a law banning the representation of violence than to prevent violent conduct. But the real causes of violence in society – such as family instability, mental illness or poverty are harder to solve. The idea that the media might play a role in making people behave badly has been well researched; there is no substantive evidence at all to support it. Criminal behaviour is most readily explained by poor background, poor parenting and a life of deprivation, and not by watching violent videos. The fact that people who watch violent videos might also be attracted to violence is a different matter. In your own research, you should think about causality. What causes something to happen? Do you think watching a television programme could cause a person to behave in a particular way?

There are media products which are designed to bring about change in people's behaviour. Anti-smoking campaigns, drink-driving campaigns and other public safety and health messages are purposefully designed with the goal of changing the attitudes and behaviour of the people who see them. Many studies have shown that the actual effect of these is very minimal: the best we can hope for is that they contribute to a gradual shift in cultural patterns. For example, we know that there has been a reduction in adult smoking over the past 20 years, but can we attribute this to anti-smoking messages in the media? I don't think anyone would be able to isolate a single factor which could be said to have caused this reduction, and, as an ex-smoker, I am unaware of anyone giving up smoking solely as a result of seeing a public information film. If purposeful messages designed to have 'effects' are so ineffective, then the argument that the media in general have deleterious effects becomes even harder to support.

Many experienced scholars have attempted to study media effects and found very little hard evidence. The relationship between media exposure and behaviour is highly complex and many other factors intervene. It has been impossible to prove that the media have direct 'effects', and yet in popular discourse the myth persists to the contrary. Students of the media will find it nigh on impossible to prove that the media have effects – you are recommended to avoid this topic in your own work.

Research in the age of the reader

In the history of academic research of the media, audience research is a relative newcomer. In the 1970s, semiotics and structuralism were trends in academia which focused on the text as the location of meaning. The importance of Marxism and debates about ideology which sprang from the work of Louis Althusser (1979; 1984) led to a focus on the modes of production, the ideological content of texts and, to a lesser extent, the processes of production. During the 1980s, some key studies shifted the attention of media scholars away from the analysis of texts and towards the investigation of the text in the mind's eye of the reader. The idea that the meaning of texts was created through reading began to gain currency with the impact of feminism and other civil rights issues on cultural studies: the idea that the personal was political led to work being focused on the way in which audiences read texts. The age of the reader emerged out of a political engagement with popular culture which was committed to empowering the users of texts. Issues of textual *reception* began to replace those of hermeneutics or production. The history of the changes in the way audiences have been researched has been discussed by Ien Ang (1991), David Morley (1992), Sonia Livingstone (1998) and others (see also, for example, Kitzinger, 1999).

David Morley and Ien Ang are both authors of key texts in the history of audience research. David Morley's work on how different audiences understood the news programme *Nationwide* (Morley, 1980) is a key study. Morley watched episodes of *Nationwide* with several different groups of people – evening-class students, school students, trades unionists – and noted how the meanings of the same text differed according to who was watching. His later research on how families watch television pays more attention to the location of reception by interviewing families in their own homes (this work is discussed in Chapter 1, pages 10–11). Morley's work has been foundational in the history of media studies.

Ien Ang is a scholar who has researched audiences from a feminist perspective, most notably the way women watch television. In the early 1980s, Ang placed the following advertisement the Dutch women's magazine, *Viva*:

> I like watching the TV serial *Dallas*, but often get odd reactions to it. Would anyone like to write and tell me why you like watching it too, or dislike it? I should like to assimilate these reactions in my university thesis. (Ang, 1985: 10)

At the time, there was a lot of public debate in The Netherlands (and elsewhere in Europe) about the status of American melodramatic series in European television. Ang wanted to find out why people liked these pro-grammes, despite official pronouncements against such examples of American cultural imperialism. In response to her advertisement, Ang received 42 letters, the majority of which were from women or girls (three were from boys or men). This is hardly a representative sample, but rather a self-selecting group of people from among *Viva* readers – which itself is likely to be unrepresentative of the Dutch population as a whole. There are lots of methodological flaws in this research. However, from the letters she received and her subsequent correspondence, Ang created a very rich study of the reasons why people like American melodramatic television. As she says, 'The central question is *how* these letter-writers experience *Dallas*, what it means when they say they experience pleasure or displeasure, how they relate to the way in which *Dallas* is presented to the public' (Ang, 1985: 11).

Researching audiences by soliciting letters from them may not be a completely reliable method, but Ang's work made a significant impact on our thinking about what people like about television genres which some may consider unworthy of serious study. By concentrating her analysis on viewers' reports of their thoughts and feelings, Ang was able to develop a theory of the 'melodramatic imagination'. This study is important because it focused on the (mainly) female viewers of soap opera. The *Dallas* study made the feminist interrogation of audiences central to the modes of enquiry in our field. Janice Radway also conducts research into readers from a feminist perspective. Radway's *Reading the Romance* (1984) contributed a great deal to shifting the emphasis of textual research from the hermeneutic study of the *text as text* to the study of the text as part of an interpretive process (see Case Study 5.1).

CASE STUDY 5.1. AUDIENCES/RADWAY

Janice Radway's study *Reading the Romance: Women, Patriarchy and Popular Literature* (1984), one of the first to examine the pleasure of the text from the point of view of the reader, is a key text in the history of audience research. Radway interviewed readers of Harlequin Romance novels – a much maligned genre – who gathered in a Dorothy Evans' bookstore in Smithton to discuss romantic novels. Radway questioned the assumptions traditionally made about readers of mass-produced fiction; assumptions made on the basis of reading the texts. Basing her own theory on the work of Clifford Geertz and other anthropologists, Radway set out to understand how the women interpreted the romances and to look at the texts as part of an interpretive process.

> A good cultural analysis of the romance ought to specify not only how the women understand the novels themselves but also how they comprehend the very act of picking up a book in the first place. The analytic focus must shift from the text itself, taken in isolation, to the complex social event of reading where a woman actively attributes sense to lexical signs in a silent process carried on in the context of her ordinary life. (Radway, 1984: 8)

Meaning, Radway is saying, lies not in the text alone, but in how readers interpret texts. Her work is in keeping with a tendency in popular culture for celebratory studies aiming to increase appreciation for works which traditionally exist well outside the canon of mainstream literature. A great deal of popular culture studies investigates genres considered to be worthless and/or lowbrow by many mainstream critics. Radway's work was significant in two related ways: because of the way it accorded respect to lowbrow women's fiction, and because the method (interview) allowed the readers to speak for themselves about why they like their preferred reading matter. She finds that her readers read the texts very much against the grain, interpreting what to many critics would appear to be very negative and repressed female figures, as strong and positive role models. This work is one which begins from a position of empowerment rather than enslavement of the audience. Radway is concerned with the means by which women negotiate with hegemonic representations of themselves without jeopardizing self-respect.

Ien Ang's method of advertising for respondents in popular magazines was adopted by Jackie Stacey in her study of how British women watched female stars of the Hollywood era (1994). In 1989, Stacey placed an announcement in the letters pages of *Woman's Realm* and *Woman's Weekly* asking readers about their favourite stars of the 1940s and 1950s, and identifying herself as a researcher at the University of Birmingham. This was followed up with a questionnaire aimed at investigating respondents' cinema-going habits and attitudes in the 1940s and 1950s.

There is a strong political motivation behind much of the feminist work on readers. This is the product of the desire to empower the reader – and to affirm that the power to interpret the text lies in the reader, and not in the producer. This idea gels with Stuart Hall's work on the encoder/decoder model which was very influential in cultural studies during the 1980s (Hall, 1981). The paradox thrown up by semiotics, that texts are polysemic and yet we need to interpret their meanings, was resolved by the idea of audience empowerment: the turn to audiences of the 1980s and 1990s placed the location of meaning firmly in the mind of the reader.

That the meaning of a text is polysemic and open to multiple (even infinite) interpretations became almost an unquestionable orthodoxy in the 1990s. Most scholars have now pulled back from this interpretive liberalism. It is generally recognized that the insistence on privileging the moment of reception over that of production distracts us from the material reality that meaning production is largely the domain of media makers. Although the affirmation that audiences create meaning is a political position with which one may have a great deal of emotional sympathy, intellectually it is non-sensical. I agree that it would be great if ordinary people had control over the meaning of media texts, but, in reality, the primary power to create meanings lies in the major corporations which produce the texts and the people they employ. Texts are, of course, *multisemic* – they are open to multiple interpretations – but I resist the word *polysemic* if that means that the text allows you to interpret it as you will. Meaning is in the relationship between the audience and the text. A television programme like *The West Wing* is liberal and patriotic at the same time because that is how the producers planned it: it would have to be deliberately read against the grain to be interpreted as a fascist tract. The fundamental meaning won't change if it is viewed by a revolutionary communist or a neo-Nazi, although the identification with the text and the sense of recognition probably avoid.

Students can research audiences for particular programmes to investigate the specific kinds of pleasures of the texts. The idea of meaning communities is interesting to research. For example, we could study the way a particular group of people use the media as part of their social interaction. The uses that people put the media to are valuable means of understanding the relationship between the reader and the text. These kinds of 'pleasures of the text' are open to investigation by researchers who take the time to ask about them.

The ethics of audience research

In each of the methods we consider in this chapter, your primary object of analysis is *people*. Before we go any further, we need to consider the special ethical considerations in researching ordinary members of the public. Audience research typically falls within the rubric of what your university probably calls 'human subjects research'. This means any form of research which involves using people as subjects in a research project. There are special rules and guidelines for dealing with 'human subjects' which your supervisor or the chair of your university ethics committee should be able to provide you with. As a general rule, though, you should never expose your subjects to any form of harm; physical or psychological. You should never embarrass or humiliate your subjects, nor should you do anything immoral or improper, or ask your subjects to do anything immoral or improper. You should always seek informed consent and never surprise or shock subjects. There is very little justification for conducting research using children, and you should only use children as subjects after ensuring you have the full and informed consent of their carers: likewise with the mentally ill or learning disabled. You should never show people potentially dangerous or pornographic material. If in doubt, ask; if you can't get an answer, don't do it. Redesign your study if you think there is any chance that you might be in violation of human subjects guidelines.

We said in the opening section of this chapter that, in the broadest definition of the term, any study of people constitutes a form of audience research. Consequently, potential subjects for audience research are all around us, and offer a valuable resource for the undergraduate researcher to exploit. Your friends, family, colleagues and neighbours all could be encouraged to participate in your research with a little charm and encouragement from you. In the following sections of this chapter, we are going to discuss some of the methods you can use to study audiences.

Choosing your method

We saw in Chapter 1 that your research method should always be selected to suit your object of analysis. The methods discussed here cover the range of approaches from the more objective to the instrumental. Much professional research is carried out for instrumental reasons, but professional research commissioned by industry will also include more subjective forms of research, such as the focus group which has become a mainstay of all audience researchers. Table 5.1 shows the way we can relate the various objects of enquiry within audience research to the appropriate method.

TABLE 5.1
Choosing Your
Method to
Match Your
Object of
Analysis

Object of analysis	Method
Memories about past behaviour	Oral history or interview
Current behaviour	Interview or survey
Attitudes and opinions	Surveys or focus groups
Behaviour	Ethnography or observation

If you are looking for factual information about audiences, the best approach is probably a closed-question survey. However, if you are interested in studying how people feel about something, then it is best to use a more nuanced method such as the in-depth interview or the focus group.

Observing audiences

Scientific method is based on observation. There are many methods of observing audience behaviour, including laboratory research, ethnography and participant observation.

Experimental research

One of the methods most directly derived from science is the laboratory experiment. In sciences such as physics or chemistry, most research is carried out in a laboratory. When scientists report their findings, they are careful to describe their method fully because one of the measures of successful research is the extent to which it is *replicable*. Scientists can say that they have a reliable experiment if the work can be repeated by others and the same findings made. In the early days of mass communication research (the 1920s and 1930s), some experiments were made within the laboratory setting. The Payne Fund Studies, conducted in the USA between 1928 and 1932, for example, included laboratory experiments among the many methods employed to investigate the impact of the cinema on children and young people (Charters, 1970). *The Emotional Responses of Children to the Motion Picture Situation* (Dysinger and Ruckmick, 1970) was one of the books to be published as a result of the Payne Fund Studies. Dysinger and Ruckmick used monitors to measure the sweating and heartbeat of children and young people while watching films. They found that the youngsters displayed physical responses while watching films, leading them to conclude that the movies did have an effect on young viewers. One of their findings was that adolescents of sixteen years of age got more excited than children of nine during scenes involving themes of a romantic or sexual nature. They warned:

When the pictures are finally shown in color . . . and when the stereoscopic effect of tridimensional perception is added . . . an irresistible presentation of reality will be consummated. When, therefore, a psychoneurotic adolescent, for example, is allowed frequently to attend scenes depicting amorous and sometimes questionably romantic episodes, the resultant effects on that individual's character and development can be nothing but baneful and deplorable. (Dysinger and Ruckmick, 1970: 119)

Another of the Payne Fund Studies looked at how the social attitudes of children were influenced by film going. Ruth Peterson and L.L. Thurstone conducted a number of studies in small towns in Chicago on changes in children's attitudes toward various social groups and problems as a result of seeing specific films. They wanted to see how the attitudes of high-school children towards issues such as nationality, race and crime changed as a consequence of seeing films addressing these issues. They used a laboratory method of measuring attitudes 'before and after' exposure to films, taking as their survey instruments *attitude scales* and *paired comparison* methods. They found very little difference in children's attitudes as a result of seeing the films, with the exception of D.W. Griffith's *The Birth of a Nation* (1915). This epic about the American Civil War shows very extreme anti-African-American sentiment. The children were given a survey which measured their attitude toward 'the Negro' both before seeing the film and one week afterwards. Peterson and Thurstone found dramatic changes and were able to conclude:

> *The Birth of a Nation* had the effect of making children less favorable to the Negro. . . . It was interesting to find that the change in attitude was so marked that, after an interval, the attitude of the group was definitely less favorable to the Negro than before the film was seen. (Peterson and Thurstone, 1976: 38)

Other studies in the series showed less dramatic results, but the findings of the Payne Fund research were exaggerated and sensationalized in the press. The public outcry supporting the interpretation that the Payne Fund Studies had showed that films were harmful to young people was one of the causes of the introduction of greater censorship in the USA.

'Before and after' studies have often been used in the past. During World War II, American soldiers were shown films explaining 'why we fight', and surveys were taken before and after the screenings to see if their willingness to fight had changed as a result of seeing the film. In general such studies are not considered very valid. People work out what they are supposed to know – the educational function cannot be removed from the effect of viewing. Within communication research, some areas such as interpersonal communication continue to use experiments as a dominant research paradigm, but within the social sciences and humanities, generally, laboratory research is not a major research method.

For most kinds of question, the laboratory experiment is not appropriate, and it has been discredited: most research into audiences today is interested in how people behave when in the real environment. For example, how do people watch television at home?

Ethnography

The most direct way of finding out how audiences behave is by observing in the field, and *ethnography* is the name given to the methods used to observe audience behaviour (Moores, 1993). Ethnography might involve observing how people behave when they are actually watching television (Lull, 1990), shopping (Miller, 1998), dancing (Rietveld, 1998) and so on. The method is derived from anthropology, which involves the study of foreign people, but while anthropology addresses the exotic, ethnography more typically involves 'making strange' the ordinary and everyday. To conduct good ethnography, you must be detached and removed from the situation, and you observe others without allowing your presence to intervene in the situation. But of course, this is impossible – while people are being observed they necessarily behave differently than they would in private.

James Lull has conducted several studies in which he looks at people watching television in various family situations and in different countries (Lull, 1990). He uses an army of researchers to do the observing for him and to report on their observations. Lull's work is exceptionally labour-intensive: he has a team of research assistants conducting the participant observation. It is very expensive to conduct this kind of research and beyond the reach of most readers of this book in terms of scale and depth. However, it is perfectly possible for you to conduct small-scale ethnographic work observing people you know (and who won't feel too awkward about your being there). It is a good method to use in conjunction with interviews so that you can observe people and then ask them about their behaviour. This combination of methods was used by Tamar Liebes and Elihu Katz in their study of Israeli television audiences.

CASE STUDY 5.2. LIEBES AND KATZ: *DALLAS*

Tamar Liebes and Elihu Katz (1990) observed the responses of different ethnic and racial groups in Israel as they watched the American soap *Dallas*. Groups of friends were observed as they watched the broadcast programme and then interviewed about what they had just seen. Groups were recruited to reflect the ethnic composition of Israeli society and included Arabs, Moroccan Jews, recent arrivals from the Soviet Union and second-generation Israelis on a kibbutz. *The Export of Meaning: Cross Cultural Readings of 'Dallas'* also includes a chapter (co-written with Sumiko Iwao) which reports on a study observing how Japanese viewers watched the programme. Liebes and Katz were concerned to appreciate how different people interpreted the programme. The researchers asked the groups to retell the episode they had just seen and coded the subsequent conversations. They found that there were two main types of viewer involvement. The first is 'referential', whereby the viewer relates the programme to reality, especially to their own life situation. In the second, which they label 'critical', viewers are conscious of the programme as a construction which they can then criticize. Most viewers slip between these different modes of involvement quite easily, although some groups of viewers specialize in one rather than the other. Liebes and Katz are able to show that the experience of viewing *Dallas* differs according to viewers' social attitudes and position.

Most readers of this book will have neither the time nor the finances to conduct research on the scale of Lull or Liebes and Katz. However, anyone can carry out a small-scale ethnographic study of an aspect of culture with which they are familiar. We discussed the use of work placements in Chapter 4 when we talked about researching industries, so I won't reiterate the stages of a participant observation. Participant observation is an equally valid method for studying producers or audiences. The best subjects for students conducting observational studies is an area of culture in which they are already participants. Victor Sampedro (1998) conducted an interesting participant observation study of overseas students' use of newspapers from their home countries while at university in the USA. Sampedro was inspired to conduct the study by his own experience of using the newspaper library to keep in touch with events back home. Sampedro observed the patterns of reading ethnographically (he was a participant observer, watching his subjects as he also read the foreign papers), and subsequently he interviewed the subjects about their use of the media. Sampedro's research prompted him to think about the role of the media in helping people to maintain their local identities despite being geographically displaced. The theoretical paradigm for the research (globalization and identity) was secondary in his thinking about this project. Clearly, the topic appealed to him because he shared a sense of identity and community with other foreign students who frequented the newspaper library.

Ethnographic methods are often used in combination with other methods, commonly the interview (as in Case Study 5.2). Ethnography requires a degree of critical distance that is sometimes difficult to attain when you are involved in the situation yourself. Take your time and give yourself plenty of 'time out' while conducting fieldwork – keep a journal of what happens at events you attend and try to update it frequently during the event.

It might militate against your enjoyment of the occasion, but it will dramatically improve your research as a consequence! Remember that you are there to observe the impact of the event on others rather than participating yourself. You should be aiming to get a more critical distance and a deeper understanding of the social milieu which you inhabit.

The stages in a participant observation of audiences are much the same as for industries (see Chapter 4, pages 120–4). But you do need to be sensitive to the fact that people feel differently about being observed in their workplace (where such things may be more acceptable; where people often feel they are 'putting on a show' anyway and where people are 'in role' as their job title) than in their homes. Observing people in their leisure-time is a much more significant invasion of privacy. Before contemplating doing such a study, you should be sure that you have the full cooperation and consent of your subjects.

If you are thinking about participant observation, you should begin by thinking about what groups you belong to and your own media use. Think about your friends and family and their media use. A good idea is to watch and then ask questions later. Observe how people behave in a particular social setting and try to reach conclusions about it. Develop a provisional hypothesis or research question and then test it in the field.

Asking questions

While ethnography and methods of observation can be useful in finding out about audience behaviour, if you want to find out about people's ideas, opinions and attitudes, there is no substitute for asking them. Most social science research is based on people's reports of their actions in surveys or some kind of questionnaire (see Deacon et al., 1999; Punch, 1998; Burns, 2000). Whether they use *questionnaires*, *interviews* or *focus groups*, researchers are not directly observing respondents to get their information, but are relying on reports of participants in the study. It is important to remember that the subjects are relaying information to the researcher about their world and are thus observing on the researcher's behalf. A key to making sure that respondents give accurate reports lies in the design of the questions asked.

Questionnaire design

One of the most common ways of asking people about their opinions and attitudes is the survey questionnaire. A survey is used to compare a number of different people along the same *variables*. A *variable* is something which you can measure, and which differs between people, such as age or gender. The term simply means 'something that can vary' and is a technical term for something which you can measure. Every item on a survey is measuring a variable of some kind, whether it be age, gender or how many beers you typically drink on a night out.

The national census is a survey of all citizens in the UK carried out every ten years. The government gathers information on all households in the country in order to determine how to allocate resources and to monitor social developments. Elections are a form of mass survey – all voters are expected to say which candidate they want to represent them. Opinion polls are surveys which are used for various things, including predicting the outcome of an election. But in opinion polls, unlike the census or a general election, we don't ask everyone in the country what they think, but only a small sample of people. Organizations like MORI and NOP make generalizations based on these samples of how we will vote in a general election (see their websites in Appendix 2, p. 179 for information on how they conduct research). However, the whole population is not surveyed until the election itself, and sometimes predictions have been wrong. In the 1992 general election, for example, the Labour Party was widely predicted to beat the Conservative Party but in fact the Conservatives held on to a majority in Parliament and went on to govern for another four years. The polling organizations had not accurately predicted the outcome of the election. Clearly, something had gone wrong with the research methodology employed. One theory about this argues that people were too embarrassed to admit to voting Tory and lied to the interviewers about their voting intention. It seems that people wanted to appear more compassionate and less selfish than they really were and didn't want to admit to a stranger that they would be voting out of self-interest. Today, polls on future voting take into account how people voted at the last election and adjust their voting intention figures accordingly.

Opinion polls, like all forms of research involving asking people about things, cannot be protected from the possibility that people might not tell the absolute truth. Respondents may misreport in order to make themselves seem to be nicer, or more sexually experienced, or more socially aware. Respondents may want to tell interviewers what they think they want to hear, skewing their answers accordingly. They might make something up to conceal the fact that they don't have a clue about what the interviewer is asking. People usually misreport to make themselves seem more important or knowledgeable than they really are. One of the problems with surveys is that people do not always tell the truth! When designing a questionnaire, you have to be aware of this possibility and take it into account.

Surveys are used in all areas of media and cultural research to find out people's opinions and attitudes. All of the major research companies and industries commission research, as we discussed in Chapters 2 and 4. The ITC conducts frequent research into the standards and mores of the viewing public. For example, Guy Cumberbatch investigated the public's attitudes toward television in his book, *Television: The Public's View* (Cumberbatch, 2000). In the following discussion of research questionnaires, we include examples from the ITC's *Attitudes to Television Questionnaire* (Independent Television Commission, 2001), which was the survey instrument used by Cumberbatch in his research.

Types of questions

The type of question you want to ask depends on the kind of variable you are trying to get at. In the ITC survey, there are more than 50 questions using a variety of forms of question.

Binary questions. If you want to know how men and women differ on a particular issue, you will need to include in your survey instrument a question to identify the gender of your respondents. Gender has only two options: male or female. It is is a *binary* variable and requires you to ask a binary question. You could also ask, 'male = yes/no?' and get the same information, but you would probably offend many people. Sometimes you just want to know a simple answer to a yes/no question. For example, Question 2a on the ITC survey asks:

Have you bought or rented a new television set in the last 12 months?

1 ☐ YES
2 ☐ NO

Source: Independent Television Commission, 2001: 1.

Binary questions, then, are those where it is possible to give one of two responses.

Open-ended and closed-end questions. In an open-ended question, respondents are asked to fill in their own responses, whereas in a closed-end question, the responses are given in the survey and respondents are required to indicate which is the appropriate response for them. If you wanted to know people's age, for example, you could ask 'What was your age last birthday?' This is an open-ended question. However, the same question could be asked as follows:

Are you:

1. Under 18
2. 18–24
3. 25–40
4. 41–65
5. 66 or over

In this case, you would not be able to do such fine analysis of the ages of your respondents. However, if you are interested in comparing the responses of 'old' people (whom you have defined as over 40) and 'young' people (whom you have defined as under 40), you will have ample detail with the above closed-end question format. The advantages and disadvantages of each type of question format are well discussed by Ranjit Kumar (1999).

Using prompts

In conducting a survey, you may want to show your subjects identifiers of particular things. In media research, for example, people may be shown the logo of a television station along with its name to see if they can identify it. This method was used in the ITC survey of people's attitudes towards television. Subjects were shown a series of cards with the logo of all the television stations that were available in their area. First, the interviewers asked the subjects to tell them which channels they watched. Then, the respondents were asked questions about the stations which they had identified. For example: 'Which of these channels would you say you personally watch most often?' (Independent Television Commission, 2001: 4). The interviewer was instructed to ask, 'and which next?' until the respondent had identified four. The answers to these questions were then coded by the researcher conducting the survey interview.

Constructing scales

Scales are used in survey research when sets of questions are used to develop a more complex picture of general attitudes. The Likert scale, named after the social scientist, Rensis Likert, elicits from respondents the strength of feeling towards something (Babbie, 1989). For example, you might present your interviewees with a series of statements and for each one ask them to say whether they 'strongly agree'; 'agree'; 'disagree'; 'strongly disagree' or are 'neutral/don't know'. The ITC survey includes several questions using Likert scale questions. For example, Question 9a asks:

How interested are you in acquiring a satellite dish?

1 ☐ VERY INTERESTED
2 ☐ SLIGHTLY INTERESTED
3 ☐ DON'T KNOW
4 ☐ NOT THAT INTERESTED
5 ☐ NOT AT ALL INTERESTED

Source: Independent Television Commission, 2001: 11.

In her study of swear words, Millwood Hargrave uses a four-point scale for people to grade the offensiveness of words as 'very severe'; 'severe'; 'mild' or 'not swearing' (see Case Study 4.4).

Semantic differentiation. In a variation on the Likert scale, a semantic differentiation question gives respondents two opposite words and asks them to place their response on the continuum between the two. Survey questionnaires must be very carefully designed to elicit the required information. They have the advantage that information can be gathered in such a way as to be readily analysed by computer programmes such as SPSS (Statistical Package for the Social Sciences).

Sampling

A census asks questions of all the people in the country, and while we might want to find out what everyone in the country thinks about certain issues, that is not usually practical. In most cases, surveys are administered to a representative sample of people, and generalizations are made about how the rest of the population would respond. The government have a responsibility to represent all the people in the country, and they therefore survey everyone in the country and do not have to make *generalizations* based on their data. If you have census information, you can make conclusions. For example, the government can definitively say how many people of a particular religion live in a particular area – certainly more accurately than if you sampled all the people living in one street and multiplied that by the number of streets in a town. But you may not be interested in finding out what everyone in the country thinks. If you are interested in studying a particular community – for example, people who attend a particular club or regular film-goers – you are not interested in the opinions of the whole country. In this case, your *population* is all the people in that group; a *sample* is the subset that you are going to study. Thus, if you know that a particular club regularly attracts 500 people and you can get 50 people to answer your survey, you have sampled ten per cent of your population. This is a very good percentage on which to make generalizations. Samples should be *random*; otherwise, you will not be able to make reliable generalizations.

Many excellent undergraduate projects have been conducted using questionnaires, and it is not difficult to design and administer your own small-scale questionnaire with some careful thinking and planning. You need to be aware of the different kinds of questionnaire and the different kinds of questions that one can ask (see Roger Sapsford, 1999, for more detailed discussion).

Some common problems in questionnaire design

There are lots of problems that can arise if your questionnaire or interview schedule is not carefully designed. Below are some common problems in question design which can easily be avoided if you are aware of them in advance.

Incomprehensible questions. Read your questions through carefully to yourself and test them on others before you administer the survey. This will help to ensure that you do not have any questions which are simply not understood by your respondents.

Double-barrelled questions. Questions which have two parts and which respondents may want to answer differently are 'double-barrelled'. Make sure that you avoid them, and that every question asks for a single response.

Leading questions. Although you might prefer people to answer in a particular way, your survey should be designed so that it is impossible for respondents to guess what they are 'supposed' to say. You must avoid indicating in the question what the answer is supposed to be. For example, the question, 'How bad a Director-General was John Birt?' suggests that respondents agree with you that John Birt was a bad Director-General, and it may not get at their true opinion of the man.

Speculative questions. Do not ask respondents to speculate on what might happen – for example, by asking, 'What do you think will be the impact of the Internet on the film industry?' People may well feel that, because they want to please you, they should have an answer, but they may know nothing about the issue. It is best to avoid speculative questions altogether.

Hypothetical questions. Likewise, hypothetical questions are problematic; it is of little value to ask people what they might do in given circumstances. Avoid questions which ask people to imagine what might happen.

Presumptuous questions. You should avoid asking anything which is presumptuous, that is, that assumes things about the person that you haven't established. 'What did you watch on television last night?' should not be asked unless you have established that the interviewee was watching television last night. Likewise, 'What kind of films do you prefer to go and see?' implies that people do go to the cinema and therefore is a presumptuous question.

Longitudinal studies

There have been many studies of audience behaviour conducted over periods of time, and we call any such study into the long-term behaviour of respondents, *longitudinal*. The British Film Institute, for example, conducted an audience tracking survey in the five years 1991–96. Some 500 respondents filled in questionnaire diaries about their television habits every day (Petrie and Willis, 1995; Gauntlett and Hill, 1999). This same sample was used by Robert Turnock (2000) in his investigation of audience responses to the death of Princess Diana on 31 August 1997. The BBC and other organizations also conduct longitudinal research into media habits. It is unlikely that readers of this book would be in a position to conduct longitudinal studies, but you should be aware of some of them.

Reliability and validity

No undergraduate study is going to meet the standards of professional research methods which these tests are designed to measure. If you want to know more, there are several good textbooks on the subject, including those by Earl Babbie (1989), Robert B. Burns (2000), Roger Sapsford (1999) and Keith F. Punch (1998).

The information you collect in your survey will not be reliable, so how can you draw conclusions? You need always to acknowledge the limitations of the piece and say how you would have done things differently with more time and resources. Your conclusions may be provisional, but they are yours. You have done your own piece of original research – say what you personally found clearly and boldly. Don't be inhibited by the strictures of what is proper survey research in stating conclusions on what you have found. Imagination and intellect are required to interpret data, and sometimes you might find that you make speculations. These could easily lead to further hypotheses, which it is a good idea to present in a section on 'future research'. Survey research is an excellent way to investigate media and cultural audiences. However, students need to take great care in designing their studies and to recognise their limitations.

Focus groups

The focus group is a good way of researching the responses, ideas and opinions of people in greater depth than a survey. A focus group is an organized discussion of a small group of people on a given topic.

Advantages and disadvantages of focus groups

If you want to find out why people believe what they do, understand more of the nuanced reasons behind their answers or question them about their opinions of particular media texts, focus groups are probably the best approach. Andrea Millwood Hargrave's team used focus groups to find out more about which words people found offensive and the impact of the context of viewing on the degree of offence. Such complex questions as 'why?' and 'in what context?' are too vague to be used in a survey and take time and empathy to elicit. Focus groups are an ideal way to study how people feel about things or to delve into the complexities of their opinions and attitudes. It is a more textured method of analysis and one plagued with problems of reliability and validity as a consequence.

CASE STUDY 5.3. SURVEY/FOCUS GROUP

Andrea Millwood Hargrave, 2000. *Delete Expletives*? The Advertising Standards Authority, British Broadcasting Corporation, Broadcasting Standards Commission and the Independent Television Commission (jointly funded research).

The research presented here combines survey research and focus groups to understand how people from various backgrounds feel about sacrilegious or otherise offensive language in the media. This research was funded by several bodies which have an interest in understanding the social mores and need to find out more about public opinion: the Advertising Standards Authority, the BBC, the Broadcasting Standards Commission and the Independent Television Commission. The researchers were required to determine public opinion with regard to swearing and obscenity on television programmes and advertise-ments, and in advertisements in magazines and on posters. Millwood Hargrave's team interviewed 1,033 in their homes, asking them to respond

TABLE 5.2

Ranked Order
of Ten Most
Offensive
Words
According to
Severity in
2000 and
1998

	Year	
	2000	(1998)
Cunt	1	(1)
Motherfucker	2	(2)
Fuck	3	(3)
Wanker	4	(4)
Nigger	5	(11)
Bastard	6	(5)
Prick	7	(7)
Bollocks	8	(6)
Arsehole	9	(9)
Paki	10	(17)

Source: Millwood Hargrave, 2000: 9.

to a list of vulgar and obscene swear words. Respondents aged over 18 from several different parts of Britain and in many diverse forms of household were interviewed. They were given a list of words and asked to say how severe in offensiveness each word was from a choice of 'very severe'; 'fairly severe'; 'mild' or 'not swearing'.

In order to analyse the responses, the researchers gave a score to each word so that 'very severe' was given three points; 'fairly severe' two; and 'mild', one, and the category 'not swearing' was given no points. With this numerical value given to each response, it was possible to calculate a mean (average) score and use this to create the ranking shown in Table 5.2.

From this information, they were able to show that 'cunt' is the word which causes most offence to most people. Because they also collected data on what groups respondents belonged to, and where they lived in Britain, they were able to correlate this information with the ranked data. Thus, they were able to report that respondents living in the south considered the term 'Jew' 'very severe' more frequently than respondents in the north of England. A similar survey had also been carried out in 1998, allowing the researchers to compare results obtained at two points in time and thus to analyse changes in standards. In this study, the researchers are able to note some changes over the years in the attitudes of people towards expletives. For example, attitudes towards words which insult people on the grounds of race, such as 'nigger' or 'Paki', had changed. People generally found these terms of racial abuse more offensive in 2000 than they had previously. However, the relative status of words of profanity had not changed.

In order to find out *why* people don't like to hear certain words on television programmes, the researchers conducted a series of *focus groups*. This method is more suited to eliciting the degree of embarrassment felt by multigenerational families in the face of offensive language on posters or on television. The focus group element looked at the reactions of 14 different groups, in a discussion lasting two hours. The groups included single white men, black parents, single women, same sex couples and families with a learning-disabled person. The focus group organizers used video and poster extracts containing offensive language as 'prompts' for the discussions, which lasted about two hours. The focus group study found that people associated swearing with aggression, vulgarity, and inability to express oneself. Participants reported that they didn't like to hear swearing around children. For example, one British Asian male said: 'If our child sees or hears that [on television], then it's going to think that's the norm' (p. 6). In general, concern over obscenity was expressed by parents of teenagers more frequently than by any other group.

Organizing your own focus group

Professional social researchers pay people to attend focus groups, but students reading this book are unlikely to have the money to do this. If you are thinking about focus group research, consider your access to potential subjects and try to design a study which allows you to use your friends and fellow students as subjects as much as possible. This will not have the academic rigour of professional research, but it will get you a set of subjects. So, once again, it is best to research an area in which you already have a lot of contacts if you want to use this method.

A focus group might be appropriate if you are interested in the responses of different people towards something. For example, you might want to study how different people respond to a television personality. Let's take Graham Norton, for example. He is an extremely camp character on British television and an openly gay performer. A good study might be to examine how gay and lesbian people respond to his persona as opposed to straight people. Dividing your subjects into different 'straight' and 'gay' focus groups would enable both groups to talk more openly about their responses. If you had gay and straight people in the same groups to talk about sensitive issues to do with sexuality, you can see that they might feel too inhibited to talk openly. However, it has also been said that getting together groups of people of like minds tends to make the ideas they express more extreme, as people may feel the need to conform to what they perceive to be group norms.

If you were interested in how people of different generations use music, you might use focus groups as a part of your study. You could compare how 'young' and 'old' people use music in their lives by, first of all, asking likely candidates to attend focus groups. Getting together about four older people and four younger people in separate groups, you could ask them what they get out of music, what live music they go to, what radio stations they listen to and so on. You should lead the discussion so that you can be sure that both groups follow the same broad subject areas, and you should have a list of topics you want to cover in front of you at the time. You should record your focus groups, but you should also take brief notes as you go along. In this case, a survey, administered in advance, would help you to select candidates for your focus group.

How many subjects?

There is no definitive answer as to how many people you should interview or survey in your audience research. No undergraduate study is going to be reliable according to the standards of professional researchers, and it is unrealistic to expect otherwise. Few postgraduate students will have the resources to do so, either. However, you cannot just interview yourself and your best friend, nor can you make up data. You need to agree with your supervisor a target number of subjects which is reasonable. The more in-depth the interview (and more time-consuming to administer and code), the fewer subjects you need. But if you are aiming to give respondents a self-administered one-page survey, you will need more responses before you can make any reasonable conclusions.

Oral history

Interviewing is a very good way of finding out about people's behaviour and their attitudes to the past as well as the present. Oral history is an approach which relies for its primary research on interviews with people about their past experiences. Oral history has been conducted on producers of the media (see, for example, Mark Williams, 1999). The method can be used to good effect to investigate audiences in the past. Two studies which explore how British people responded to media technologies are Tim O'Sullivan's essay, 'Television Memories and Cultures of Viewing, 1950–65' (1991), and Shaun Moores's study, 'The Box on the Dresser: Memories of Early Radio and Everyday Life' (1988). O'Sullivan's study sets out to fill a gap in the existing literature on early television viewing. Most published research focuses on the institutions involved in television production, and, with the exception of some studies conducted by the BBC (Silvey, 1974; Briggs, 1979), O'Sullivan found that very little work had been done on how audiences experienced television viewing. He concludes that

> Increased understanding of the domestic conditions and cultures which govern personal television viewing and use has a vital part to play in gaining greater critical insight into the shifting historical and contem-

porary significance of television and other communication technologies in the transformation of post-war British culture. (O'Sullivan, 1991: 178)

However, very little work has been done in this area and there are lots of potential research topics for students to investigate using this method.

The place to begin to look for subjects for oral history is at home. Asking the older generation about their media use at certain times can be very informative – for example, their recollections of the music scene when they were young. A good research question might be, 'How influential was punk music on people growing up in the 1970s?' If you have family or friends who grew up in a different country, an interesting research area is the way they used the media when they first came to this country. Here you might ask, 'How important is access to "news from home" to first-generation British citizens?' You could research what media were available from your subjects' background country (videos, newspapers, etc.) and ask them which of these they used. You could find out if they used any British media and whether these were useful in helping them to acclimatize to life in their new country. Individual interviews or focus groups would be useful approaches to take in gaining the information required from subjects, but oral history also requires a great deal of historical research. Case study 5.4 involved a focus group of older people recollecting the early years of radio (Moores, 1988).

CASE STUDY 5.4. MOORES: EARLY RADIO

Shaun Moores, 1988. The box on the dresser: memories of early radio and everyday life. *Media, Culture and Society*, 10: 23–40.

In this oral history study about the early days of radio, Shaun Moores interviewed people at the Norris Street Old People's Day Centre and the Community Room at the Beaumont County Infant School in his home town of Warrington. Moores does not say how many people he interviewed for the study, but credits ten subjects by name and thanks several others. The study is based on the recollections of older people about their use of radio in the 1920s and 1930s.

Moores is investigating what happened to the status of leisure and entertainment during a crucial period in the social history of the British working class. Most of Moores's subjects were working-class people who lived in the Orford and Quay Bay areas of Warrington. Moores uses historical sources to set the scene of working-class life during this period. The key part of his study investigates the way radio contributed to a withdrawal of working-class social life into the interior. He shows how, with the introduction of the radio, a family audience was constructed, sometimes for the first time. Entertainment and leisure became centred around the household and the family during the 1920s and 1930s, as Moores demonstrates in this very engaging study.

Combining methods

We have seen how the use of more than one method can be quite illuminating in studying audiences. Andrea Millwood Hargrave's study (discussed above) uses survey research and focus groups to study the mores and attitudes of today's television audiences. Often a survey is a good way to find out general information about a large population before focusing on a smaller sample for in-depth interviews or focus groups. This was also the method employed by the Global Disney Audiences Project, which investigated the meaning of Disney in audiences around the world (Wasko et al, 2001).

The audience research methods discussed in this chapter can also be combined with other methods discussed elsewhere in this book. For example, you could conduct a semiotic analysis of a film and then conduct focus groups to find whether your own interpretation is shared, or whether other people can provide different insights. Here you would be combining textual analysis with audience research.

Discussion

In this chapter, we have discussed some of the main ways in which audiences have been researched and have given you some guidelines for conducting your own audience research. In dealing with audiences, we come closest in media and cultural studies to the ethical considerations faced by many other researchers who use people in their research. We must always be wary of doing harm to people and remember that there are serious ethical considerations to be taken into account. You should never ask people to do anything that might cause them the least harm, physical or psychological. So you should not get into areas that people might find upsetting. Always get informed consent to anything and make sure that the subject knows what is going to happen. You don't necessarily have to give away what the survey is about if that might jeopardize your results, but always debrief the subjects and tell them as much as you can about your work.

Audience research has been very controversial within media and cultural studies, largely because there are so many possible paradigms for research. There is no right or wrong way to conduct audience research; you must just find the right method for your research question. The study of audiences is one of the most fruitful and productive areas of researching media and culture.

6 Presenting Your Work

Chapter overview

In this, the final chapter of *How To Do Media and Cultural Studies*, we look at how you should present your work for submission. In order to understand exactly what is expected of you in writing your project, you must be familiar with the criteria for assessment in your university or college. This chapter offers some general criteria: your own institution will probably have similar ones. We discuss some strategies to help you plan your work and organize your time to the optimum. Some consideration is given to the contents of the project: although these will vary according to the precise nature of your study, there are some commonalities to these. In this chapter, we list the various sections which projects should normally contain. We also offer some advice on matters of style, picking up on some general problem areas for students, and give guidance on how to find further assistance. This chapter comes at the end of the book, but the information it contains will be of relevance to you throughout the time you spend writing your project. If you have a clear idea of where you are heading with your project, you will have a better sense of what you should concentrate on during the preparation, research and writing stages.

Introduction

How you present your work is absolutely crucial in determining how well you are going to do in the project. You need to think about presentation and style while you are working on your project, and think about how you are going to organize and submit your work while you are conducting the research. You have to give evidence that you have done work: you don't get any marks for anything which is not actually submitted. Your tutor is able to give you credit only for what you actually submit. This chapter will guide you through the main principles you should bear in mind when writing a project. It also includes some examples of tables of contents and how to present your information in a professional and scholarly way. The success of your project depends on how well you can convey to the reader what you have done and why. Other works which can help you in writing up your project include books by Judith Bell (1999) and David Silverman (2000).

Criteria for assessment

The criteria for marking projects are likely to be similar in most institutions, but make sure that you know what they are in your case – they should be in the course documentation. Marks are usually given for each of the following.

Originality of idea

How far is your research going into new territory? Are you researching something which hasn't been done before? Are you researching something different from the rest of your classmates? If your tutor is reading ten other projects on the same topic, no matter how original your approach is, you are going to have a hard time standing out from the crowd. Your idea should be topical – but not so much so that everyone else is also doing it! You need to be able to state how and why your idea is original and include this in your introduction.

Conceptualization

The design and planning of the project will provide an important element of most assessments. Your tutor will want to know that you have thought carefully about the design and execution of your project. Whether your project is *valid* and *reliable* is also likely to be a criterion (see discussion in Chapter 1, pages 19–22). You should ensure that your project investigates what you claim it does and does so in a manner which is appropriate. You will need to demonstrate that you have thought about the relationships among your object of analysis, the theoretical paradigm you are working within and your methodology. How to design your research question is discussed in greater depth in Chapter 1.

Organization and structure

Your tutor will want to be able to appreciate the point of your project. This will be made much easier if your work is well organized and clearly presented. Give your chapter and section headings clear and simple names.

Think through the overall logic of your argument and make sure that this is reflected in the way you order and organize your work. An important part of the assessment will depend on whether you can organize your ideas and findings clearly and accurately.

Research

You will be assessed on the quality of your research and also the amount of research you have done. This book has given you some guidelines on how to conduct a good research project. Make sure that you have a well thought out research design and that you have discussed it carefully with your tutor at various points during the conduct of the project. The main part of your assessment will be based on how well you have executed the research you have planned. In addition, there is the crude matter of the amount of work you have done. The work should look as if it has taken the time that you were given to do it. If it is a final year project, the marker will be asking if you have demonstrated that you spent a whole year doing the study. Be assured that your tutor is experienced enough to know whether you have written the entire thing over the Easter holidays or a long weekend; not only will your work suffer if you leave it until the last minute but your grades will, too. So make sure you give yourself plenty of time to do the work and the time to write up your findings.

Presentation

Although you don't get any extra marks for having brightly coloured binders and professionally bound dissertations, it is important to take care over presentation. Make sure that your work is neat and tidy and that you have structured and organized the chapter headings and subheadings neatly. Your work should be typed, double-spaced, on one side of the paper, and clearly labelled. Any illustrations or supplementary material (such as a videotape or audiotape) should be carefully labelled and firmly attached, including your student name or number. Include a cover sheet with the title of your dissertation, the name and number of the unit or module, your course title and your name. You should make sure that you meet all the criteria for submission at your own university and understand what is expected of you. Consult your module guide and/or tutor if in doubt.

Style

Carefully proofread your work before submitting it. It is a good idea to give yourself a week or so to go through the final text carefully before you submit to check your grammar and punctuation. You should also confirm the spelling of any unfamiliar words or names. Your work will benefit from being well written, so make sure that you check your style – often it helps to read it out loud to see if it makes sense.

The way that marks are allocated should be discussed in the relevant course guide. It is worth spending some time thinking about the criteria for assessment and ensuring that you demonstrate that you have met them all in your final draft. Remember that everything you want to count towards the final mark should be included in the project you submit – don't expect the lecturer to take into account work you did but did not present in the final piece of work. The criteria for assessment exist for a reason – they are there to help you to understand the makings of a good project. Think about how they relate to your particular project and make sure that you take them into account at all stages in your project.

Planning your work

You need to think ahead to the presentation stage while you are conducting your study. You can begin to write elements which will go into the final version of the essay from the beginning. Make sure you keep a full record of every book, article, journal and television programme of relevance to your project as you come across them. Keep an annotated provisional bibliography – jot down everything you *should, could* or *might* refer to in your final essay. Go back to this list frequently and keep tabs on what you have managed to get hold of. If something turns out to be no good, make a note of why. If something is very useful, make a more detailed note of why and think about how it relates to the other things you have on your list.

Keep a log or diary of what you do towards the project. Include things like making telephone calls (even if they weren't productive), going to the library and talking with your supervisor. This will help you to reflect on how you are progressing. The diary can provide a good basis for discussion with your supervisor in the early stages of the project.

It is very important to write an outline of your project as early as possible in the process, as we discussed in the first chapter of this book (see Chapter 1, pages 33–36). Time spent at the beginning of the project will save you time in the long run. The more research you do on the planning stage, the less likely you are to encounter obstacles later in the process.

Remember to keep very good bibliographic notes, including details of all information you use from whatever source.

The project contents

You need to be aware of the elements that your project should contain. For example, do you need a table of contents? What should be in the main body of the text and what in the appendices? Your tutor will probably provide you with guidelines on what is required at your university, so you should check with the teaching staff if there are any particular requirements. In general, though, your final project should contain the following elements:

The table of contents

The presentation of your material in clear sections is very important. It helps you to organize your material and helps readers find their way through the work. The table of contents should list the main chapter or section headings and, if necessary, the subheadings without going into too much detail. As a general rule, the table of contents should not exceed one page in length and need not comprise more than five lines. Remember that the most important function of the table of contents is to ensure that readers can find their way to specific sections if they wish, so do include page numbers. Table 6.1 gives an example of a generic table of contents which could be used for almost any kind of project! Use this as a template for organizing your own research project. The headings used in Table 6.1 will be discussed in the following sections. Of course, the exact nature of the table of contents will vary from project to project and needs to reflect what you actually did in the project. Table 6.2 shows a hypothetical table of contents of a project analysing the representation of femininity in magazines for black women.

Introducing your work

It may sound obvious, but the introduction is the first thing the reader is going to read about your work, and it is important that it does several things clearly and concisely. First, it must specify what the project is about, indicating what the reader can expect from the rest of the essay. The introduction needs to give a very concise précis of what you have done in researching your project. It also needs to state clearly why you have done the research that the reader is about to spend a couple of hours reading. You need to explain the value of your work and its significance up front. Tell the reader *what* you are interested in and *why*. Don't be afraid to be personal here; it is always interesting to share in the motivation of other people. Clearly, you are not going to be able to write the introduction until you have finished the project. When it comes to writing your research up, I

TABLE 6.1 A Generic Table of Contents	Title 1. Introduction 2. Literature review 3. Hypothesis 4. Method 5. The Study 6. Discussion 7. Conclusion 8. Bibliography 9. Appendices
TABLE 6.2 A Hypothetical Table of Contents	The Representation of Femininity in Magazines for Black Women 1. Introduction 2. Previous literature on women's magazines and representations of femininity 3. Research question: Is the discourse of femininity in magazines for black women empowering? 4. Content analysis and discourse analysis: discussion of the method 5. Analysis of six issues of *Pride* 6. Discussion 7. Conclusion 8. Bibliography 9. Appendix: coding sheet

recommend that you write the introduction very quickly at first – spend no more than ten to fifteen minutes on it just to get down on paper where you intend to go with the project. Later, when you have finished the entire project and written the conclusion, go back to the introduction and rewrite it completely, bearing in mind where you have actually gone with the project. Keep it brief and keep it interesting, and, although it is the first thing the reader sees, it should be the last thing you write. In our example in Table 6.2 the introduction should state why the researcher wants to study the representation of femininity in magazines for black women. The introduction should indicate to the reader where the researcher is going to take them and what is at stake in the project.

Reviewing the literature

In any project, you will need to show that you have read widely by reviewing the literature on the topic. This could include books, journal articles, trade literature, videos or lectures. Whatever has informed your thinking needs to be discussed and reviewed here. Sometimes it will be called a 'literature review', but it more of a survey. In other words, you are not supposed to evaluate whether the literature is good or bad, as you would in a book review, for example, but you should say what the literature says that is of relevance to what you are going to say. In our hypothetical project (Table 6.2) we would include the literature on women's magazines and on feminist debates about the representation of women generally. We would also have to include discussion of literature about the representation of black women, whether related specifically to magazine representations or not. We would have to comment on the strengths and weaknesses of the literature overall. We would need to draw out of the literature some key themes and comment on the extent to which we agree with the authors discussed.

You should give credit to the source of your ideas – show you have read widely. Think about what others have said on the subject. It is a good idea to write the literature review early on in the project – you may come across something in your reading which makes you change your mind about the project. So read widely and give a draft of your literature review to your tutor as soon as possible.

The literature discussed should be organized thematically. Think about the main subject areas that the literature falls into: how can you categorize all the literature that you have read? You may want to put all the researchers of one persuasion together, or to discuss all the trade literature separately from the academic. For example, 'literature about women's magazines' might be one section, while 'black feminist' perspectives' could be another. The literature review should present all the arguments which you are going to get into.

It is a good idea to show the literature review to your supervisor at an early stage to ensure that you are covering enough ground and that your work is going in the right direction. Don't expect to change the literature review much once you get into the research, unless you come across some new literature during your research. The point of the literature review is for you to find out what has been said before and to set out how you are going to push forward the sum of our knowledge in this area.

The literature review section should explain how your reading and knowledge of the field, allied with your personal interest discussed in the introduction, have informed the design of your project. The literature review section of your project should lead logically into your research question or hypothesis.

Stating your research question or hypothesis

Whatever the nature of your study, you need to be able to state in a clear, single sentence what you wish to demonstrate or test. It may or may not be in the form of a hypothesis, but should be emphasized in the text in boldface or underlining to indicate its importance. The research question should follow on from the literature review, and the relationship between the two needs to be spelled out clearly. In our example the research question is: 'Is the discourse of femininity in magazines for black women empowering?' The researcher would need to demonstrate how the question follows on from the literature discussed.

Explaining your method

Having stated your research question, the next step is to say how you are going to conduct your research. Here you are specifying how you have *operationalized* the question or hypothesis. You need to be very clear about the relationship between the hypothesis and the method(s) employed. You must show that the method chosen is a valid and appropriate test of the question. Explain exactly what you did, when and why. Do not worry that you do not always see this in published research – for the purposes of the project, the conventions are different and you are expected to show how you conducted your study. You should be sure to include discussion of any false paths you have followed – the reader will want to see that you have learned from your mistakes and that your ideas have developed in the process of designing and conducting your study.

If it is a film study, state what films you looked at and why you chose those, and not others. If it is an interview-based method, explain how you found your interview subjects and what kind of interview you used (for example, open-ended or close-ended questions). Justify each design decision you made in academic terms, not expediency. 'I only interviewed five people because that was all I could be bothered to get' or 'that was how many people came over on Friday' is not an academic justification. However, 'small groups of close friends feel more comfortable talking about sensitive issues' may be a perfectly acceptable academic rationale for a focus group of five. In our example, content analysis of the kinds of women represented in conjunction with a discourse analysis of the context of representation are perfectly justifiable methods. Content analysis is a tried and tested method of analysing the content of media while discourse analysis answers nuanced questions around issues of empowerment.

Arguing your case/presenting your findings

The next stage in the project is to say what you found when you conducted your study. If you have done a more empirically based study, you will have to come up with facts and figures that you need to present in an uncluttered manner. Here you should expand on the findings to relate them to your original hypothesis or research question. Think carefully about what you have learned in researching the project and be clear and logical about presenting what you have found. This is the most important part of the write-up and the one that the reader will focus on the most, so make sure you bring out all the main points in this section. Content analysis is a quantitative method which will generate tables of data which you should present. You will produce one coding sheet for each issue of *Pride* you analyse in our example, and one summary sheet of the overall findings.

The conclusion

The final part of the text should conclude your work, showing how you have done what you set out to do in the introduction. The conclusion should briefly summarize the whole project, so make sure that you do refer to what you did in the previous sections. The conclusion should link in neatly with the introduction. Show in the conclusion how, having reached the end of your research, you have addressed the questions raised in the introduction. If necessary, go back and rewrite the introduction. It may seem like a cheat, but in fact it is just good writing style to telegraph to the reader what is going to happen and why. Only when you know the whole plot from beginning to end can you sit down and write the first scene. The conclusion needs to relate directly to the introduction and to tie up any loose ends.

The bibliography

Your bibliography should include everything that has informed your dissertation. It is a statement of the books (and other) material that you have read. By including something in the bibliography, you are saying that you have read it; although it is not expected that you have read every word of the works it lists, the bibliography should include everything that you mention in the body of the text. It is correct academic procedure to include *only* those items that you have referred to in the text. But it is also essential that you include in your bibliography everything that you have mentioned in the project.

It is very important that you give full and proper references at the end of your project. You need to give credit to every source, primary and secondary, that you have used in your work. Whenever you reference something, you are saying that you have used that work – never reference something that someone else has referenced. If you come across a quotation within an article, for example, you may not quote it in your work. If you think it is indispensable to your research to use that quotation, you should go to the original source. Find out if the person who actually used those words intended that they should be used in that way. Read the context in which they were first written. Maybe this is a better resource than the one you first found it in – great! Read the quotation in the original form and then you can use it in your own work; you have not actually accessed the work until you have read and understood it for yourself. Your first source may well have misunderstood or taken out of context the quotation.

All statements of fact usually need to have a source: you should give a bibliographic reference for any statistic you use in your essay so that readers can verify your source. You do not have to include in your bibliography sources of information which may be considered 'general knowledge'. Therefore, if you need to use a reference book to find out when the Queen ascended to the throne or who directed *Sixth Sense*, you don't need to give a reference for your source or list it in your bibliography.

See 'Style Matters' below for details of how to list your bibliographic and other material.

Appendices

Footnotes are the notes at the bottom of the page: in general, it is best to avoid these. As a matter of style, if you have something to say, say it in the body of the text. Appendices are not usually included in your final word count (but check with your supervisor). Here you should include transcripts of interviews, samples of your questionnaire or 'instrument'. The appendix should include full details of data collected in the project.

Style matters

Let's consider some of the ways in which your presentation and style can be enhanced and improved. In this section, we look first of all at what not to do and consider the problems of plagiarism and poor grammar and punctuation which so often let students down. Then we present a guide to writing your bibliographic and other reference information.

A note on plagiarism

When you submit your essay, you are effectively saying that the work is yours. You put your name to it and you submit it for assessment along with all the other people in your class. If you present someone else's work as if it were your own, this is *plagiarism*. Plagiarism means copying and it is a form of cheating by stealing. When you copy work without giving the author credit for it, you are breaking the codes by which academics work – you are defying a professional norm which protects people's work from being appropriated by someone else. *Never copy.* Plagiarism can result in expulsion from the university.

Quotations

You should use quotations in your essay, but take care not to use too many or to quote too much. It is fine to quote up to about five lines. But anything longer should be paraphrased. Be wary of relying on quotations for the main part of your work. Remember, your tutors want to know your ideas and opinions. You need to demonstrate that you have read and understood the relevant literature. You can show this best by putting ideas in your own words. Use direct quotations when an author's words cannot be easily sumarized.

Frequently asked questions on punctuation, spelling and grammar

Media or medium?   By the time you reach the third year of your degree, you should know that the word *media* is plural. By the same token never use the form 'mediums'; although this is becoming acceptable in everyday speech, it is still anathema to many of the more old-fashioned lecturers on your course. If there are more than one medium, they should be referred to as 'media'. Never use 'medias'.

Use of the apostrophe.   The use of the apostrophe (') is very simple and easy, yet many students do not know how to use it properly. The most common misuse of apostrophes is overuse – people tend to stick them in when they think they might be needed and end up putting in too many! So always ask yourself if an apostrophe is really necessary. Apostrophes are used in two ways – to show ownership or possession (e.g. *Peter's* pencil), and to indicate where letters have been omitted (sometimes called contraction or elision), as in *don't* or *can't*.

Using the apostrophe to indicate possession is the most common use. We use it when we indicate that the letter *s* is being used to show ownership rather than a plural. For example, in the sentence 'These are John's drawings', the apostrophe between *John* and *s* indicates that the drawings referred to belong to John. The *s* after *drawing* indicates a plural. If we wanted to discuss the colour of a drawing, we might write: 'The drawing's colours are very vivid.' If we could rephrase our sentence such that we could say the object belonged to the subject, e.g. 'The drawings belong to John' or 'The colours are elements of the drawing', then we know that the apostrophe is being used to indicate possession.

The apostrophe is also used to show *elision* or to indicate that something has been left out. Use this for words like *they're* to mean *they are* and *don't* when we are contracting together the two words, *do* and *not*.

One common mistake is to use the apostrophe with the third person singular pronoun showing possession as in *it's*. The correct way to express 'of it' is 'its' – never it's. This is consistent with the way we use other personal pronoun possessives, such as *his, hers* and *theirs*. It's is only used to mean 'it is'.

You should refer to a style book such as *The Guardian Style Book* or a good grammar book if you are in any doubt. There are useful self-administered quizzes on the Internet, too. Try looking at the BBC's revision website (www.bbc.co.uk/education/revisewise/english/spelling) to get you started.

Notes on references

There are two different ways in which bibliographical information is presented in published work. One uses numerical notes in the text to refer the reader to a reference at the end of the page or document. This is sometimes called a 'note system' and includes the Chicago style, Modern Language Association (MLA) style and Harvard style. This note system is mostly widely used in the humanities (Gibaldi, 1999). The other form uses the author's name and date of publication in parentheses in the text and provides full bibliographic details in alphabetical order of the author's last name in the bibliography at the end of the document. This style is used by the American Psychological Association (APA) among others and is often referred to as APA style.

The note system method is most fully explained in *The Chicago Manual of Style* (1993) and in Kate Turabian's *Manual for Writers* (Turabian, 1996). This method uses notes at the end of the essay to present a list of references in the order in which they are cited. Commonly used in humanities journals, especially history and literature, this system has the advantage that all the references are presented in the order in which they are mentioned in the essay – this can give a more fluid feel to the references. Its disadvantages are that it can be quite repetitive – a reference is separately listed each time it is mentioned, and it can be difficult to find specific references. *The Chicago Manual of Style* should be available in your university library. You can also consult its website to find out the answers to frequently asked questions; go to: www.press.uchicago.edu/Misc/Chicago/cmosfaq.html.

The more commonly used style in the social sciences (a variation of which I have used in this book) is the author/date reference or APA style. In this system, the author and date of publication are mentioned in the body of the text, and the reader can find the specific reference by looking up the author's name in the alphabetical list of references at the end of the work. This system has the disadvantage that the greater level of information in the body of the text can be distracting to some readers. It has the advantage that the precise citations are easier to find in the bibliographic list of references. It is strongly recommended that you keep careful track of your sources in order to be sure that the referencing does not go astray.

Citations in the text

In the author reference style, the name of the author is the one that should be given in the text. If you are referring to a book by one author you should always give that name in the text:

(Scannell, 1999)

If you are giving a quotation you should also give the page number:

(Scannell, 1999: 126)

Where you are citing an essay in an edited volume, you do not refer to the editors in the body of the text, but to the author of the particular essay you have read:

(Meech, 1999)

The above could refer to Peter Meech's essay in a collected volume, a journal article or a book. The author reference system makes no distinction in the body of the text – you have to go to the bibliography to find out about the actual publication. Remember that it is only necessary in your essay to give the name of the author and the date of publication – the reader should then be able to consult the bibliography to get further information. Where there are two pieces by the same author published in the same year in your bibliography you should refer to one as

(Scannell, 1999a)

and the other as

(Scannell, 1999b)

In the bibliography, they should also be listed as 'a' and 'b'.

Wherever possible, you should cite the author of the exact piece. In some cases, as in some magazines and several websites, the precise author of the piece is not given. In these instances, you should cite the institution publishing the piece as the author – for example, *The Economist* or the Periodical Publishers' Association. These institutional authors should be treated like any other and listed alphabetically alongside other authors in the bibliography.

Writing your bibliography

Note carefully the use of punctuation and italics below. It is very important to follow the exact order. List the author's surname first in the bibliography, followed by a comma and then the first name.

Single-author books. Where there is one author of a book, you should use the following format:

Stokes, Jane, 1999. *On Screen Rivals: The Cinema and Television in Britain and the US*. London: Macmillan.

Edited volumes. Where you are citing the whole volume, the format should be as follows:

Stokes, Jane and Anna Reading (eds.), 1999. *The Media in Britain: Current Debates and Developments*. London: Macmillan.

Note that, although the first author is listed surname first and given name second, subsequent editors should be listed with their names in the usual order. It is necessary to invert the normal order of names only when you are making an alphabetical list by authors' last names. More frequently, you are likely to be referring to an individual essay in a collection, in which case you should use the following form:

Meech, Peter, 1999. Advertising. In Jane Stokes and Anna Reading (eds.), *The Media in Britain: Current Debates and Developments*. London: Macmillan, pp. 25–40.

Note that you should always give the page numbers for an essay in a collected volume, although this is not necessary for a whole book. The abbreviation used for *pages* is *pp*.

Journal articles. For journal articles, you need to list also the page numbers of the relevant volume. This is the format to follow:

Dayan, Daniel, 2001. The peculiar public of television. *Media, Culture and Society*. Volume 23, number 6: pp. 743–765.

Note that the titles of articles in journals and of essays in collected volumes are given without capitalization; however, the titles of books and journals are capitalized. Sometimes the words 'volume' and 'number' are omitted and the volume number italicized or emboldened as in the Sage style used in the bibliography of this book.

Newspaper articles.   The entry for a newspaper article is as follows:

Greenslade, Roy, 2002. Give the money back, Tony. The *Guardian* 3 June 2002. Media section. pp. 4–5.

Most newspaper articles have bylines showing the author of the piece and you should always give the author's name whenever possible. In cases where no author is given, you should refer to the publication as the institutional author. Thus an article in the *Guardian* with no given author (for example, the editorial) would be listed with *Guardian* as its author in the bibliography.

Broadcast material.   When citing broadcast material, you should always give the name of the series or producer. Give sufficient information about the production: company, title of the programme, title of the series, and the date and channel of first transmission. In long-running series, such as soaps or the news, always give the date of transmission. For a videotape or DVD, give the publication date.

Websites.   When doing research on the Internet, always write down the URL or web address of every site you visit (for example, www.ppa.co.uk). URL stands for Uniform Resource Locator and appears in the address bar of your browser. You should also write down the name of the author whether an institutional one (for example, the Periodical Publishers' Association) or a person. If you want to reference a page on the site with a named author, such as the director's message, you should use the person's name as the first part of your reference. For example, if referring to Derek Carter's message in the Annual Report of the Periodical Publishers' Association, you should do so as follows:

Carter, Derek, 2002. A message from the PPA Chairman. *Periodical Publishers' Association* http://www.ppa.co.uk/annualreview/index.htm Date accessed: 7 February 2002.

If, however, you want to refer to information on the same website which does not have any named author, you should use the name of the organization publishing the information as the author. In the following example, the Periodical Publishers' Association is the *institutional author*:

Periodical Publishers' Association, 2002.

Note that you should always give the URL as it appears in the address bar. The easiest way to do this is to copy that data directly into your document, making sure that the punctuation remains unchanged. Any line breaks should be made after a dash or full stop, and no other punctuation (such as hyphens) should be added.

Wherever possible, you should cite the author of any Web page and list the author's name as the first field in your references. This should be followed by the year of access, with the rest of the date following later; for example:

Paik, Nam June 2002. Context. http://www.geocities.com/namjunepaik/context.html. Date accessed: 7 February 2002.

In the body of your text, there is no need to treat your electronic references differently from any other. If you are using a footnote style, you just list the reference as a number; if you are using an author reference, you use the author/date index. Thus, the references above would be cited in your text as follows: (Carter, 2002); (Periodical Publishers' Association, 2002) and (Paik, 2002).

The American Psychological Association gives details of how to reference electronic sources on its website: http://www.apastyle.org/elecmedia.html#link.

As a general principle, remember that you are giving reference to the authors of the work you have read. As far as possible, you should always list the author in your bibliography and in your reference in the text. In the case of books, book chapters, journal articles and so on, it is usually pretty clear who the author is. But sometimes it is not possible to identify a person as an author. In magazines, journals and newspapers where no author is given, you should cite the title of the publication as the author: the author is almost certainly an employee of the publication and is speaking with the voice of the publication. In the case of a website or an official publication such as a company report, the author will be the company providing the website (e.g. nua) or report (e.g. Granada). Again, these are official mouthpieces of organizations that need to be referenced. It is never appropriate to use 'anon' or 'anonymous' as an author except in very rare examples such as quoting from traditional rhymes and poems. Almost everything you are likely to quote comes from a specific source that must be credited and acknowledged.

Several American universities have excellent writing centres which provide students with help with all aspects of essay writing. Dartmouth College has an excellent guide for students to use when writing their term papers. Dartmouth's site is very useful in giving information on how to reference different kinds of material. It is very easy to use and find your way around in: www.dartmouth.edu/~sources/. Another useful site is that of the University of Purdue's On-Line Writing Lab (OWL), which has readily printable data on a wide range of presentation topics, including using the APA and MLA styles: www.http://owl.english.purdue.edu/handouts/research/index.html. Your own study skills department should be able to provide you with further guidance and support.

Concluding comments

This book has aimed to help you write your project. I hope you find it useful and instructive. The most important thing to remember about conducting your own research is to find something you enjoy doing. The scholars you read in books and who teach you in your classes probably study the media and culture because they interest and fascinate them. You probably chose to study this subject at university because you, too, are highly motivated to study the topic. Your research project is a wonderful opportunity for you to research something that interests you personally. When you are working on a subject in which you have a personal interest, you will find solving problems and digging out resources pleasurable and fulfilling. I hope this book has encouraged you to think about your own interests and concerns. I will be very happy if this book inspires some of you to go ahead and research something your teachers would never have thought of! When you have a genuine interest in the topic, you can communicate that to others and you will write a thoughtful, engaging work which others want to read, and which contributes to the level of knowledge in our field.

Appendix 1: Libraries and Archives of Relevance

This appendix lists some libraries and archives which may prove useful to students of media and cultural studies. You should use your own college or university library as your first point of reference and ask the librarians about how to find specific information.

British Broadcasting Corporation

The British Broadcasting Corporation (BBC) has a vast archive of material about the workings of the BBC housed in its archive in Reading. Access has to be arranged in advance and users must identify the specific information they wish to view before their visit.

> British Broadcasting Corporation
> Written Archives Centre
> Caversham Park
> Reading
> Berkshire RG4 8TZ
>
> Tel: 01734 472742

The British Film Institute

The British Film Institute Library contains a wide range of books, journals and periodicals on film and television studies. The collection is international in focus and includes material in several languages relevant to film and television around the world. The library contains a comprehensive stock of material on the media industries more broadly, in Britain and internationally.

There are charges to use the library which is reference only. Contact the library in advance to find out about current charges.

British Film Institute (BFI) National Library
British Film Institute
21 Stephen Street
London WIP 1LN

Tel: 020 7255 1444
Fax: 020 7436 2338
E-mail: library@bfi.org.uk

The British Film Institute collection includes some films which are available for students to view on the premises, contact the 'Research Viewings' department for further information.

British Film Institute Research Viewings
(address as above)

Tel: 020 7957 4726
Fax: 020 7580 5830

The latest information about access and charges can be found on the British Film Institute website: www.bfi.org.uk.

The British Film Institute also houses the Independent Television Commission (ITC) Library which it acquired in 2002.

The British Library

The British Library is home to several diverse collections in various media of relevance to readers of this book (www.bl.uk). Their main collection is the book and periodical library which is housed in Euston Road. Access to the library is normally restricted to researchers at a postgraduate level. However, much of the collection is available via inter-library loan (ask your university librarian for details). If you are doing research which can only be done at the British Library you may get permission to use it, and should contact Reader Admissions on 020 7412 7677 or e-mail: Reader-Admissions@bl.uk.

The British Library
96 Euston Road
London NE1 2DB

The British Library Newspaper Library at Colindale in London contains a wide range of material of relevance to the historian of newspapers and periodicals. In addition, it contains several collections of a more specialized nature such as the British and Irish Cinema and Film Periodicals Collection.

British Library Newspaper Library
Colindale Avenue
London NW9 5HE

Tel: 020 7412 7353

The British Library also houses a large collection of music which is available
for researchers in their music collections library:

Music Collections
The British Library
96 Euston Road
London NW1 2DB

Tel: 020 7412 7772
Fax: 020 7412 7751
E-mail: music-collections@bl.uk

The National Sound Archive is housed in the British Library. They can be
reached at:

The Recorded Sound Information Service
The British Library
National Sound Archive
96 Euston Road
London NW1 2DB

Tel: 020 7412 7440
Fax: 020 7412 7441
E-mail:nsa@bl.uk

The British Unversities Film and Video Council (BUFVC)

The BUFVC promotes the study of British film and television. Its archive
includes recordings of television programmes and provides a back-up service
recording programmes off-air for researchers and teachers. The BUFVC is
also home to the British Universities Newsreel Project and to a number of
other special collections.

The British Universities Film and Video Council (BUFVC)
77 Well Street
London W1T 3QJ

Tel: 020 7393 1500
Fax: 020 7393 1555
E-mail: ask@bufvc.ac.uk

Centre for the Study of Cartoon and Caricature

The Templeman Library at the University of Kent at Canterbury is home to the Centre for the Study of Cartoon and Caricature. It houses a growing collection of over 85,000 cartoons and 5,000 books and other material relating to cartoons and caricature. Much of the collection is searchable via the on-line database at: www.library.ukc.ac.uk/cartoons. The Head of the Centre is Dr Nick Hiley, N.P. Hiley@ukc.ac.uk.

> The Centre for the Study of Cartoon and Caricature
> Templeman Library
> University of Kent
> Canterbury
> CT2 7NU

> Tel: 01227 823127
> Fax: 01227 823127
> E-mail: cartoon-centre@ukc.ac.uk

The History of Advertising Trust Archive (HAT ARCHIVE)

The History of Advertising Trust (HAT) is a registered charity charged with preserving the history of advertising. The HAT archive contains a wide range of advertising, public relations and marketing material dating from 1800 to the present day and is housed at the University of East Anglia. The archive includes copies of advertisements as well as books and other material about advertising. This is an expanding collection and it is not fully catalogued at the time of writing, but access to the catalogue is available via the University of East Anglia's website at: www.lib.uea.ac.uk/hatwelc/welcome.htm. HAT's homepage is at: www.hatads.co.uk/collection.htm.

> HAT House
> 12 Raveningham Centre
> Raveningham
> Norwich NR14 6NU

> Tel: 01508 548623
> Fax: 01508 548478
> E-mail: hat@uea.ac.uk

The UK Data Archive (UKDA)

The UK Data Archive is housed at the University of Essex and collects and makes available the largest collection of digital data in the social sciences and humanities in the United Kingdom. It also contains two specialist units: the History Data Service and the Qualitative Data Service. The UKDA also provides access to international data sets via agreements and partnerships with other archives in different countries. It can be accessed online at: www.data-archive.ac.uk.

UK Data Archive
University of Essex
Wivenhoe Park
Colchester
Essex CO4 3SQ

Tel: 01206 872001
Fax: 01206 872003
E-mail: archive@essex.ac.uk

The Printing Historical Collection

Housed at the London College of Printing and Distributive Trades, the Printing Historical Collection is devoted to the art and history of books. The collection contains five thousand items relating to the physical, technical and aesthetic evolution of the book in western cultures. The collection provides greater access to rare materials than is usually available. Specialist subjects within the collection include: children's books, illustration techniques and illustrators, printing processes, and typography and book design. More information can be found at: www.linst.ac.uk/library/special_collections.

London College of Printing and Distributive Trades
Department of Learning Resource
Elephant and Castle
London SE1 6SB

Tel: 020 7514 6638
E-mail: s.mahurter@lcp.linst.ac.uk

The Mass-Observation Archive

The Mass-Observation project was founded in 1937 in order to create 'an anthropology of ourselves'. The project continued until the early fifties, and the archive of data is held as part of Special Collections at the University of Sussex Library. The collection consists of 3000 typed reports by the team of observers/investigators; the raw materials underlying the investigations; and diaries and other personal materials. Detailed information about the project and data is available at: www.sussex.ac.uk/library/massobs.

The Mass-Observation Archive
Special Collections
The Library
University of Sussex
Brighton BN1 9QL

Tel: 01273 678157
Fax: 01273 678441
E-mail: library.specialcoll@sussex.ac.uk

National Museum of Photography, Film and Television

Opened in Bradford in 1999, the museum hosts an extensive collection of materials relating to photography, film and television. The large collection of photographs includes some of the earliest experimental work from the 1830s to the present day. There are also major collections of items of photographic, cinematic and televisual technology, handbooks and technical manuals. An on-line guide to the museum's collection and facilities, known as Insight, is located at: www.nmpft.org.uk/insight/home.asp.

The Collections Department
The National Museum of Photography, Film & Television
Bradford BD1 1NQ

Tel: 01274 202030
E-mail: enquiries.nmpft@nmsi.ac.uk

North West Film Archive

The North West Film Archive is kept by the Library Service of the Manchester Metropolitan University. It contains a collection of film and video footage about Greater Manchester, Lancashire and Cheshire providing a social history resource for scholars of the region. It was established in 1977 and now forms the largest British film archive outside London.

North West Film Archive
Manchester Metropolitan University
Minshull House
47–49 Chorlton Street
Manchester M1 3EU

Tel: 0161 247 3097
E-mail: n.w.filmarchive@mmu.ac.uk

Appendix 2: Websites of Interest to Researchers in Media and Culture

The Internet and the World Wide Web provide an invaluable resource to researchers of media and culture. The amount of material available is expanding at a rapid rate and the exact number and composition of sites is undergoing constant change. This appendix lists some of the most useful sites at the time of writing. It is worth while spending time experimenting and investigating what is available of relevance to your topic.

When beginning your project it is a good idea to spend some time taking stock of what is available to you through your university home pages. Most universities have information of direct relevance to your courses with links to other useful websites. The communications or media studies department at your university may well have a website containing relevant information for your research, so make sure you are familiar with the information services provided for you. The Communications and Media Studies degree at the University of Aberystwyth does a particularly good job of providing on-line information for all students; Daniel Chandler runs a very useful website at Aberystwyth with several extremely useful links: www.aber.ac.uk/media. If you are unsure of what your university has or how they can help you, go along to see your subject librarian or talk to the person at the information desk and find out whether there are any sessions on web research aimed at students on your course.

Public libraries are another good source of information about the Internet and many have free open access facilities. If you do not have access to a good library at your place of work or study, then try your local library. The British Library website has information about access to its book collection and special collections. Wherever in the world you are studying, The Library of Congress in Washington houses the largest collection of books and provides a good place to search for bibliographic information.

Many of the sites that you will come across in your research are put up by commercial organizations or private companies as part of their public relations effort: make sure you take these with the appropriate pinch of salt. One of the biggest problems with the web is that you can't always check the veracity of the sources: therefore you always have to be mindful of who is the publisher of the site. Although more and more organizations are putting information on the web, many are also now charging for accessing their information. What was once freely available is now often subject to subscription charges. All of the major trade journals have sites, some of them are available on a subscription-only basis or have some functions and search facilities which must be paid for. If you need to use one which requires a subscription find out from your library or information services department whether it is possible for them to subscribe.

The following list is indicative of publications and organizations of relevance to readers of this book. It would be impossible to include everything of potential relevance to students and this list is provided to get you started on your own web-based research.

List of websites of relevance to students of British media and culture

Advertising, marketing/opinion and trade organizations

Adbusters: www.adbusters.org
The Advertising Association: www.adassoc.org.uk
Association of Market Survey Organizations: www.amso.co.uk
British Market Research Association: www.bmra.org.uk
BRAD: www.intellagencia.com
Campaign: www.campaignlive.com
Gallup: www.gallup.co.uk
ICM: www.icmresearch.co.uk
The Market Research Society: www.mrs.org.uk
Media Week: www.mediaweek.co.uk
MORI (Market and Opinion Research International): www.mori.com
NOP Research Group: www.nop.co.uk
YouGov: www.yougov.com
Zenith Media: www.zenithmedia.co.uk

Advocacy and alternative media organizations

The Bulletin Board on Film Censorship: www.bbfc.org.uk.
Campaign for Freedom of Information: www.cfoi.org.uk
The Centre for Media Education: www.cme.org
Free Speech TV: www.freespeech.org
Index on Censorship: www.indexonline.org
Undercurrents: www.undercurrents.org

Broadcast media

BBC: www.bbc.co.uk
Broadcast: www.broadcastnow.co.uk
The Broadcast Education Association: www.beaweb.org
The Broadcasting Standards Commission (BSC): www.bsc.org.uk
Broadcasters' Audience Research Board (BARB): www.barb.co.uk
Carlton: www.carlton.co.uk
Channel 4: www.channel4.com
Channel 5: www.channel5.co.uk
Commercial Radio Companies Association: www.crca.co.uk
Granada: www.granadamedia.com
ITN Archive: www.itnarchive.com
ITV: www.itv.co.uk
Pearson: www.pearson.com
The Radio Authority: www.radioauthority.org.uk
Radio Joint Audience Research Ltd (RAJAR): www.rajar.co.uk
Sky Television: www.sky.com

Cinema

The British Board of Film Classification (BBFC): www.bbfc.co.uk
The British Film Institute: www.bfi.org.uk
British Universities Film and Video Council (BUFVC): www.bufvc.ac.uk
Film Finance: www.filmfinance.com
United International Pictures: www.uip.co.uk

Digital media

Audit Bureau of Circulations (electronic) (ABCe): www.abce.org.uk
Internet Trends and Statistics: www.nua.com
Hobbes' Internet Timeline: www.zakon.org/robert/internet/timeline
Slashdot: www.slashdot.org
Wired: www.wired.com

Government agencies and organizations

The Department of Media, Sport and Culture: www.culture.gov.uk
Hansard: www.parliament.the-stationery-office.co.uk/pa/cm/cmhansrd.htm
The Office for National Statistics: www.statistics.gov.uk
United States Government Statistics: www.fedstats.gov

Museums, galleries and libraries

The British Museum: www.thebritishmuseum.ac.uk
The Library of Congress: www.lcweb.loc.gov
The National Museum Directors' Conference: www.nationalmuseums.org.uk
The National Museum of Photography, Film and Television: www.nmpft.org.uk
The Photographers' Gallery: www.photonet.org.uk
The Science Museum: www.sciencemuseum.org.uk
The Victoria and Albert Museum: www.vam.ac.uk

Print media

Books/publishing
The Bookseller: www.thebookseller.com
Editor and Publisher: www.mediainfo.com.
Publisher's Weekly: www.publishersweekly.com
Whitaker's BookTrack: www.booktrack.co.uk

Magazines
BBC Worldwide: www.bbcworldwide.com/categories/magazines.asp
Condé Nast: www.condenast.co.uk
EMAP: www.emap.com
IPC: www.ipcmedia.co.uk
The Periodical Publishers Association: www.ppa.co.uk

Newspapers/journalism
Audit Bureau of Circulations (ABC): www.abc.org.uk
The *Daily Mail*: www.dailymail.co.uk
Daily Mail and General Trust: www.dmgt.co.uk
Daily Express: www.express.co.uk
The *Daily Telegraph* www.telegraph.co.uk
Drudge Report: www.drudgereport.com
The *Financial Times*: www.ft.com.
The *Gay Times*: www.gaytimes.co.uk
The *Guardian*: www.guardian.co.uk
The *Independent*: www.independent.co.uk
The Los Angeles Times: www.latimes.com
The *Mirror*: www.mirror.co.uk
The National Readership Survey: www.nrs.co.uk
The Newspaper Society: www.newspapersoc.org.uk
The National Union of Journalists: www.nuj.org.uk
The New York Times: www.nytimes.com

The Press Association: www.pa.press.net
The Press Complaints Commission: www.pcc.org.uk
The *Star*: www.megastar.co.uk
The *Sun*: www.thesun.co.uk
The Times: www.timesonline.co.uk
Variety: www.variety.com
The Voice: www.voice-online.net
The Washington Post: www.washingtonpost.com

Scholarly writing skills

American Psychological Association (APA): www.apastyle.org
BBC Revisewise: www.bbc.co.uk/education/revisewise/english/spelling/index.
shtml
Chicago Style: www.press.uchicago.edu/Misc/Chicago/cmosfaq.html
English Plus+: www.englishplus.com
Online Writing Lab: www.owl.english.purdue.edu/handouts/research/index.html

References

Adorno, Theodor W., 1991. *The Culture Industry. Selected Essays on Mass Culture*. Edited by J.M. Bernstein. London: Routledge.

Adorno, Theodor W., 1994. *Adorno: The Stars Down to Earth and Other Essays on the Irrational in Culture*. Edited by Stephen Crook. London: Routledge.

Adorno, Theodor and Max Horkheimer, 1993. The culture industry: enlightenment as mass deception. In Simon During (ed.), *The Cultural Studies Reader*. London: Routledge.

Aitchison, Jean, 1991. *Communications and Information Thesaurus*. The Hague: UNESCO.

Alasuutari, Pertti, 1995. *Researching Culture. Qualitative Method and Cultural Studies*. Thousand Oaks, CA/London: Sage.

Allen, Robert C., 1992. Audience-oriented criticism and television. In Robert C. Allen (ed.), *Channels of Discourse, Reassembled*. London: Routledge, pp. 101–37.

Allen, Robert C. and Douglas Gomery, 1985. *Film History. Theory and Practice*. New York: Alfred Knopf.

Althusser, Louis, 1979. *For Marx*. London: Verso.

Althusser, Louis, 1984. *Essays on Ideology*. London: Verso.

Altman, Rick, 1981. *Genre: The Musical*. London: Routledge and Kegan Paul.

Altman, Rick, 1999. *Film/Genre*. London: British Film Institute.

Ang, Ien, 1985. *Watching 'Dallas'. Soap Opera and the Melodramatic Imagination*. London: Methuen.

Ang, Ien, 1991. *Desperately Seeking the Audience*. London: Routledge.

Babbie, Earl, 1989. *The Practice of Social Research* (5th edn). Belmont, CA: Wadsworth.

Balio, Tino, 1976a. The stars in business: the founding of United Artists. In Tino Balio (ed.), *The American Film Industry*. Madison, Wisconsin: University of Wisconsin Press, pp. 135–52.

Balio, Tino (ed.), 1976b. *The American Film Industry*. Madison, Wisconsin: University of Wisconsin Press.

Balio, Tino, 1976c. *United Artists. The Company Built by the Stars*. Madison, Wisconsin: University of Wisconsin Press.

Balio, Tino (ed.), 1990. *Hollywood in the Age of Television*. Boston: Unwin Hyman.

Balio, Tino, 1993. *Grand Design: Hollywood as a Modern Business Enterprise 1930–1939*. New York: Charles Scribner and Sons.

Balio, Tino, 1998. 'A major presence in all of the world's important markets'. The globalization of Hollywood in the 1990s. In Steve Neale and Murray Smith (eds.), *Contemporary Hollywood Cinema*. London/New York: Routledge, pp. 58–73.

Barker, Martin and Julian Petley (eds.), 1997. *Ill Effects. The Media/Violence Debate*. London: Routledge.

Barthes, Roland, 1967. *Elements of Semiology*. Translated by Annette Lavers and Colin Smith. New York: Hill and Wang.

Barthes, Roland, 1973. *Mythologies*. Translated by Annette Lavers. London: Paladin Books.

Barthes, Roland, 1984. *Image, Music, Text*. Translated by Stephen Heath. London: Fontana.

Barthes, Roland, 1987. *S/Z*. Translated by Richard Miller. New York: Hill and Wang.

Barthes, Roland, 1990. *The Fashion System*. Translated by Matthew Ward and Richard Howard. Berkeley and Los Angeles, CA: University of California Press.

Bauer, Martin W., 2000. Classical content analysis: a review. In Martin W. Bauer and George Gaskell (eds.), *Qualitative Researching with Text, Image and Sound: A Practical Handbook*. London: Sage, pp. 131–51.

Beharrell, Peter, 1993. AIDS and the British press. In John Eldridge (ed.), *Getting the Message. News, Truth and Power*. Glasgow Media News Group. London: Routledge, pp. 210–49.

Bell, Allan, 1991. *The Language of News Media*. Oxford: Blackwell.

Bell, Allan and Peter Garrett, 1998. *Approaches to Media Discourse*. Oxford: Blackwell.

Bell, Judith, 1999. *Doing your Research Project. A Guide for First-time Researchers in Education and Social Science* (3rd edn). Buckingham: Open University Press.

Berger, Arthur Asa, 1987. Semiological analysis. In Oliver Boyd-Barrett and Peter Braham (eds.), *Media, Knowledge and Power*. London: Open University Press, pp. 132–55.

Berger, Arthur Asa, 1998a. *Media Research Techniques*. Thousand Oaks, CA/London: Sage.

Berger, Arthur Asa, 1998b. *Media Analysis Techniques*. Thousand Oaks, CA/London: Sage.

Bignell, Jonathan, 1997. *Media Semiotics. An Introduction*. Manchester/New York: Manchester University Press.

Bordwell, David, 1985. *Narration in the Fiction Film*. Madison, Wisconsin: University of Wisconsin Press.

Bordwell, David, Kristin Thompson and Janet Staiger, 1985. *The Classical Hollywood Cinema: Film Style and Mode of Production to 1960*. London: Routledge.

Bourdieu, Pierre, 1984. *Distinction. A Social Critique of the Judgement of Taste.* London: Routledge and Kegan Paul.

Branigan, Edward, 1992. *Narrative Comprehension and Film.* London: Routledge.

Briggs, Asa, 1961. *The History of Broadcasting in the United Kingdom. Volume 1: The Birth of Broadcasting.* London: Oxford University Press.

Briggs, Asa, 1965. *The History of Broadcasting in the United Kingdom. Volume 2: The Golden Age of Wireless.* London: Oxford University Press.

Briggs, Asa, 1970. *The History of Broadcasting in the United Kingdom. Volume 3: The War of Words.* London: Oxford University Press.

Briggs, Asa, 1979. *The History of Broadcasting in the United Kingdom. Volume 4: Sound and Vision.* London: Oxford University Press.

Briggs, Asa, 1995. *The History of Broadcasting in the United Kingdom. Volume 5: Competition.* London: Oxford University Press.

British Broadcasting Corporation, 2000. Annual Report. London: BBC. Available also on BBC website: www.bbc.org.uk.

Burns, Robert B., 2000. *Introduction to Research Methods* (4th edn). Sage: London.

Cameron, Ian (ed.), 1992. *The Movie Book of Film Noir.* London: Studio Vista.

Cameron, Ian and Douglas Pye (eds.), 1996. *The Movie Book of the Western.* London: Studio Vista.

Castells, Manuel, 1996. *The Information Age: Economy, Society and Culture. Volume 1: The Rise of the Network Society.* London: Blackwell.

Castells, Manuel, 1997. *The Information Age: Economy, Society and Culture. Volume 2: The Power of Identity.* London: Blackwell.

Castells, Manuel, 1998. *The Information Age. Economy, Society and Culture. Volume 3: End of Millennium.* London: Blackwell.

Castells, Manuel, 1999. An introduction to the information age. In Hugh Mackay and Tim O'Sullivan (eds.), *The Media Reader: Continuity and Transformation.* London: Sage/Open University Press, pp. 398–410.

Caughie, John, 1981. Dossier on John Ford in *Theories of Authorship.* London: Routledge and Kegan Paul.

Cawelti, John G., 1976. *Adventure, Mystery and Romance. Formula Stories as Art and Popular Culture.* Chicago: University of Chicago Press.

Charters, W.W., 1970. *Motion Pictures and Youth. A Summary.* New York: Arno Press. Originally published 1933, New York: Macmillan.

Chibnall, Steve and Robert Murphy (eds.), 1999. *British Crime Cinema.* London: Routledge.

The Chicago Manual of Style, 1993. 14th edn. Chicago: University of Chicago Press.

Childs, Peter and Mike Storry, 1999. *Encyclopaedia of Contemporary British Culture.* London: Routledge.

Collins, Richard, 1999. European Union media and communication policies. In

Jane Stokes and Anna Reading (eds.), *The Media in Britain. Current Debates and Developments*. London: Macmillan, pp. 158–69.

Corner, John (ed.), 1991. *Popular Television in Britain. Studies in Cultural History*. London: British Film Institute.

Corner, John, 1998. *Studying Media: Problems of Theory and Method*. Edinburgh: Edinburgh University Press.

Cresser, Frances, Lesley Gunn and Helen Balme, 2001. Women's experiences of on-line e-zine publication. *Media, Culture and Society*, **23**: 457–73.

Crisell, Andrew, 1999. Broadcasting: television and radio. In Jane Stokes and Anna Reading (eds.), *The Media in Britain. Current Debates and Developments*. London: Macmillan, pp. 61–73.

Cumberbatch, Guy, 2000. *Television: The Public's View*. An ITC Research Publication. London: ITC.

Curran, James, 2000a. Introduction. *Media Organizations in Society*. London: Arnold, pp. 9–16.

Curran, James, 2000b. Literary editors, social networks and cultural tradition. In James Curran (ed.), *Media Organizations in Society*. London: Arnold, pp. 215–39.

Curran James and Jean Seaton, 1991. *Power Without Responsibility. The Press and Broadcasting in Britain* (4th edn). London: Routledge.

Deacon, David, Michael Pickering, Peter Golding and Graham Murdock, 1999. *Researching Communications. A Practical Guide to Methods in Media and Cultural Analysis*. London: Arnold.

Dorfman, Ariel and Mattelart, A., 1975. *How to Read Donald Duck: Imperialist Ideology in the Disney Comics*. New York: International General.

Duffy, Brendan, 1999. The analysis of documentary evidence. In Judith Bell, *Doing Your Research Project. A Guide for First-time Researchers in Education and Social Science*. Buckingham: Open University Press, 106–17.

During, Simon (ed.), 1993. *The Cultural Studies Reader*. London: Routledge.

Dyer, Richard, 1982. *Stars*. London: British Film Institute.

Dyer, Richard, 1987. *Heavenly Bodies*. London: British Film Institute.

Dyja, Eddie, 2001. *BFI Film and Television Handbook 2002*. London: British Film Institute.

Dysinger, W.S. and C.A. Ruckmick, 1970. *The Emotional Responses of Children to the Motion Picture Situation*. New York: Arno Press. Originally published 1933, New York: Macmillan.

Eco, Umberto, 1984. *Semiotics and the Philosophy of Language*. London: Macmillan.

Eldridge, John (ed.), 1993. *Getting the Message. News, Truth and Power*. Glasgow University Media Group. London: Routledge.

Eldridge, John, Jenny Kitzinger and Kevin Williams, 1997. *The Mass Media and Power in Modern Britain*. Oxford: Oxford University Press.

Ferguson, M. (ed.), 1990. *Public Communication*. London: Sage.

Feuer, Jane, 1982. *The Hollywood Musical*. London: Macmillan/British Film Institute.

Feuer, Jane, 1992. Genre study and television. In Robert C. Allen (ed.), *Channels of Discourse, Reassembled*. London: Routledge, pp. 138–59.

Feuer, Jane, 1999. Averting the male gaze. Visual pleasure and images of fat women. In Mary Beth Harolovich and Lauren Rabinovitz (eds.), *Television, History and American Culture. Feminist Critical Essays*. Durham, North Carolina and London: Duke University Press, pp. 181–200.

Friedman, Lawrence S., 1999. *The Cinema of Martin Scorsese*. Oxford: Roundhouse Publishing.

Garber, Marjorie, 1992. *Vested Interests. Cross-Dressing and Cultural Anxiety*. London: Routledge.

Garnham, Nicholas, 1990. *Capitalism and Communication: Global Culture and the Economics of Information*. London: Sage.

Garnham, Nicholas, 1997. Political economy and the practice of cultural studies. In Marjorie Ferguson and Peter Golding (eds.), *Cultural Studies in Question*. London: Sage, pp. 56–73.

Garrett, Peter and Allan Bell, 1998. Media and discourse: a critical overview. In Allan Bell and Peter Garrett, *Approaches to Media Discourse*. Oxford: Blackwell, pp. 1–20.

Gauntlett, David, 1995. *Moving Experiences. Understanding Television's Influences and Effects*. London: John Libbey.

Gauntlett, David and Annette Hill, 2000. *TV Living: Television, Culture and Everyday Life*. London: Routledge.

Geertz, Clifford, 1973. *The Interpretation of Cultures*. New York: Basic Books.

Geraghty, Christine, 1998. Audiences and 'ethnography': questions of practice'. In Christine Geraghty and David Lusted, *The Television Studies Book*. London: Arnold, pp. 141–57.

Gibaldi, Joseph, 1999. *MLA Handbook for Writers of Research Papers* (5th edn). Modern Language Association of America.

Glasgow University Media Group, 1976. *Bad News*. London: Routledge and Kegan Paul.

Glasgow University Media Group, 1980. *More Bad News*. London: Routledge and Kegan Paul.

Glasgow University Media Group, 1982. *Really Bad News*. London: Routledge and Kegan Paul.

Gledhill, Christine, 1991. *Stardom: Industry of Desire*. London: Routledge.

Goldsmiths Media Group, 2000. Media organizations in society: central issues. In James Curran (ed.), *Media Organizations in Society*. London: Arnold, pp. 19–65.

Goodwin, Peter, 1999. The role of the state. In Jane Stokes and Anna Reading (eds.), *The Media in Britain: Current Debates and Developments*. London: Macmillan, pp. 130–42.

Gramsci, Antonio, 1971. *Selections from the Prison Notebooks of Antonio Gramsci*. Edited and translated by Quintin Hoare and Geoffrey Nowell-Smith. London: Lawrence and Wishart.

Gramsci, Antonio, 1985. *Selections from Cultural Writings*. Edited by David Forgacs and Geoffrey Nowell-Smith. Translated by William Boelhower. London: Lawrence and Wishart.

Granada plc., 2000. Annual Report. Available on website: www.granadamedia.com.

Gunter, Barrie, 2000. *Media Research Methods. Measuring Audience Reactions and Impact*. London: Sage.

Gunter, Barrie, Jane Sancho-Aldridge and Paul Winstone, 1993. *Television: The Public's View*. London: John Libbey.

Habermas, Jürgen, 1989. *The Structural Transformation of the Public Sphere*. Cambridge: Polity Press.

Hall, Stuart, 1981. Encoding/decoding. In S. Hall, D. Hobson, A. Lowe and P. Willis (eds.), *Culture, Media, Language*. London: Hutchinson.

Hall, Stuart, 1986. Media power and class power. In James Curran, Jake Ecclestone, Giles Oakley and Alan Richardson (eds.), *Bending Reality: The State of the Media*. London: Pluto, pp. 5–14.

Halloran, James D., 1998. Mass communication research: asking the right questions. In Anders Hansen, Simon Cottle, Ralph Negrine and Chris Newbold (eds.), *Mass Communication Research Methods*. London: Macmillan, pp. 9–34.

Hansen, Anders, Simon Cottle, Ralph Negrine and Chris Newbold, 1998. *Mass Communication Research Methods*. London: Macmillan.

Hardy, Phil, 1998. *Gangsters*. London: Aurum Press.

Harrison, Jackie, 2000. *Terrestrial TV News in Britain. The Culture of Production*. Manchester/New York: Manchester University Press.

Hebdige, Dick, 1988. *Hiding in the Light. On Images and Things*. London: Comedia/Routledge.

Held, David, 1980. *Introduction to Critical Theory. Horkheimer to Habermas*. London: Hutchinson.

Henderson, Lesley, 1999. Producing serious soaps. In Greg Philo (ed.), *Message Received. Glasgow Media Group Research 1993–1998*. Harlow, Essex: Addison Wesley Longman, pp. 62–81.

Herman, Edward S. and Noam Chomsky, 2002. *Manufacturing Consent. The Political Economy and the Mass Media*. New York: Pantheon Books.

Hobson, Dorothy, 1982. *Crossroads: The Drama of a Soap Opera*. London: Methuen.

Holmes, Susan, 2001. 'As they really are, and in close-up': film stars on 1950s British television. *Screen*, **42**: 167–87.

Hornig Priest, Susanna, 1996. *Doing Media Research. An Introduction*. Thousand Oaks, CA/London: Sage.

Independent Television Commission, 2000. Annual Report. London: ITC. Available on website of ITC: www.itc.org.uk.

Independent Television Commission, 2001. *1999 Attitudes to Television Questionnaire*. London: ITC.

Inglis, Fred, 1990. *Media Theory: An Introduction*. Oxford: Blackwell.

Inglis, Fred, 1993. *Cultural Studies*. Oxford: Blackwell.

International Visual Communication Association (IVCA), 2001. *The IVCA Business Media Handbook*. London: IVCA.

Jenkins, Henry, 1992. *Textual Poachers*. London: Routledge.

Jensen, Klaus Bruhn, 1991a. Introduction: the qualitative turn. In Klaus Bruhn Jensen and Nicholas W. Jankowski (eds.), *A Handbook of Qualitative Methodologies for Mass Communication Research*. London/New York: Routledge, pp. 1–11.

Jensen, Klaus Bruhn, 1991b. Reception analysis: mass communication as the social production of meaning. In Klaus Bruhn Jensen and Nicholas W. Jankowski (eds.), *A Handbook of Qualitative Methodologies for Mass Communication Research*. London/New York: Routledge, pp. 135–48.

Johnson, Rachael, 2001. Playing fathers and monsters. The classical appeal of Anthony Hopkins. *CineAction*, 55: 24–30.

Kitzinger, Jenny, 1999. A sociology of media power: key issues in audience reception research. In Greg Philo (ed.), *Message Received. Glasgow Media Group Research 1993–1998*. Harlow, Essex: Addison Wesley Longman, pp. 3–20.

Krippendorff, Klaus, 1980. *Content Analysis. An Introduction to Its Methodology*. Beverly Hills, CA/London: Sage.

Kumar, Ranjit, 1999. *Research Methodology. A Step-by-Step Guide for Beginners*. London: Sage.

Larkin, Colin, 1999. *The Virgin Encyclopaedia of Stage and Film Musicals*. London: Virgin Books.

Liebes, Tamar and Elihu Katz, 1990. *The Export of Meaning: Cross Cultural Readings of 'Dallas'*. New York/Oxford: Oxford University Press.

Lindlof, Thomas R., 1995. *Qualitative Communication Research Methods*. London: Sage.

Livingstone, Sonia, 1990. *Making Sense of Television: The Psychology of Audience Interpretation*. Oxford: Pergamon.

Livingstone, Sonia, 1998. Relationships between media and audiences. Prospects for audience research studies. In Tamar Liebes and James Curran (eds.), *Media, Ritual and Identity*. London/New York: Routledge, pp. 237–55.

Livingstone, Sonia and Peter Lunt, 1994. *Talk on Television: Audience Participation and Public Debate*. London: Routledge.

Lothe, Jakob, 2000. *Narrative in Fiction and Film. An Introduction*. Oxford: Oxford University Press.

Lull, James, 1990. *Inside Family Viewing: Ethnographic Research on Television's Audiences*. London: Routledge.

Mackay, Hugh and Tim O'Sullivan, 1999. *The Media Reader: Continuity and Transformation*. London: Sage/Open University Press.

Mann, Robin (ed.), 2000. *The Blue Book of British Broadcasting 2000*. London: Taylor Nelson Sofres Telex.

Marc, David and Robert J. Thompson, 1995. *Prime Time, Prime Movers. From 'I Love Lucy' to 'L.A. Law' – America's Greatest TV Shows and the People who Created Them*. Syracuse, NY: Syracuse University Press.

Marshall, Bill and Robynn Stilwell, 2000. *Musicals: Hollywood and Beyond*. Exeter, England/Portland, OR: Intellect Books.

Martín-Barbero, Jesús, 1993. *Communication, Culture and Hegemony. From the Media to Mediations*. Translated by Elizabeth Fox and Robert A. White. London: Sage.

Marx, Karl and Friedrich Engels, 1964 [1848]. *The Communist Manifesto*. New York: Simon and Schuster.

Marx, Karl and Friedrich Engels, 1974. *The German Ideology*. Edited by C.J. Arthur. London: Lawrence and Wishart.

Mast, Gerald and Marshall Cohen, 1985. *Film Theory and Criticism. Introductory Readings* (3rd edn). Oxford: Oxford University Press.

MacKenzie, Donald and Jude Wajcman, 1999. *The Social Shopping of Technology* (2nd edn). Buckingham: Open University Press.

McLeod, Kembrew, 1999. Authenticity within hip-hop and other cultures threatened with assimilation. *Journal of Communication*, **49**, Autumn: 134–50.

McLuhan, Marshall, 1995. *Understanding Media* (new edn). London: Routledge.

McQuail, Denis, 1994. *Mass Communication Theory. An Introduction* (3rd edn). London: Sage.

Messenger Davies, Máire Mosdell and Nick Mosdell, 2001. *Consenting Children?: The Use of Children in Non-Fiction Television Programmes*. London: Broadcasting Standards Commission.

Miller, Daniel, 1998. *A Theory of Shopping*. Cambridge: Polity Press.

Miller, Toby, 2000. Stars and performance. In Robert Stam and Toby Miller (eds.), *Film and Theory: An Anthology*. Oxford: Blackwell.

Millwood Hargrave, Andrea, 2000. *Delete Expletives?* The Advertising Standards Authority, British Broadcasting Corporation, Broadcasting Standards Commission and the Independent Television Commission (jointly funded research).

Monk, Claire, 1999a. From underworld to underclass. Crime and British cinema in the 1990s. In Steve Chibnall and Robert Murphy (eds.), *British Crime Cinema*. London: Routledge, pp. 172–88.

Monk, Claire, 1999b. Heritage films and the British cinema audience in the

1990s. *Journal of Popular British Cinema*. Volume 2: *Audiences and Reception in Britain*, pp. 22–38.

Moores, Shaun, 1988. The box on the dresser: memories of early radio and everyday life. *Media, Culture and Society*, 10: 23–40.

Moores, Shaun, 1993. *Interpreting Audiences. The Ethnography of Media Consumption*. London: Sage.

Morley, David, 1980. *The 'Nationwide' Audience*. London: British Film Institute.

Morley, David, 1986. *Family Television: Cultural Power and Domestic Leisure*. London: Comedia.

Morley, David, 1992. *Television, Audiences and Cultural Studies*. London: Routledge.

Morley, David and Roger Silverstone, 1991. Communication and context: ethnographic perspectives on the media audience. In Klaus Bruhn Jensen and Nicholas W. Jankowski (eds.), *A Handbook of Qualitative Methodologies for Mass Communication Research*. London: Routledge, pp. 149–62.

Morley, David and Kuan-Hsing Chen (eds.), 1996. *Stuart Hall: Critical Dialogues in Cultural Studies*. London: Routledge.

Morrison, D. 1998. *The Search for Method: Focus Groups and the Development of Mass Communication*. Luton: University of Luton Press.

Mottram, James, 2000. *The Coen Brothers: The Life of the Mind*. London: BT Batsford.

Munby, Jonathan, 1999. *Public Enemies, Public Heroes*. Chicago: University of Chicago Press.

Murdock, Graham, 1997. Base notes: the conditions of cultural practice. In Marjorie Ferguson and Peter Golding (eds.), *Cultural Studies in Question*. London: Sage, pp. 86–101.

Neale, Steve, 1992. The big romance or something wild? Romantic comedy today. *Screen*, 33: 284–99.

Neale, Steve, 2000. *Genre and Hollywood*. London: Routledge.

Neale, Steve and Frank Krutnik, 1990. *Popular Film and Television Comedy*. London/New York: Routledge.

Neale, Steve and Murray Smith (eds.), 1998. *Contemporary Hollywood Cinema*. London/New York: Routledge.

Nichols, Bill, 1991. *Representing Reality: Issues and Concepts in Documentary*. Bloomington, Indiana: Indiana University Press.

O'Sullivan, Tim, 1991. Television memories and cultures of viewing, 1950–65. In John Corner (ed.), *Popular Television in Britain: Studies in Cultural History*. London: British Film Institute, pp. 159–81.

PACT (Producers Alliance for Cinema and Television), 2001. *The PACT Directory of Independent Producers*. London: PACT.

Peterson, Ruth C. and Louis Leon Thurstone (1976). *Motion Pictures and the Social Attitudes of Children*. New York: Arno.

Petrie, Duncan and John Willis (eds.), 1995. *Television and the Household. Reports from the BFI's Audience Tracking Study*. London: British Film Institute.

Philo, Greg (ed.), 1996. *Media and Mental Distress*. Glasgow Media Group. Harlow, Essex: Addison Wesley Longman Ltd.

Philo, Greg (ed.), 1999. *Message Received. Glasgow Media Group Research 1993–1998*. Harlow, Essex: Addison Wesley Longman Ltd.

Pines, Jim (ed.), 1992. *Black and White in Colour: Black People in British Television Since 1936*. London: British Film Institute.

Propp, Vladimir, 1968. *Morphology of the Folktale*. Austin, Texas: University of Texas Press.

Punch, Keith F., 1998. *Introduction to Social Research. Quantitative and Qualitative Approaches*. London: Sage.

Rabinovitz, Lauren, 1999. Ms.–Representation. The politics of feminist sitcoms. In Mary Beth Harolovich and Lauren Rabinovitz (eds.), *Television, History and American Culture. Feminist Critical Essays*. Durham, North Carolina/ London: Duke University Press, pp. 145–67.

Radway, Janice, 1984. *Reading the Romance: Women, Patriarchy and Popular Literature*. Chapel Hill, North Carolina: University of North Carolina Press.

Ramamurthy, Anandi, 1997. Constructions of illusion: photography and commodity culture. In Liz Wells (ed.), *Photography A Critical Introduction*. London/New York: Routledge.

Riessman, C., 1993. *Narrative Analysis*. Newbury Park, CA: Sage.

Rietveld, Hillegonda, 1998. *This is Our House*. Hampshire: Ashgate Publishing.

Riffe, Daniel, Stephen Lacy and Frederick G. Fico, 1998. *Analyzing Media Messages. Using Quantitative Content Analysis in Research*. London/ Mahwah, New Jersey: Lawrence Erlbaum.

Rigby, Jonathan, 2000. *English Gothic. A Century of Horror Cinema*. London: Reynolds and Hearn Ltd.

Rosengren, Karl Erik (ed.), 1981. *Advances in Content Analysis*. London: Sage.

Rubin, Martin, 1999. *Thrillers*. Cambridge: Cambridge University Press.

Sampedro, Victor, 1998. Grounding the displaced: local media reception in a transnational context. *Journal of Communication*, **48**: 125–43.

Sapsford, Roger, 1999. *Survey Research*. London: Sage.

Saussure, Ferdinand de, 1983. *Course in General Linguistics*. Translated by Roy Harris. London: Gerald Duckworth.

Scannell, Paddy (ed.), 1991. *Broadcast Talk*. London: Sage.

Scannell, Paddy, 1996. *Radio, Television and Modern Life. A Phenomenological Approach*. Oxford: Blackwell.

Scannell, Paddy and David Cardiff, 1991. *A Social History of Broadcasting. Volume 1: 1922–1939. Serving the Nation*. Oxford: Basil Blackwell.

Schatz, Thomas, 1981. *Hollywood Genres: Formulas, Filmmaking and the Studio System*. Philadelphia: Temple University Press.

Schlesinger, Philip, 1987. *Putting Reality Together: BBC News* (2nd edn). London: Methuen.

Scholes, Robert, 1985. Narration and narrativity in film. In Gerald Mast and Marshall Cohen (eds.), *Film Theory and Criticism*. New York/Oxford: Oxford University Press, pp. 390–403.

Seale, Clive (ed.), 1998. *Researching Society and Culture*. London: Sage.

Seiter, Ellen, 1992. Semiotics, structuralism and television. In Robert C. Allen, *Channels of Discourse Reassembled*. London: Routledge, pp. 31–66.

Seymour-Ure, Colin, 1996. *The British Press and Broadcasting Since 1945* (2nd edn). Oxford: Blackwell.

Silvey, Robert, 1974. *Who's Listening? The Story of BBC Audience Research*. London: Allen and Unwin.

Silverman, David, 2000. *Doing Qualitative Research. A Practical Handbook*. London: Sage.

Silverstone, Roger, 1994. *Television and Everyday Life*. London: Routledge.

Smith, Chris, 1998. *Creative Britain*. London: Faber and Faber.

Smith, Murray, 1995. *Engaging Characters. Fiction, Emotion and the Cinema*. Oxford: Clarendon Press.

Sparks, Colin, 1986. The media and the state. In James Curran, Jake Ecclestone, Giles Oakley and Alan Richardson (eds.), *Bending Reality: The State of the Media*. London: Pluto, pp. 76–86.

Sparks, Colin, 1999. The press. In Jane Stokes and Anna Reading (eds.), *The Media in Britain: Current Debates and Developments*. London: Macmillan, pp. 41–60.

Stacey, Jackie, 1994. *Star Gazing. Hollywood Cinema and Female Spectatorship*. London: Routledge.

Stam, Robert and Toby Miller (eds.), 2000. *Film Theory: An Anthology*. Oxford: Blackwell.

State University of New York at Albany. *Film Literature Index*. Quarterly.

Stokes, Jane, 1999a. Use it or lose it: sex, sexuality and sexual health in magazines for girls. In Jane Stokes and Anna Reading (eds.), *The Media in Britain. Current Debates and Developments*. London: Macmillan, pp. 209–18.

Stokes, Jane, 1999b. Anglo-American attitudes: affirmations and refutations of 'Americanicity' in British television advertising. In Yahya Kamalipour (ed.), *U.S. Image Around the World*. Albany, NY: State University of New York Press.

Stokes, Jane, 1999c. *On Screen Rivals. The Cinema and Television in Britain and the US*. London: Macmillan.

Stokes, Jane and Anna Reading (eds.), 1999. *The Media in Britain: Current Debates and Developments*. London: Macmillan.

Storey, John, 1993. *An Introductory Guide to Cultural Theory and Popular Culture*. London: Harvester Wheatsheaf.

Storey, John, 1994. *Cultural Theory and Popular Culture: A Reader*. London: Harvester Wheatsheaf.

Sweeney, Gael, 2001. The man in the pink shirt: Hugh Grant and the dilemma of British masculinity. *CineAction*, 55: 57–67.

Stratton, Jon, 2001. Not really white – again: performing Jewish difference in Hollywood films since the 1980s. *Screen*, 42: 142–66.

Thomas, Sari, 1997. Dominance and ideology in culture and cultural studies. In Marjorie Ferguson and Peter Golding (eds.), *Cultural Studies in Question*. London: Sage, pp. 74–85.

Thompson, John B., 1995. *The Media and Modernity. A Social Theory of the Media*. London: Polity.

Thompson, Kristin and David Bordwell, 1994. *Film History: An Introduction*. New York: McGraw-Hill.

Todorov, Tzvetan, 1981. *Introduction to Poetics*. Translated by Richard Howard. Minneapolis, Minnesota: University of Minnesota Press.

Tulloch, John, 2000. *Watching Television Audiences: Cultural Theories and Methods*. London: Arnold.

Tulloch, John and Henry Jenkins, 1995. *Science Fiction Audiences: Watching 'Doctor Who' and 'Star Trek'*. London: Routledge.

Tunstall, Jeremy, 1983. *The Media in Britain*. London: Constable.

Tunstall, Jeremy, 1993. *Television Producers*. London: Routledge.

Tunstall, Jeremy, 1996. *Newspaper Power. The National Press in Britain*. Oxford: Clarendon Press.

Tunstall, Jeremy and Michael Palmer, 1991. *Media Moguls*. London: Routledge.

Turabian, Kate, 1996. *A Manual for Writers of Term Papers, Theses and Dissertations*. Chicago: University of Chicago Press.

Turner, Graeme, 1996. *British Cultural Studies. An Introduction* (2nd edn). London: Routledge.

Turnock, Robert, 2000. *Interpreting Audiences and the Death of a Princess*. London: British Film Institute.

van Dijk, Teun, 1988. *News as Discourse*. Hillsdale, New Jersey: Erlbaum.

Wasko, Janet, Mark Phillips and Eileen R. Meehan (eds.), 2001. *Dazzled by Disney? The Global Disney Audiences Project*. London/New York: Leicester University Press.

Weber, R.P., 1985. *Basic Content Analysis*. Beverly Hills, CA: Sage.

Wheeler, Mark, 1997. *Politics and the Mass Media*. Oxford: Blackwell.

Williams, Kevin, 1998. *Get Me a Murder a Day! A History of Mass Communication in Britain*. London: Arnold.

Williams, Mark, 1999. Considering Monty Margetts's *Cook's Corner*: oral history and television history. In Mary Beth Harolovich and Lauren Rabinovitz (eds.), *Television, History and American Culture. Feminist Critical Essays*. Durham, North Carolina/London: Duke University Press, pp. 36–55.

Williams, Raymond, 1963. *Culture and Society 1780–1950*. Harmondsworth: Penguin Books.

Williamson, Judith, 1978. *Decoding Advertisements. Ideology and Meaning in Advertising*. London/New York: Marion Boyars.

Winner, Langdon, 1977. *Autonomous Technology. Technics-out-of-Control as a Theme in Political Thought*. Cambridge, MA: MIT Press.

Winston, Brian, 1986. *Misunderstanding Media*. London: Routledge and Kegan Paul.

Winston, Brian, 1998. *Media, Technology and Society. A History: From the Telegraph to the Internet*. London: Routledge.

Wollen, Peter, 1998. *Signs and Meaning in the Cinema*. Expanded edition. London: British Film Institute.

Wood, Robin, 1981. *Howard Hawks*. London: British Film Institute.

Wood, Robin, 2001. Hawke ascending. *CineAction*, 55: 2–13.

Wright, Will, 1979. *Six-Guns and Society*. Berkeley, CA: University of California Press.

Index